本书的出版受到上海市教委第五期重点学科国际贸易法学科项目（J51204）的大力支持，特此致谢。

Legal Theory of International Arbitration

国际仲裁的法理思考和实践指导

〔法〕伊曼纽尔·盖拉德（Emmanuel Gaillard） 著
黄 洁 译
陈晶莹 审校

图书在版编目(CIP)数据

国际仲裁的法理思考和实践指导/(法)盖拉德(Gaillard, E.)著；黄洁译. —北京：北京大学出版社, 2010.6
ISBN 978-7-301-17180-6

Ⅰ.国… Ⅱ.①盖… ②黄… Ⅲ.国际仲裁-法理学-研究 Ⅳ.D994

中国版本图书馆 CIP 数据核字(2010)第 081373 号

书　　　名：	国际仲裁的法理思考和实践指导
著作责任者：	〔法〕伊曼纽尔·盖拉德(Emmanuel Gaillard) 著 黄　洁 译　陈晶莹 审校
责任编辑：	王　晶
标准书号：	ISBN 978-7-301-17180-6/D·2589
出版发行：	北京大学出版社
地　　址：	北京市海淀区成府路 205 号　100871
网　　址：	http://www.pup.cn
电　　话：	邮购部 62752015　发行部 62750672　编辑部 62752027 出版部 62754962
电子邮箱：	law@pup.pku.edu.cn
印　刷　者：	北京宏伟双华印刷有限公司
经　销　者：	新华书店
	890 毫米×1240 毫米　A5　5.5 印张　153 千字 2010 年 6 月第 1 版　2010 年 6 月第 1 次印刷
定　　价：	20.00 元

未经许可，不得以任何方式复制或抄袭本书之部分或全部内容。
版权所有，侵权必究
举报电话：010-62752024　电子邮箱：fd@pup.pku.edu.cn

目　　录

导论 ·· （1）

第一章　国际仲裁的表现形式 ··· （11）
　（一）国际仲裁归为单个国家法律秩序的一部分 ········· （14）
　　A. 两大理由 ··· （15）
　　B. 哲学前提 ··· （20）
　（二）国际仲裁根植于多个国家法律秩序 ···················· （23）
　　A. 哲学前提 ··· （24）
　　B. 批判分析 ··· （29）
　（三）国际仲裁是自治的法律秩序：仲裁法律秩序 ······ （32）
　　A. 哲学前提 ··· （36）
　　B. 对仲裁法律秩序存在的认可 ································ （47）

第二章　国际仲裁表现形式的后果 ································· （59）
　（一）国际仲裁表现形式对仲裁员裁决权的影响 ········ （61）
　　A. 禁诉令 ·· （63）
　　B. 在国家法院和仲裁庭之间的平行程序问题 ········· （77）
　（二）国际仲裁表现形式对仲裁员裁决的影响 ············ （82）
　　A. 国际仲裁表现形式对仲裁员自由进行仲裁程序和识别
　　　 解决争议的实体规则的影响 ································ （83）
　　B. 国际仲裁表现形式对限制当事人自由选择解决争议的
　　　 实体规则的影响 ·· （100）
　（三）国际仲裁表现形式对裁决效力的影响 ················ （118）
　　A. 被仲裁地的法律秩序撤销的裁决的效力 ············· （118）
　　B. 仲裁地的法律秩序作出的不撤销裁决的决定的效力 ··· （125）

结论	(130)
About the Author	(132)
Bibliography	(141)
Table of Abreviations	(155)
索引	(157)
译后记	(171)

导　　论

1. 每当人们论及国际仲裁的法学理论总是不能不提到 Henri Batiffol 及他对国际私法法理发展有着显著贡献的经典文章[1]。但是,这一褒奖实际上是自相矛盾的。因为如果人们追溯历史经典,首先应当想到的是 Berthold Goldman,因为 1963 年他在海牙国际法学院关于国际仲裁冲突法的基础课程奠定了重建国际仲裁法理的基础。与当时的主流观点截然不同的是[2],Goldman 创造性地提出"仲裁员没有仲裁管辖地(forum)",如果一定要为仲裁员找一个仲裁管辖地的话,这个地点是全世界[3];从法学的理论角度讲,这意味着需要探讨国际仲裁和国家法律秩序的关系。此外,我们还需要肯定 Phocion Francescakis 对此作出的贡献——在 1960 年他对自然法和国际私法的关系作出了精辟的分析[4]。至于 Henri Batiffol,他致力于证明国际私法这个技术性很强的领域,在识别或者国际公共政策等问题上,如何从源自自然法的普遍主义(universalist)概念中受益。

---

[1] See H. Batiffol, *Aspects philosophiques du droit international privé*, Paris, Dalloz, 1956.

[2] 在 1957 年,国际法研究所(Institute of International Law)在 G. Sauser-Hall 报告的基础上采纳了《阿姆斯特丹决议》。该决议建议仲裁员适用仲裁地的冲突法,该法可以被称为"裁判地法"(lex fori)(Institute of International Law, *Yearbook*, 1952, volume 44, part I, p. 469, at p. 571)。就此问题的诸观点的演变,参见 *infra*, §§ 89 *et seq.*

[3] B. Goldman, Les conflits de lois dans l'arbitrage international de droit privé, *Collected Courses*, volume 109 (1963), p. 347, at p. 374. See also Comité français de droit international privé, Session of November 23, 1985, *Travaux du Comité français de droit international privé, Journée du cinquantenaire*, 1988, p. 117.

[4] Ph. Francescakis, Droit naturel et droit international privé, *Mélanges offerts à Jacques Maury*, Paris, Dalloz, 1960, volume I, p. 113.

2. 与国际私法相比较,国际仲裁法更适合法学理论的分析。自治(autonomy)和自由(freedom)这对基本的哲学概念处于这一领域的核心地位。同样至关重要的是以下因素带来的正当性问题:当事人可以自由选择私人的争议解决方式而非国家法院,还可以选择仲裁员,制定他们认为合适的争议解决程序,确定争议适用的准据法,即使选择的规则并非来自某个法律制度。仲裁员的自由裁量权也同样重要,例如,仲裁员可以自由决定自己的管辖权和仲裁程序,若当事人没有选择,仲裁员还可以选择解决争端的实体法。意义更深远的是,仲裁员有权力基于当事人的仲裁协议作出裁决,仲裁裁决和当事人的仲裁协议一样具有私人属性,这就引发了一个根本性的问题:仲裁员的权力以及仲裁程序和裁决的法律性质来自何处?这个问题可以被称为国际仲裁的法律属性(juridicity)问题。因为仲裁的渊源问题——一些人称其为"基本规范"(basic norm)问题[5],其他人谓之"承认规则"(rule of recognition)问题[6]——是法学理论中最复杂的问题之一。因此国际仲裁应当是特别吸引法理学家的领域。如果确实"一个法学理论是否能够带来丰硕成果还是毫无作用是由它能否解决实在法(positive law)的渊源问题来衡量的"[7],国际仲裁绝对不会让法理学家们兴趣索然。

3. 然而,到目前为止,我们对国际仲裁和法学理论的交叉研究仍然非常有限。

除了 Bruno Oppetit 发表了一部关于仲裁理论的重要的著作之

---

[5] H. Kelsen, *Pure Theory of Law*, N.J., Lawbook Exchange, transl. Max Knight, 2002, p.193.

[6] H. L. A Hart, *The Concept of Law*, Oxford, Oxford University Press, 2nd ed., 1994, p.95.

[7] G. Gurvitch, *L'expérience juridique et la philosophie pluraliste du droit*, Paris, Pedone, 1935, p.138, author's translation. 关于法哲学和一般法学理论的区别,例见,F. Rigaux, *Introduction à la science du droit*, Brussels, Ed. Vie ouvrière, 1974, p.137.

外[8],许多年轻的学者对这一领域日益表现出浓厚的兴趣[9],但是国际仲裁的专家们基本上仅仅局限于对实在法的介绍和批判性评价。国际仲裁专家和法学理论家们仅仅在商人习惯法(lex mercatoria)的论战中交换过意见,商人习惯法指的是专门适用于"商人社会"的一套规则,关于它的论战贯穿了 20 世纪下半叶的整个理论讨论中。[10] 看来商人习惯法理论的奠基者们——至少默示地[11]——借鉴了法律秩序(legal order)的制度观念(institutional conceptions)来论证在国家法律秩序的规范之外,还存在着其他规范。Paul Lagarde 教授是最不支持商人习惯法的学者之一,他依据 Santi Romano 的法律秩序定义的标准,来分析商人习惯法。Maurice Hauriou 的制度理论[12]在 20 世纪下半叶已经显得陈旧过时,与此相反,Santi Romano 的著作虽然同样以制度理论为基础,并且最早面世于 1918 年,其法

---

[8] B. Oppetit, *Théorie de l'arbitrage*, Paris, PUF, 1998;参照同一作者的,Philosophie de l'arbitrage commercial international, *JDI*, 1993, p. 811.

[9] See, *e.g.*, S. Bollée, *Les méthodes du droit international privé à l'épreuve des sentences arbitrales*, Paris, Economica, 2004; Homayoon Arfazadeh, *Ordre public et arbitrage international à l'épreuve de la mondialisation*, Geneva, Schulthess, 2nd ed., 2006.

[10] 对商人习惯法的论战源自 B. Goldman 出版于 1964 年的作品(Frontières du droit et "lex mercatoria", *Archives de philosophie du droit*. No. 9, *Le droit subjectif en question*, 1964, p. 177)。从不同的角度对此问题的论述,参见 C. Schmitthoff (The Law of International Trade, its Growth, Formulation and Operation, *The Sources of the Law of International Trade*, London, Stevens & Sons, 1964, p. 3)。1982 年以纪念 B. Goldman 为名的论文集的发表引发了争论的高潮(*Etudes offertes à Berthold Goldman*)。特别参见 Ph. Kahn, Droit international économique, droit du développement, lex mercatoria: concept unique ou pluralisme des ordres juridiques?, p. 97, of M. Virally, Un tiers droit? Réflexions théoriques, p. 373,就批判性分析参见 P. Lagarde, Approche critique de la lex mercatoria, p. 125。这场争论持续到了 20 世纪 90 年代,特别体现在以下著作中,F. Osman, *Les Principes généraux de la lex mercatoria. Contribution à l'étude d'un ordre juridique anational*, Paris, LGDJ, 1992, and F. de Ly, *International Business Law and Lex Mercatoria*, Amsterdam, North-Holland, 1992. 在 20 世纪末,涉及商人习惯法的著作,无论是对其持反对或支持观点的,数不胜数。就本书对商人习惯法的总体观点,请参见后文,§§ 52 *et seq.*

[11] B. Goldman, Frontières du droit et "lex mercatoria", *op. cit.* footnote 10, p. 190.

[12] M. Hauriou, *La Théorie de l'institution et de la fondation*, Paris, Coll. Cahiers de la nouvelle journée, Bloud & Gay, 1925.

语版本直到 1975 年才出现[13],却仍然被认为是内容新颖并且引人入胜的。[14] 这番比较是为了说明即使制度主义者的设想摒弃了法律和国家的共存关系,商人习惯法也绝对不具有法律秩序的尊贵特征。[15] 结果,无论是为了佐证跨国规则的存在,还是在国家法律秩序不承认它们的情况下,否认跨国规则的法律性质,绝大多数国际仲裁专家们都参考了 Santi Romano 对法律秩序的定义。这表明 Santi Romano 至少在这个层面上,在法国的实在法领域的专家中享有迟来的声誉。

社会学家们已经开始分析国际仲裁[16],相反,法学理论家对国际仲裁和国际仲裁专家对法学理论一样仍然毫无兴趣。好在近来一些仲裁专家参考了商人习惯法,提出了以法律属性具有相对性和在一个网络中相互联系的多元化的法律制度为基础的新理论。[17] 这些专家希望以此取代 Hans Kelsen 提出的法律的金字塔模型理论。然而,我们会发现,通过参考商人习惯法,国际仲裁并没有被当做一个私人的争议解决模式,相反国际仲裁被认为有能力创设并非来自国家法律秩序的规则。可惜的是,这些理论研究仅仅是国际仲裁所涉及的哲学问题的冰山一角。

---

〔13〕 See S. Romano, *L'ordinamento giuridico*, Pisa, Spoerri, 1st ed., 1918。法语版为 *L'ordre juridique*,由 Lucien François 和 Pierre Gothot 翻译,导论由 Phocion Francescakis 撰写,Paris, Dalloz, 1975. 法语第二版在 2002 年出版,Pierre Mayer 撰写前言。

〔14〕 将两个理论联系起来的著作,特别参见 G. Fassò, *Histoire de la philosophie du droit. XIXe et XXe siècles*, Paris, LGDJ, 1976, translated from the third edition, *Storia della filosofia del diritto*. volume III, *Ottocento e Novecento*, Bologna, Società editrice il Mulino, 1974.

〔15〕 P. Lagarde, Approche critique de la *lex mercatoria*, *op. cit.* footnote 10, pp. 133—134 and footnote 31. 又见 2005 年,P. Lagarde 给 A. Kassis 的书题写的前言,*L'autonomie de l'arbitrage commercial international. Le droit français en question*, Paris, L'Harmattan, 2005.

〔16〕 此领域的先行者是 Y. Dezalay 和 B. G. Garth, Y. Dezalay and B. G. Garth, *Dealing in Virtue: International Commercial Arbitration and the Construction of a Transnational Legal Order*, Chicago, The University of Chicago Press, 1996(前言由 P. Bourdieu 撰写)。

〔17〕 See F. Ost and M. van de Kerchove, *De la pyramide au réseau? Pour une théorie dialectique du droit*, Brussels, Publications des Facultés universitaires Saint-Louis, 2002, for example at pp. 14 and 111.

4. 这并不意味着国际仲裁专家们对价值标准不感兴趣,或者他们对仲裁领域的构建和仲裁与其他法律领域的关系无所谓。显然,法学界的出版物并未完全局限于描述某个法律制度或仲裁员采用的解决方法。法学家们经常论证应当采用哪个解决方法,而且仲裁法中最意义深远的问题通常是产生最重大分歧的地方。同样,法学家们并未忽视道德规范,相反他们认为国际仲裁应当尊重并且从道德规范中得到启发,这些规范包括合同诚信、公共政策或者友好仲裁(amiable composition)等。[18] 但是国际仲裁的根本的哲学前提仍旧不甚明了。

5. 即使仲裁专家用法学理论家的成果证明自己的观点,他们的分析往往存在着很高的主观主义风险。这种在法学理论中寻找最好的意见来证明自己的观点的正确性的做法,若非仲裁专家们下意识所为,的确很冒险。这个方法预期的好处是可以为实体法提供稳固的理论支持,或者为改变实体法提供建议。以下几个例子说明了这一点。

如果某学者认为除非"真正的国际公共政策"(truly international public policy)被国内法律制度所接纳,否则它就不具有法律性质,该学者就会借用 Kelsen 或者 Hart 的理论,而非 Santi Romano 或者 Ost 和 van de Kerchove 的思想。这表现在一篇题为"仲裁员、法官和国际商事交易的非法行为"的博士论文中:

> 根据 Hart 所代表的最传统的理论,一个完整的法律制度建立于两种规则之上。第一,**首要规则**(*primary rules*)是不可或缺的。它们是个人之间的行为准则,为法律规范的对象设定义务规则。第二,必须存在所谓的**次要规则**(*secondary rules*)。这种规则有三个作用:它们允许产生、改变和评判首要规则,这包括

---

[18] See in particular P. Mayer, La règle morale dans l'arbitrage international, *Etudes offertes à Pierre Bellet*, Paris, Litec, 1991, p. 379; V. Heuzé, La morale, l'arbitre et le juge, *Rev. arb.*, 1993, p. 179.

违反首要规则的惩罚措施。但是,商人习惯法不幸缺乏这种次要规则。更确切地说,为了满足这三种功能,商人习惯法必须从规范国与国之间关系的国际法和管理国际商事交易的国内法(national law)中借用规则。结果,如果真正的国际公共政策规则禁止某行为,但是它却无法惩戒该行为。惩戒功能实际上是可适用的国内法或国与国之间的法律规则的特征。[19]

认为真正的国际公共政策是无力惩戒非法行为的观点仅仅是一个简单的假设,但是却带来一连串的问题。由于这个观点以 Hart 权威思想的正当性为武装,它变成了一个从中可以得出法律后果的结论。这个观点实质上仍然是一个假设,但是它的假设存在于作为论据的哲学理论而非最后提出的结论中。简单而言,通过选择作为论据的哲学理论,它将一个没有证据支持的命题表达成能够通过有说服力的分析得出的必然结论。换句话说,真正的国际公共政策是无力惩戒非法行为的观点纯粹基于 Hart 这位权威专家的哲学理论。我们只要选择其他哲学理论作为前提,结论会截然相反。例如,如果用美国哲学家 Holmes 的理论代替 Hart 的理论,我们就会轻而易举地得出相反的结论。Holmes 认为,法律不过是"法院实际上将做什么的预测"[20]。因为国际商事仲裁的仲裁员愿意在判案时参考"真正的国际公共政策"的要求,所以根据 Holmes 对法律的定义,仲裁员赋予这些要求在裁决中享有不可否认的法律属性。仲裁员依据国际公共政策因素进行裁决,例如,不适用不符合真正的国际公共政策的强行规则[21],或者宣布一个执行起来会导致滥用权力的秘密协议无

---

[19] A. Court de Fontmichel, *L'arbitre, le juge et les pratiques illicites du commerce international*, Paris, Editions Panthéon-Assas, 2004, p. 102, author's translation.

[20] O.W. Holmes, The Path of the Law, *Harvard Law Review* 457 (1897), p. 461. Holmes 法官对法律著名的定义可以总结如下:"法律对我来说,不过是对法院实际上将做什么的预测,仅此而已。(The prophecies of what the courts will do in fact, and nothing more pretentious, are what I mean by the law.)"

[21] 例见,ICC 第 6379 号案件的裁决,被引用于 A. Court de Fontmichel, *L'arbitre, le juge et les pratiques illicites du commerce international*, op. cit. footnote 19, § 314 and footnote 94.

效[22];这一切都表明真正的国际公共政策规则能够惩戒非法行为[23]。考虑到它的可预见性,这种能够惩戒非法行为的能力毫无疑问地说明法律制度应当接受 Holmes 的哲学前提。

另一个例子是对商人习惯法的争论。学者们策略性的选择哲学参考文献来解释商人习惯法的法律本质。[24] 支持商人习惯法的学者们从 Maurice Hauriou 或者 Santi Romano 的著作中分别找到默示的或明示的证据。[25] 今天,这些学者自然转向 François Ost 和 Michel van de Kerchove 等的法学思想[26]。这些法学理论家把一个规则的有效性定义为它能产生法律效果的能力,他们认为有效性需要满足形式的、实证的和价值论的三个标准。和这三个标准相应的是合法性(legality)、有效性(effectiveness)和正当性(legitimacy)三大支柱,它们不可避免地相互作用,或者互相促进或者互相阻碍。[27] 这个模式的灵感源自古典文献中提出的法的三层面理论,其中的代表是巴西哲学家 Miguel Reale 的著作。在这个模式中,各种组合都有可能。[28] 例如,一个正当却无效且不合法的规则仅仅有供立法者或者法官参考的价值;一个合法但还没生效且不正当的规则只会被弃之不用;一个有效但却既不合法也不正当的规则,可能是强权者推行的规则;一

---

〔22〕 例见,ICC 第 6248 号案件的裁决,被引用于,A. Court de Fontmichel, *L'arbitre, le juge et les pratiques illicites du commerce international*, op. cit. footnote 19, § 215 and footnote 100.

〔23〕 就此问题的一般论述,参见后文,§ 215 and footnote 100.

〔24〕 参见后文,footnote 15。

〔25〕 就在 S. Romano 提出的概念基础上对商人习惯法的深入分析的例子,see F. Osman, *Les Principes généraux de la lex mercatoria. Contribution à l'étude d'un ordre juridique anational*, op. cit. footnote 10.

〔26〕 See, for example, J-B. Racine, Réflexions sur l'autonomie de l'arbitrage commercial international, *Rev. arb.*, 2005, p. 305, at p. 341.

〔27〕 F. Ost and M. van de Kerchove, *De la pyramide au réseau? Pour une théorie dialectique du droit*, op. cit. footnote 17, at p. 309.

〔28〕 M. Reale, *Teoria Tridimensional do Direito: preliminares históricas et sistemáticas*, São Paulo, Saraiva ed., 4th ed., 1986; in French, see M. Reale, La situation actuelle de la théorie tridimensionnelle du droit, *Archives de philosophie du droit. Le droit international*, 1987, p. 369. 就更加全面的书目,see F. Ost et M. van de Kerchove, *De la pyramide au réseau? Pour une théorie dialectique du droit*, op. cit. footnote 17, at p. 310, footnote 2 and p. 364.

个既正当又有效的规则代表了传统自然法的特点;另一个例子是,一个既合法又有效但却不正当的规则是一个非正义的规则。这个设想的目的是综合法学家的方法(合法性支柱)、包括 Holmes 和 Ross[29] 在内的现实主义原则的支持者(有效性支柱)、和自然法原则(正当性支柱)。这个模式虽然复杂,但是它对法哲学的重大贡献在于提出了一个法律的动态观点,因为它强调"规则和法律制度是具体存在的,它们由特殊的运动驱动着"[30],例如这三大支柱之间总是可以互换位置。在这个法律属性——或具有作为法律的资格——具有动态性质的框架内,商人习惯法的法律属性是无可争议的。这个结论并不令人惊讶,因为这些学者借用了"由某些强大的经济部门所建立的自我管理现象(人们会特别借鉴商人习惯法……)"来支持有必要"从金字塔的架构过渡到网络架构"的观点。这个论证实际上存在着循环论证的毛病:商人习惯法现象,作为现实,支持了法的某个设想,这个法的设想,反过来,又为它的支持者佐证了商人习惯法的法律属性。

6. 以上讨论仅仅是为了提醒读者注意,法律理论不关心是否能够区分正误和能将假设证明为事实的科学真理;相反,它仅仅反省社会关系的组织方式。

意识形态(ideology)这个概念表明论证的证据总是或多或少地具有自然的或人为的本质特征。在这个方面,Bruno Oppetit 引用了 Jean Baechler 的观点[31],观察到

> 如果意识形态真的"是一个偏见,借此激情以价值观念的形式出现",如果激情和价值观念真的是武断的,因为它们不是以理性为基础的,从这个观点引出的一个主要的结论就是:意识形态既不能

---

[29] A. Ross, *On Law and Justice*, London, Stevens & Sons Ltd., 1958.

[30] F. Ost and M. van de Kerchove, *De la pyramide au réseau? Pour une théorie dialectique du droit*, op. cit. footnote 17, p.354, author's translation.

[31] J. Baechler, *Qu'est-ce que l'idéologie?*, Paris, NRF coll. Idées, Gallimard, 1976, p.60.

被证明又不能被驳倒;所以,它不能以对错论断,它只能以有效率或者无效率的,内在连贯的或者不连贯的标准来评判[32]。

对意识形态的批判大量出现在对商人习惯法的辩论中。在1982年,Wilhem Wengler强烈反对法律的一般原则这个概念,认为它是"伪法律、善变、时常内容不明的"[33]。所以国家法院不应当执行根据法律的一般原则这个幻想作出的裁决。[34] 将某个学说表述为某种意识形态实际上表明了它追求的目的和它主张的不同。实际上,我们要紧的是不应该被带有意识形态色彩的语言和思想所欺骗;换句话说,不要忽略它的涵义和真正目的。

那些认为"意识形态"这个术语在20世纪下半叶已经被滥用了的人,倾向于使用"神话"(myth)这个词。这些人强调"不一目了然的事情就是难以形容或者荒谬反常的"是不正确的,在某种程度上法律神话(legal myths)"是知识的间接助手"。我们不应当指责这些人;相反,我们需要仔细分析和解释他们的观点,"甚至不放过这些观点的每一点微小异处"。[35]

7. 本书正是要从基本的观点、哲学或者,更确切地说,思想表现的角度分析仲裁法。在实在法中,尽管国际仲裁的"表现形式"(representations)*从未引人瞩目,然而它们却毫无疑问地构建了仲

---

[32] B. Oppetit, La notion de source du droit et le droit du commerce international, *Archives de philosophie du droit*. No. 27, "*Sources*" *du droit*, 1982, p. 43, at p. 45, author's translation.

[33] W. Wengler, Les Principes généraux du droit en tant que loi du contrat, *Rev. crit. DIP*, 1982, p. 467, at p. 501, author's translation.

[34] W. Wengler强烈批评某些法律顾问,他们"坚持达成仲裁协议"并"说服当事人相信法律的一般原则是一个和国内私法体系一样完整的法律系统",*ibid*., at p. 500, author's translation.

[35] Ch. Atias, *Philosophie du droit*, Paris, PUF, 2nd ed., 2004, pp. 317—318, author's translation.

＊ 法语"représentation",英语为"representation",意思为"An image or idea formed by the mind. An idea that is the direct object of thought and the mental counterpart or transcript of the object known by means of it"。参见Webster's Third New International Dictionary of the English Language Unabridged (1993), p. 1926。译者就此词的翻译也请教过多人,曾考虑用"表象"、"本质"、"法相"(佛教的术语),最终选定"表现形式"。——译者注

裁这个领域。所以,很自然的某些学者之间观点类似,但是却和其他学者的观点相左。思想阵营的形成并非偶然。例如,就以下仲裁的基础性问题而言,本书的作者在与他人合著的关于国际商事仲裁的著作[36]中提出的解决方案和 Jean-François Poudret 和 Sébastien Besson 在他们对国际仲裁比较法的卓越的研究[37]中提出的解决方案截然不同。这些问题包括:确定解决实体问题适用的法律、接受在仲裁庭和国家法院之间的平行程序(lis pendens)的概念、或者承认已经被仲裁地所在国的法院撤销的仲裁裁决。尽管在一个特定的国家制度或者仲裁案例法中,对实在法的描述总是会——或者应当会——有科学的趋同之处,但是分歧肯定存在于如何将仲裁领域系统化、对各种方法的评价或者对仲裁发展趋势的建议等问题中。[38] 这种分歧对某一思想的内在价值并无影响。它仅仅证明了,该思想是以某个国际仲裁的表现形式为基础发展起来的,也证明了,在本质上为什么在各个思想阵营之间存在准体系(quasi-systematic)的差异。

本书旨在揭示处于幕后但却至关重要的国际仲裁的表现形式,以及说明它们在实在法中的后果[39]。

---

[36] See E. Gaillard and J. Savage (eds.), *Fouchard Gaillard Goldman On International Commercial Arbitration*, The Hague, Kluwer, 1999. 关于国际仲裁的各种观点的内在连贯性,特别参见 O. Sandrock, To Continue Nationalizing or to De-nationalize? That is Now the Question in International Arbitration, *The American Review of International Arbitration* 301 (2001).

[37] J-F. Poudret and S. Besson, *Comparative Law of International Arbitration*, London, Sweet & Maxwell, 2007.

[38] See, *e.g.*, E. Gaillard, La reconnaissance, en droit suisse, de la seconde moitié du principe d'effet négatif de la compétence-compétence, *Global Reflections on International Law, Commerce and Dispute Resolution. Liber Amicorum in honour of Robert Briner*, Paris, ICC Publishing, 2005, p. 311, and J.-F. Poudret, Exception d'arbitrage et litispendance en droit suisse. Comment départager le juge et l'arbitre?, *ASA Bull.*, 2007, p. 230. 就此问题,一般参见,后文, § § 82 *et seq.*

[39] 2006 年 11 月 1 日在巴伊亚州的萨尔瓦多市举行的第 6 届巴西仲裁委员会上的主题发言对这些表现形式进行了第一次分析。后来演讲稿原文在 the *JDI*, 2007, p. 1182 以"主权或自治:对国际仲裁表现形式的反思"为题发表。

第一章　国际仲裁的表现形式

（一）国际仲裁归为单个国家法律秩序的一部分
（二）国际仲裁根植于多个国家法律秩序
（三）国际仲裁是自治的法律秩序：仲裁法律秩序

8. 将国际仲裁的各种表现形式系统化是很困难的,因为思想的表现形式通常只隐含在仲裁专家针对专业问题的法律思考中,而我们又很少能够把它定义出来。

9. 多年来,仲裁法已经成为许多学术讨论的主题,人们很想知道这些讨论在多大程度上涉及国际仲裁的表现形式。

在 20 世纪上半叶仲裁是司法属性还是合同属性成为一场大讨论的焦点。[40] 在那时,愿意促进仲裁发展的学者们强调它的合同属性,然而司法属性的支持者们强调仲裁和国家法院之间应当是对立的。[41] 同样,强调仲裁的合同属性就是要让"外国"裁决免于服从针对承认外国司法决定而设计的严格的程序。在法学家们达成了广泛的共识,采用日益自由的方式对待仲裁之后,这场大讨论以毫无意义的结论收场,即认为仲裁具有混杂司法和合同的"混合"(mixed)属性或者仲裁的属性既非司法也非合同,而是"独一无二的"(sui generis)[42]。从意识形态的角度看,这场演变表明了,因为表现形式是这些概念的基础,所以当概念的目的已经达到,或者它们的目的已经不存在的时候,表现形式也变得毫无意义了。在现实中,这场讨论的主题也是不充分的,因为仲裁的合同属性自身不能回答仲裁员的裁决权来自仲裁协议,但仲裁协议效力的渊源是什么这个根本问题。

这样的问题也同样存在于某些国际私法专家提出的如何区分国际仲裁的地域性理论和合同理论中。地域性和当事人自治之间并不总是存在清楚的分界线,它们的差别在多数时候仅仅是程度上的差

---

[40] 关于这个问题,例见,H. Motulsky, *Ecrits*, volume II, *Etudes et notes sur l'arbitrage*, Paris, Dalloz, 1974, pp. 5 *et seq* 中讨论仲裁本质的章节。

[41] 具有悖论的是,今天许多作者通过强调仲裁裁决的纯粹私法性质,来推崇一个老的观点,其关注的是在仲裁地作出的针对某仲裁的司法决定,而不是仲裁裁决本身。例见 S. Bollée, *Les méthodes du droit international privé à l'épreuve des sentences arbitrales*, op. cit. footnote 9. 就此问题的讨论,一般参见后文 § §130 *et seq*.

[42] 就此问题,例如参见 David, *Arbitration in International Trade*, Deventer, Kluwer Law and Taxation Publishers, 1985, § § 83 *et seq*. 又见 1957 年在国际法研究所阿姆斯特丹会议上的讨论。*Yearbook*, 1957, volume 47, part II, p. 394, at pp. 398—401.

别而已。例如,在一个以"地域性和自治"为题的研究中,Roy Goode 教授在这两个观点的极端之间划分了 6 个中间层次。[43] 这里,问题再一次被不确切地归结为合同识别问题,因为这个定义不能够解决许多与仲裁协议的效力的渊源有关的问题。从这个角度来说,强调合同理论实际上增强了对国际仲裁地域性的支持。"地域性"这个概念很不清晰,因为裁决执行地规定的承认外国仲裁裁决条件的法律,和仲裁进行地规范仲裁程序的法律一样带有地域偏见。因此,各种仲裁法所具有的实际存在的或是假定的地域性,以及仲裁的合同性质,都不能充分地展现一个结构分明而且完整的国际仲裁观点。

10. 本书仅仅讨论能够完整地解释国际仲裁的现象、渊源、目的和结构的三大基础性的表现形式。第一种将国际仲裁归为单个国家法律秩序的一部分。第二种认为国际仲裁根植于多个国家法律秩序。这门课的作者最赞同的是第三种表现形式,它承认国际仲裁的自治属性,并认为已经产生了一个真正的法律秩序:仲裁法律秩序。

(一) 国际仲裁归为单个国家法律秩序的一部分

11. 第一种表现形式是这样全面解释国际仲裁的:它简单地将仲裁员等同于在一个单个国家法律秩序中行使职责的国内法官,这里法律秩序指的是仲裁地的法律秩序。在这种表现形式中,仲裁地(seat)被当作仲裁管辖地(forum):仲裁裁决的法律效力完全来自仲裁地所在国的法律。因为仲裁程序是在哥伦比亚或者英国进行的,所以这个裁决被认为是"哥伦比亚的"或者"英国的",而非"国际的"。尽管这种表现形式的历史可以追溯到国际仲裁发展的早期,它仍然在当代学说中占有一席之地。

---

[43] R. Goode, The Role of the *Lex Loci Arbitri* in International Commercial Arbitration, *Arbitration International* 19 (2001).

A. 两大理由

12. 这种表现形式把国际仲裁归为仲裁地的法律秩序的一部分,并且把仲裁员看成仲裁地法律秩序的代言人。有两大理由可以支持这种表现形式,它们是:客观主义和主观主义的观点。尽管从严格的逻辑角度讲,这两大理由互相排斥,然而它们有时又共同存在于许多学者的著作中。

(1) 客观主义的观点

13. F. A. Mann 在 1967 年发表的一篇题为《调整仲裁的法律》(*Lex Facit Arbitrum*)的文章中有力地阐述了客观主义的观点。[44] 在整篇文章中,他都在谴责 Berthold Goldman 在 1963 年于海牙国际法学院关于国际仲裁的冲突法的课程中提出的仲裁的全面国际主义的观点[45]。在讨论了历史因素后,作者毫不隐讳地拒绝了以下理论:

> Goldman 教授清晰的阐述极具权威性,他说:"探寻国际仲裁属性的特有连接点毫无例外地揭示不可避免地必然存在一个自治的,而非国家的,体系。"[46]

作者也引用了持同样国际主义观点的 Charalambos Fragistas[47] 和 Philippe Fouchard[48] 的著作。这些著作的观点至今仍然处于理论

---

[44] F. A. Mann, *Lex Facit Arbitrum*, *International Arbitration. Liber Amicorum for Martin Domke* (P. Sanders ed.), The Hague, Martinus Nijhoff, 1967, p. 157, reprinted in *Arbitration International* 241 (1986).

[45] B. Goldman, Les conflits de lois dans l'arbitrage international de droit privé, *op. cit.* footnote 3.

[46] F. A. Mann, *Lex Facit Arbitrum*, *op. cit.* footnote 44, p. 158. Berthold Goldman 的原文是法语,翻译成英文是"any search for connecting factors specific to the nature of international arbitration results in the inescapable necessity of an autonomous, not national, system", author's translation.

[47] Ch. N. Fragistas, Arbitrage étranger et arbitrage international en droit privé, *Rev. crit. DIP*, 1960, p. 1.

[48] Ph. Fouchard, *L'arbitrage commercial international*, Paris, Dalloz, 1965.

前沿,它们作出的主要贡献之一是推动了反对派观点的系统化,在这之前,这些反对派观点特别是在英国的某些专业领域已经被广泛接受,但是仍旧缺乏条理性。

这种表现形式的基础是将仲裁员等同于仲裁地所在国的法院的法官。它假定仲裁庭仅仅是构成各个法律秩序的各类法院之一。例如,位于法国的仲裁庭就相当于法国的其他法院,比如高级初审法庭(*Tribunal de Grande Instance*)或者商业法庭(*Tribunal de Commerce*)。F. A. Mann 认为:

> 国家法院的法官与仲裁员之间有明显的相同之处,即他们都受到当地主权的控制。即使与国内法官不同,仲裁员在许多方面,虽然不是统一的,被当地立法者允许甚至命令去接受当事人的主张,这是因为,并且在一定的程度上是,当地主权要求的结果。
>
> 这也驳斥了某些持有仲裁和司法程序根本不同观点的学者,他们认为仲裁"从未融入国家司法的因素……也没有代表过或行使过国家主权",由此仲裁不能"等同于它的地理所在地的国家司法机关的活动"(B. Goldman,上述课程)。难道在一个国家领土上进行的每一个活动不受到这个国家的管辖吗?难道这个国家不能决定仲裁员是否和以何种方式与法官类似,并且仲裁员就像法官一样,接受它的法律管辖吗?每个国家对这个问题都有不同的回答,但是毫无疑问的是每个国家都有权利,并且确实能够行使自由裁量权作出回答。[49]

---

[49] F. A. Mann, *Lex Facit Arbitrum*, *op. cit.* footnote 44, p. 162, quoting B. Goldman, Les conflits de lois dans l'arbitrage international de droit privé, *op. cit.* footnote 3. Berthold Goldman 的文章原文是法文,英文翻译如下:" arbitration ' in no way involves the public service of justice … nor does it illustrate or exercise sovereignty'; and for these reasons it cannot be ' assimilated to the functioning of the public service of justice in the State in which it is geographically found' ", author's translation.

即使在英国,F. A. Mann 的观点也并非得到一致赞同。在修改英国仲裁法和制定1996《仲裁法》的过程中,Lord Wilberforce 指出:

F. A. Mann 甚至否认了"国际仲裁"这个概念的所有正当性,他认为:

> 这个名称用词不当。从法律角度而言国际商事仲裁并不存在。尽管它有一个臭名昭著的令人误会的名字,但是和每个国际私法体系均是国内法体系一样,每个仲裁都是国内仲裁,即每个仲裁都受到一个特定的国内法体系的调整。[50]

这个理论最突出之处在于它无条件地否认了当事人可以自由选择规范仲裁的法律:

> 同样的回答[在一个国家内发生的任何活动不可避免地受到这个国家的管辖]也适用于驳斥持以下观点的人,他们认为仲裁法(*lex arbitri*)不包括仲裁地的法律,而是当事人明示或者默示地在合同中选择的法律,例如合同自体法(proper law of the contract)。[51]

F. A. Mann 认为当事人可以自由选择法律的观点是一个"完全行不通的学说",因为它没有指明哪个规则授予当事人有权利选择他们认为最合适的法律制度规范仲裁。[52]他认为与当事人的意愿完全无关,只有仲裁地的法律制度才能够客观地提供一个让仲裁兴旺发

> 我想在一个我个人认为有些重要的问题上花点时间。这个问题是仲裁和法院之间的关系。我从来不认为仲裁程序是法院程序的一种类型,或者一种附属,要么二者关系不佳。我总是希望看到仲裁尽可能的被认为是一个独立存在的体系,仲裁毫无疑问的受到成文法的规范,但是它应当能够自由决定自己的程序和自由发展自己的实体法——是的,实体法。我总是希望看到仲裁法朝这个方向发展。但是,这不是英国法的通常主张,英国法采用了对仲裁广泛监督的态度,并且赋予法院纠正仲裁的巨大权力,但是却从未真正定位仲裁员和法院的关系。其他国家以及《联合国国际贸易法委员会国际商事仲裁示范法》采纳了不同的态度。我相信,我们的制度和其他制度的区别一直在相当程度上使得当事人不敢到我国仲裁……

Lord Steyn 在 *Lesotho Highlands*, [2006] AC 221, § 18 一案中重申了上述观点。

[50] *Ibid.*, p. 159.
[51] *Ibid.*, p. 162.
[52] *Ibid.* and footnote 27.

展的环境。[53]

（2）主观主义的观点

14. 认为国际仲裁的法律属性只能够来自仲裁地的法律秩序的观点也体现在更富有主观主义色彩的言论中。主观主义者认为通过选择某个特定的国家作为仲裁地，当事人或者，在缺乏当事人合意的情况下，仲裁机构或者仲裁员有意将仲裁交给仲裁地所在国的法律秩序独家调整。

所以，Roy Goode 教授在 2001 年发表了一篇题为"国际商事仲裁中的仲裁地法（*Lex Loci Arbitri*）的角色"的论文，在文中他极力强调，与通说不同的是，仲裁地的选择绝非偶然，更不是简单地为了便利。当当事人选定仲裁地的时候，实际上他们表达了自己接受某个国家法律秩序管辖的意愿。类似的，支持将仲裁当地化的客观主义观点的 F. A. Mann 也认为：

> 仲裁地往往是由当事人明示选择的："在伦敦仲裁"；这样的选择通常远非偶然，而是出于好的和完全可以理解的原因和目的。

并且，F. A. Mann 在没有提供进一步证据证明自己的观点的情况下，严厉地批评相反的观点为"错误的和缺乏证明的"[54]。即便当事人没有达成协议，仲裁地是由仲裁机构或者仲裁员自己选择的，它们的这种行为仍然相当于表达了当事人将仲裁交与某个法律制度调整的意愿。[55]

Jean-François Poudret 和 Sébastien Besson 在他们的《国际仲裁的

---

[53] 就提倡客观主义观点的当代法律著作，例见，有细微区别，W. W. Park, The *Lex Loci Arbitri* and International Commercial Arbitration, *International and Comparative Law Quarterly* 21 (1983), p. 22.

[54] F. A. Mann, *Lex Facit Arbitrum*, op. cit. footnote 44, p. 163 and footnote 30.

[55] R. Goode, The Role of the *Lex Loci Arbitri* in International Commercial Arbitration, *op. cit.* footnote 43, p. 32.

比较法》专著中也赞成这种国际仲裁的观点。[56] 虽然他们仔细地避免使用仲裁地法（lex loci arbitri）或者裁判地法（lex fori）的术语，他们将调整仲裁的整个法律制度——包括仲裁协议形式上的有效性、可仲裁性、仲裁庭的组建、根本的程序保证、国内法官提供的协助和对裁决的审查等——均建立在"仲裁法"（loi d'arbitrage 或者 lex arbitrii）之上，"仲裁法"本身被理解为仲裁地的法律。[57] 这里，"lex arbitrii"被定义为仲裁员的裁判地法，其相当于国内法官的裁判地法。[58] 仲裁和仲裁地的法律秩序之间的联系取决于当事人的意愿多于仲裁程序的实质行为，并且在每个仲裁和单个国家法律秩序之间建立了一个排他性的相互关系，结果是该国家法律秩序变成了仲裁法律效力的唯一渊源。这个相互关系也成为与仲裁程序、适用于实体问题的法律和裁决的效力等等有关的所有分析的明示或默示的前提。[59]

15. 我们需要承认，即使当事人作出了选择仲裁地的决定，并且所有条件保持不变，但是我们在事后所作出的对当事人选择仲裁地动机的推测是非常主观的行为。唯一可以确定的是当事人决定通过仲裁解决纠纷，所以，他们没有把同样的纠纷提交任何国家法院。但是，这样就认为当事人默示地接受了他们争议的最终解决将取决于仲裁地的法律秩序对仲裁的规定——或者，在实践中，仲裁地的法院会如何裁断——这个观点看起来至少是有问题的[60]。

---

[56] J.-F. Poudret and S. Besson, *Comparative Law of International Arbitration*, op. cit. footnote 36.

[57] *Ibid.*, §§ 112 *et seq.*, pp. 83 *et seq.*

[58] 类似的，see e.g. A. Hirsch, The Place of Arbitration and the *Lex Arbitri*, 34 *The Arbitration Journal* 43 (September 1979, no. 3)，作者公开承认"对仲裁程序而言，仲裁法（lex arbitri）等同于裁判地法（lex fori）"。值得注意的是，在仲裁著作和实践中经常提到的 lex arbitri，其字面意义是"仲裁员的法律"（the law of the arbitrator），而不是"仲裁法"（lex arbitrii，字面意义是 the law of the arbitration）。尽管作者意识到就含义而言，正确的术语应当是 lex arbitrii，但是本书将使用 lex arbitri，因为它是国际仲裁中普遍使用的术语。

[59] Regarding this reasoning, see *infra*, II.

[60] On this issue, see also *infra*, §§ 90 and 102.

16. 对本书而言,重要的是识别作为客观主义的观点或者从当事人真实或者假定的意愿中衍生出来的主观主义的观点的基础的哲学前提。

B. 哲学前提

17. 国际仲裁的第一个表现形式认为仲裁排他性地以仲裁地所在国的法律秩序为基础,它的主要依据是国家实证主义和对法律和谐的极度渴求。换句话说,国际仲裁只能扎根于一个国家,而且为了避免"混乱",这个国家必须是一个特定的国家。

(1) 国家实证主义(State Positivism)

18. 国际仲裁的第一个表现形式认为国内或国际仲裁均排他性地扎根于仲裁地的法律秩序,它的基础是深受 Kelsen 和 Hart 的思想影响的严格的国家实证主义,这是这个表现形式的第一个特点。一个权利由某规则产生,同时该规则又源自另一规则,虽然这些权利构成的体系看起来结构完美,但是它的基础却不清楚。Poudret 和 Besson 在他们的分析中并不隐瞒这一点:

> 无须涉及哲学争论,我们认为当事人意愿的效力必然来自一个法律制度。仲裁法是仲裁协议有效性的基石(*Grundnorm*)。它与国际公法一起构建了仲裁的两大潜在基础。[61]

F. A. Mann 对这个问题清楚地表示:

> 私人所享有的每个权利或者权力都是由当地法(municipal law)客观赋予的或者来源于该法的。以简便起见并根据传统可以将该法称为裁判地法,虽然更确切地说(但是较少使用)该法应当被称为仲裁法或者,在法语中称为 *la loi de l'arbitrage*(中文译仲裁法)。[62]

---

[61] J.-F. Poudret and S. Besson, *Comparative Law of International Arbitration*, op. cit. footnote 36, § 112, p. 83.

[62] F. A. Mann, *Lex Facit Arbitrum*, op. cit. footnote 44, p. 160.

19. 然而,正如被广泛接受的,国家实证主义自身不能证明国际仲裁只扎根于仲裁地的法律秩序中。但是如果将国家实证主义和国际和谐的诉求相结合,就可以得出这个结论。这种诉求指的是通过单方面努力以保证各国对待仲裁裁决的方法可以实现难以达到的国际和谐。

(2) 国际和谐的诉求

20. 假定仲裁员的权力的渊源只来自一个国家法律秩序,将仲裁地(seat of the arbitration)和法院的管辖地(forum of a national court)等同起来的学者们实质上通过论证仲裁地的法律秩序对仲裁有最完整和最有效的控制来证明他们的观点。[63] F. A. Mann 青睐这个观点,它的基础是古典国际私法方法论,其目的是选择和某案有最密切联系的法律。Mann 表示"除了仲裁地法之外的任何法律都不可成为仲裁法"[64]。由于仲裁员的国籍国和住所地国不太可能有效地调整仲裁,"明显,只有一个国家有资格制定仲裁法"[65]。这里,Mann 的观点不过是他的信仰而非令人信服的事实。

21. 这个仲裁的表现形式,虽然源自传统的法律选择方法论,将每个仲裁和一个单一的法律秩序相联系,并且只有该秩序可以调整仲裁。今天,它也体现了一个更加现代的考虑因素,即希望在国际层面上协调各国对仲裁的不同调整措施,或者用 Batiffol 的话说,希望尽可能最好地实现不同法律制度之间的"合作"。近年来,这个仲裁的表现形式得到 Sylvain Bollée 教授的热切推崇。由于该表现形式认为仲裁排他性地扎根于仲裁地的法律秩序,仲裁地法院可以对裁决进行集中控制,"这带来了一个……特别有价值的好处:调整仲裁的措施有了至关重要的可预见性"[66]。Antoine Kassis 在他的《国际

---

[63] *Ibid.*, p.161.
[64] *Ibid.*
[65] *Ibid.*
[66] S. Bollée, *op. cit.* footnote 9, at p.367, author's translation.

商事仲裁的自治性》一书中提出了同样的观点。[67] 在这本书的前言中，Lagarde 教授也强调了，如果根据承认和执行外国仲裁裁决的一般规则，仲裁地的法院作出的与某仲裁有关的决定得不到所有其他法律秩序的认可的话，国际仲裁会充满"混乱"。

22. 在现实中，调整仲裁的措施可以实现国际和谐的唯一方法是所有的国家采用同样的仲裁法，并且最重要的是，该法被每个国家的法院统一应用。尽管，国际社会为实现这种和谐进行了努力[68]，我们必须承认，现实地说，不同国家的仲裁法之间和，更显著的是，不同国家的法院对待仲裁的心态之间，有很大的差别。正是由于这种差别的存在，决定哪个法律适用于仲裁才显得格外重要。从这个方面来说，人们无法赞同那些倾向于将仲裁法律适用问题的重要性最小化的学者。这些学者认为，由于国内立法的现代化，没有必要为避免仲裁受到落后的国内法或敌视仲裁的国家法院的限制而强调仲裁的国际性。[69] 如果借用美国国际私法术语的话，这相当于认为在这个问题上仅仅存在"假冲突"。实践证明，现实中，在国际仲裁中存在一个双重矛盾的趋势：一方面是立法的现代化，另一方面是违反主流（idiosyncrasies）的司法特例剧增。近来法院广泛地采用禁诉令以保护当地企业的现象足以驳斥认为没有必要将仲裁从仲裁地的法律秩序中解放出来的观点。[70] 在各国立法不同和国家法院适用这些立法的方法也存在差异的情况下，唯一有价值的问题是是否仅仅因为仲裁恰巧正在或者已经在某国境内进行，该国的法律，无论有多么保守和当地法院如何适用该法，都有权规

---

[67] A. Kassis, *L'autonomie de l'arbitrage commercial international. Le droit français en question*, Paris, L'Harmattan, 2005.

[68] 就仲裁协议，特别参照 1958 年《纽约公约》第 2 条和《联合国国际贸易法委员会国际商事仲裁示范法》。

[69] See R. Goode, *op. cit.* footnote 43, p. 38.

[70] 就此问题参见，see *infra*, §§ 72 et seq. 这并不意味着立法有时候不会表达出对仲裁的敌视态度。例子之一是，玻利维亚关于废除 1997 年 3 月 10 日第 1770 号仲裁和调解法的 2007 年法律草案（Bolivia's preliminary draft law of 2007 on the abrogation of Law No. 1770 of March 10, 1997 on arbitration and conciliation）把仲裁从被接受的争议解决方式中删除，并且对于待决争议，该法认为如果当事人没有更新仲裁协议的话，旧的仲裁协议无效。

范仲裁。这样做,就秩序而言,好处是实实在在的。但就正义而言,根本没有好处。读者们只需要简单地想一想在数不清的案件中仲裁地的法院经常采纳违反主流的理论以帮助仲裁中的一方,该方常是该国国民。[71] 这个问题会在下文中讨论。[72] 这里,认识到将仲裁员裁决权的渊源集中化的设想属于愿为秩序牺牲正义的哲学传统就足够了[73]。

(二)国际仲裁根植于多个国家法律秩序

23. 国际仲裁的第二种表现形式认为裁决的法律属性的渊源不是一个单一的法律秩序——仲裁地的法律秩序——相反,是愿意在某种条件下承认裁决有效性的所有法律秩序。与单独地区(monolocal)的表现形式不同,在这个多地区的(multilocal)表现形式中,仲裁地法,虽然没有被完全忽视,但是仅仅是调整仲裁的许多法律秩序中的一员。它不再是仲裁员裁决权力的唯一渊源。所有可能与某仲裁有关联的法律在决定裁决有效性方面具有同等的重要性。执行裁决的国家或国家们的法律实际上与仲裁进行地所在国的法律有同样的资格规范仲裁。[74] 正是这种表现形式,让我们不难认同"仲裁员没有仲裁管辖地",或者说,全世界,而不是包括仲裁地在内的某个确定的国家,是仲裁员的仲裁管辖地。所以,裁决不再被特别称为"哥伦比亚的"或者"英国的"。裁决的"国际"属性胜过了认为裁决完全扎根于仲裁地的法律的观点,后者实际上拟人化地赋予裁决一个国籍。换句话说,多地区的表现形式强调仲裁的非集中性,然而认为仲裁地是裁决效力的唯一渊源的表现形式强调仲裁的集中性。

---

[71] See examples *infra*, II, § § 73 *et seq.* and § § 77 *et seq.*

[72] See *infra*, § 75.

[73] 这种以实证主义为特点的传统并非完全不存在于自然法流派的思想中。就人们为了避免丑闻或者混乱以至于可能容忍不公平规则的适用(*propter vitandum scandalum vel turbationem*), see Thomas Aquinas, *Summa Theologica*, 1.2, 9.96, al.

[74] On this issue, see E. Gaillard, L'interférence des juridictions du siège dans le déroulement de l'arbitrage, *Liber Amicorum Claude Reymond. Autour de l'arbitrage*, Paris, Litec, 2004, p.83. See also *infra*, § 36.

24. 从方法论的角度看,这两种表现形式是相对的,因为它们从两个不同的角度解释同一个现象:一个从这个现象的起点入手,另一个强调它的结果。第一种表现形式按照时间的先后顺序分析仲裁程序,认为仲裁员能够完成裁断纠纷的使命的前提是他们事先得到仲裁地法的授权。第二种表现形式通过仲裁的最终结果,即对双方当事人都有约束力的裁决,来分析仲裁过程。承认裁决相当于溯及既往地追认整个仲裁过程的有效性。这个可以被誉为哥白尼革命的逆向思考成为整个推理的基石。[75]

25. 在批判性分析之前,先来简单看看第二种表现形式的哲学前提。

A. 哲学前提

26. 认为仲裁过程扎根于多个国家法律秩序的表现形式和上文讨论的第一种表现形式一样基于严格的国家实证主义。唯一的区别是,前者认为国家之间的关系是一个威斯特伐利亚(Westphalian,又译为"多地区")的主权模式。

(1) 国家实证主义

27. 与它有时受到的讽刺不同,仲裁的法律属性扎根于多个国家法律秩序的表现形式并不赞同当事人的意志是仲裁协议、仲裁程序各个阶段和最终裁决的约束力的唯一渊源。它不认为裁决是"漂浮(floating)在跨国的天空中,与任何国内法体系都没有联系"[76]。相反,它认为实际上是国家法律秩序认可了仲裁这个私人的争端解

---

[75] 关于哥白尼革命, see E. Gaillard, Souveraineté et autonomie: réflexions sur les représentations de l'arbitrage international, *op. cit.* footnote 39, at p. 1173. See also L'interférence des juridictions du siège dans le déroulement de l'arbitrage, *op. cit.* footnote 74, p. 89.

[76] 在 *Bank Mellat v. Helliniki Techniki SA* 一案中,Kerr LJ 指出:"尽管一些外国知名学者持相反态度,我国的案例法不承认仲裁程序是漂浮在跨国的天空中并与任何国内法体系都没有联系。"[1984] 1 *QB* 291, at p. 301.

决方法的正当性,并且决定了要符合什么条件作为仲裁过程的最终结果的裁决才是有效的。因此,它完全符合严格的实证主义法学。

28. 一位支持仲裁的集中化观点的学者曾经作出如下不适当的批评:

> 即使最热切的支持当事人自治观点的人也认为仲裁必须在某个法律制度中进行。他们认为唯一有关的法律制度是裁决执行地的制度。但是这个观点站不住脚,因为它预先假设**在申请把裁决当作外国裁决执行之前,仲裁是在法律真空中进行的**。如果真是这样,在作出仲裁裁决之时,裁决没有任何法律基础。毫无疑问,裁决来自当事人同意接受约束的仲裁协议,但是就如先前所论述的,当事人的合意不过是一纸协议,没有任何法律效力,除非相关的国内法认为它有约束力;唯一有可能的国内法是仲裁地法。[77]

即使假设,如实证主义法学要求的那样,有能力通过国家方式来制裁某行为或者执行某规范是决定某程序的法律属性的标准;在违法行为发生后才进行制裁并不否定制裁的存在。根据定义,进行制裁的能力是实证主义的法律设想中固有的,这种能力实施与否,取决于调整的对象是否自动履行他或她的义务。可能不采取制裁的事实并不意味着法律规则不存在。如果在裁决没有被最终认可之前就否认仲裁过程的法律性质,这就像债务人在他或者她的财产被收缴之前清偿了债务,就否认债务的法律性质一样缺乏说服力。

29. 这就是为什么 Pierre Mayer 教授等学者认为无法在理论上反驳根据仲裁程序的结果来评价裁决的法律属性的方法。[78] 但是,

---

[77] R. Goode, The Role of the *Lex Loci Arbitri* in International Commercial Arbitration, *op. cit.* footnote 43, pp. 29—30, emphasis added.

[78] P. Mayer, The Trend Towards Delocalisation in the Last 100 Years, *The Internationalisation of International Arbitration. The LCIA Centenary Conference*, London, Graham & Trotman, 1995, p. 37.

他对该方法是否适宜存在疑问,他认为在实践中更为可取的是将仲裁地当做仲裁管辖地,集中用仲裁地的法律来规范仲裁。[79]

(2) 威斯特伐利亚模式:国家之间互不干涉

30. 仲裁的多地区表现形式的基础是一个令人信服的观点,即无论其他国家的决定如何,每个国家都可以就裁决作出自己的决定,这种表现形式意味着需要追溯既往地评价裁决所依据的仲裁协议的有效性以及仲裁程序的规范性。

31. 1986年在特拉维夫市大学的一次演讲中,Arthur Taylor von Mehren 在讨论了根据当事人的意愿,仲裁程序可以在单个或多个国家进行后,指出:

> 当代仲裁程序是漂移(ambulatory)的,这是因为它们不需要在地理上定位。在实践中,仲裁的进行不需要得到仲裁地所在国的政治团体的事先授权。进一步而言,尽管国家法院在各方面能够协助仲裁,但是仲裁常常可以在没有法院协助的情况下顺利开展。当被要求承认和执行裁决之时,奥斯汀主权国家(Austinian sovereign)可以要求必须满足什么条件后才承认和执行裁决。**但是,没有一个主权国家享有排他性地对待一个裁决的权利,单个或多个主权国家拒绝承认或者执行裁决的事实不会剥夺该裁决的正当性或使得该裁决丧失价值。**
>
> 在司法程序中,主权是集中的;**但是在国际商事仲裁中,主权是分散的**。结果,与法官截然不同的是,仲裁员没有裁判地法。[80]

---

[79] On this line of reasoning, see *supra*, § 21.

[80] A. T. von Mehren, Limitations of Party Choice of the Governing Law: Do They Exist for International Commercial Arbitration? *The Mortimer and Raymond Sackler Institute of Advanced Studies*, Tel Aviv University, 1986, pp. 19—20, emphasis added. "奥斯汀主权国家"暗指奥斯汀理论,其本质上将法律看做命令,并且认为这种命令只能由国家发出。就这个观点,参见, e.g G. Fassò, *Storia della filosofia del diritto. Ottocento e Novecento*, *op. cit.* at footnote 14.

换句话说，将仲裁和国家法院进行类比已经过时了，所以由单个法律秩序集中调整国际仲裁并不是唯一可能的模式。因为，每个国家可以平等自主地决定如何对待本质上具有私密性、载有国际仲裁裁决的文件。

32. 这个模式被称为威斯特伐利亚模式，它类似于1648年《威斯特伐利亚和约》(*1648 Peace of Westphalia*)签订之后建立的国际社会所采纳的以国家主权的并列为基础的国际秩序。[81] 对许多人而言，当代国际法就是以这个模式为基础建立起来的。根据这个模式，国家——而不是任何超国家的秩序——是主权的唯一渊源，国际组织本身的正当性来自它们作为主权国家意志的产物的事实。当然，这个模式不排除国家之间的合作。

33. 在仲裁法中，1958年6月10日签订的《承认和执行外国仲裁裁决的公约》(即《纽约公约》)反映了国际仲裁的威斯特伐利亚模式。虽然它没有如国际商会(International Chamber of Commerce, ICC)在1953年的公约初稿中所希望的那样，用更加现代的"国际裁决"的概念来取代在1927年9月26日制定的《日内瓦公约》中使用的"外国裁决"的概念，《纽约公约》明确了每个缔约国必须在其领土上承认和执行在其他国家境内作出的仲裁裁决的条件。[82] 与1927年的《日内瓦公约》相比，《纽约公约》大大地减弱了仲裁地的重要性。虽然《纽约公约》允许仲裁地自由规范在其领土上进行的仲裁活动，但是公约将注意的焦点引向仲裁执行地的法律秩序制定的承认裁决的条件。就像ICC建议的那样，在仲裁庭的组成或者仲裁程序的进行方面，仲裁地的法律变得次要了，并且可以被当事人的协议所

---

[81] 就和所谓的"联合国宪章"模式相对的，"威斯特伐利亚"模式的理论，参见 A. Cassese, *International Law and Politics in a Divided World*, Oxford, Oxford University Press, 1986, §§ 225 *et seq.*

[82] Enforcement of International Arbitral Awards: Report and Preliminary Draft Convention adopted by the Committee on International Commercial Arbitration at its meeting of March 13, 1953, Brochure No. 174 of the International Chamber of Commerce, published in *ICC Bull.*, May 1998, p. 32.

取代(第 5 条第 1 款 d 项)。当涉及这些重要问题,只要当事人的意愿得到尊重,仲裁地之外的其他国家不再审查仲裁是否符合仲裁地的法律。同样的逻辑也适用于仲裁协议:当事人意思自治优先于仲裁地的法律(第 5 条第 1 款 a 项)。并且,执行地的法律决定争议的可仲裁性和裁决是否符合公共政策(第 5 条第 2 款)。公约本身还规定了和执行国审查裁决有关的其他所有实质条款。因此,公约明显不认为仲裁地的法律秩序是仲裁裁决的法律效力的唯一渊源。如果仲裁地的法律秩序真是仲裁裁决的法律效力的唯一渊源的话,当根据当事人的愿望,仲裁员违反仲裁地关于仲裁协议、仲裁庭的组成和仲裁程序的规定作出裁决,该裁决就不应当在其他所有的缔约国内得到公约的保护。

从方法论的角度看,《纽约公约》的意义在于它鼓励裁决执行地的法官将注意力集中在裁决本身,而非仲裁地的法院对该裁决的看法。这与 1927 年 9 月 26 日达成的《日内瓦公约》截然不同。在 1927 年建立的体系中,承认和执行仲裁裁决取决于如下条件:

> 裁决在裁决作出地国已经是终局的了。也就是说,如果裁决仍然可以被抗诉或者起诉(opposition, appel or pourvio en cassation)(在有这些程序的国家中)或者任何对仲裁裁决效力提出异议的程序还悬而未决的时候,裁决就不是终局的(第 1 条 d 款)。

所以,1927 年公约所采纳的裁决的法律效力来自当地主权授权当事人进行仲裁的观点已经过时了。这个观点,符合本书讨论的仲裁的第一种表现形式,但是它已经被 1958 年的《纽约公约》摒弃。即便出于妥协,《纽约公约》不保护被仲裁地撤销的裁决(第 5 条第 1 款 e 项),但是公约完全中立的立场反映在它允许执行国根据本国法自由决定是否承认这种裁决(第 7 条)。重要的是,公约已经清楚地摒弃了仲裁的法律效力只来自仲裁地的法律秩序的陈旧观点。

34. 在威斯特伐利亚模式中,每个国家至少在《纽约公约》等国际条约允许的范围内保留审查仲裁裁决的权利,同时每个国家不把自己对于仲裁的观点强加于他国,这是因为每个国家都享有平等的主权。与此相反的例子是仲裁地或者其他国家的国家法院使用禁诉令,试图将它们对仲裁协议有效性的看法或者仲裁员没有资格进行仲裁的观点,强加于其他国家。禁诉令的例子反衬出威斯特伐利亚模式的合理性,因为在这个模式中每个国家作出的决定只局限在它自己的法律秩序内。[83] 和在许多其他领域中一样,在仲裁领域中,国家之间互不干涉值得提倡。

B. 批 判 分 析

35. 国际仲裁的第二种表现形式与第一种不同,因为它认为仲裁的法律属性来源于一个或者多个执行地的法律。表现形式的定义要求我们只能够根据其内在的一致性或者效率,而不是对或者错,来评价它。[84] 所以应当用一致性和效率来评价国际仲裁的第二种表现形式,并且在分析中我们还要避免机械理解的风险。

(1) 比较仲裁地和单个或者多个裁决执行地决定仲裁法律属性的相应资格

36. 如果用单纯的国际私法术语来评判各个法律解决某个案件的相应资格,人们可能发现裁决执行地所在国比仲裁地所在国的法律更有资格来决定什么样的仲裁值得法律保护。对这个结论进一步研究发现,其认为裁决执行地所在国和仲裁地所在国的法律是不同的。仲裁地所在国有时可能是裁决执行地所在国或裁决执行地所在国之一的事实,并不意味着我们不能在二者不同的情况中比较它们决定仲裁法律属性的资格。

---

[83] 对于用禁诉令以阻碍仲裁和——同样是治外法权的——对抗禁诉令的措施,参见 *IAI Series on International Arbitration No. 2. Anti-Suit Injunctions in International Arbitration* (E. Gaillard ed.), Huntington, Juris Publishing, 2005, and *infra*, §§ 72 *et seq.*

[84] See *supra*, § 6.

考虑到这一点,我们的分析有了清楚的答案。一个国家仅仅为仲裁程序提供了位于其境内的酒店或者会议中心,一个国家需要授权收缴或者强制出售位于其境内的财产,后者明显地更有资格来决定什么样的仲裁裁决值得法律保护,并且追溯既往地认定什么是有效的仲裁协议和正当的仲裁程序。[85] 由于,执行地所在国有这样强的资格,所以用仲裁地对裁决的审查来代替执行地的审查是既无法想象又不理想的(de lege ferenda)。仲裁裁决的执行地可能需要使用国家强制力才能实现裁决,因此除非是在一个联邦中,否则非常难想象裁决执行地愿意在执行裁决之前放弃除了国际公共秩序要求之外的其他审查裁决的标准。若一个执行地所在国在任何情况下都可以拒绝执行不符合它的国际公共秩序要求的裁决,同时又如某些学者坚持的那样,裁决的法律属性只来自仲裁地的法律秩序,结果会不可避免地导致裁决需要同时满足仲裁地和仲裁执行地的要求。从技术上来说,即使这种双重审查不产生《纽约公约》的起草者所要避免的双重执行许可证(exequatur)制度,二者也明显地相去不远。与每个国家在国际条约许可的范围内独立地审查国际仲裁裁决的可执行性相比,这种双重审查,无论如何冠名,都毫无疑问是一大退步。在当今世界,国际仲裁日益被作为一种常用的解决国际纠纷的途径,这种对仲裁的法律属性的双重要求至少是落伍和不合时宜的。

(2) 避免执行法主义(Lex Executionism)

37. 国际仲裁的法律属性可以来自所有愿意在一定的条件下承认裁决效力的法律秩序,这个事实并不意味着仲裁员必须服从所有这些法律秩序的总和。机械地看待裁决执行国所扮演的角色是对仲裁的第二种表现形式的错误理解,还可能会大大损害国际仲裁。

---

[85] See E. Gaillard, L'exécution des sentences annulées dans leur pays d'origine, *JDI*, 1998, p.645.

38. 仲裁地所在国或者有可能执行仲裁的一个或所有国家的法律对仲裁员的职责有何影响呢？该问题的重要性体现在某些仲裁规则鼓励仲裁员竭尽所能作出"法律上可以执行的"裁决的事实上。[86] 裁决需要是"法律上可以执行的"，这对所有关心裁决效力的仲裁员而言是个默示的责任，但是有时候它却被理解为正式地要求仲裁员保证仲裁符合所有与争议可能有关的国内法。ICC1990年第6697号裁决涉及这个问题。[87] 在讨论了《ICC仲裁规则》(*ICC Rules of Arbitration*)第26条（现第35条）后，仲裁庭指出：

> 在一些案件中，裁决执行地的法律可能在以下情况中影响仲裁员的管辖权。比如，执行地的法律要求仲裁员具有特定的国籍或者宗教信仰；或者在仲裁进行之前，仲裁协议得到当地相关权力机关的批准；或者执行地的法律认为争议标的是不可以仲裁的。若裁决执行地的公共政策禁止将某争议提交仲裁，该事实表明仲裁员不能裁决在性质上属于法院专属管辖的争议。这一点特别体现在涉及腐败和竞争法的案件中，也可能出现在破产案件中。[88]

仲裁庭认为，就本案而言，仲裁裁决的执行国的法律对仲裁员的管辖权没有进行上述限制。但是裁决执行地的法律明显是一个重要的考虑因素。

39. 如果认为每个可能会执行仲裁裁决的法律秩序都可以平等地规范仲裁协议的有效性和随后进行的仲裁，所以每个法律秩序，

---

[86] 参见《ICC仲裁规则》第35条规定："对于该规则没有明示规定的问题，国际商会仲裁院和仲裁庭必须……采取所有方法保证仲裁裁决在法律上是可以执行的。"又见《伦敦国际仲裁院(London Court of International Arbitration, LCIA)仲裁规则》的第32条第2款规定："伦敦国际仲裁院、仲裁庭和当事人……必须采用所有合理的方法保证仲裁裁决在法律上是可以执行的。"

[87] ICC Award No. 6697 of December 26, 1990, *Casa v. Cambior*, *Rev. arb.*, 1992, p. 135, note by P. Ancel.

[88] *Ibid.*, p. 141, author's translation.

就个体而言,都有资格将自己对有效性的看法强加给其他所有法律秩序。这个观点会引起误解,即通过富有悖论的执行法主义,仲裁的有效性建立在所有有关国家的国内法之间的最小公分母之上。[89] 这个观点就像认为仅仅因为仲裁碰巧在某地进行,该地的法律就能对仲裁的有效性产生绝对的国际影响一样不可接受。这个观点通常也不被仲裁庭所接受。[90] 所有可能承认裁决的国家都有资格决定裁决是否有效,并不意味着与某仲裁有各种联系的所有国家的法律都应当被累加在一起适用。累加适用意味着适用最严格的法律,这对仲裁无益。**所有**可能和仲裁有联系的国家的法律秩序都有被适用的资格并不意味着**每个**法律秩序,就个体而言,可以超越其他所有法律秩序。在仲裁的威斯特伐利亚表现形式中,每个国家只能在自己的法律秩序内决定什么样的仲裁值得法律保护。

(三)国际仲裁是自治的法律秩序:仲裁法律秩序

40. 国际仲裁的第三种表现形式认为仲裁的法律效力应当基于一个独特的跨国法律秩序。它可以称为仲裁法律秩序,并不同于仲裁地和单个或多个裁决执行地的国家法律秩序。这种表现形式符合国际仲裁员根深蒂固的观点:他们不代表任何国家主持正义,但是他们仍然为了国际社会的利益发挥司法作用。考虑到国际仲裁被日益广泛地当作解决国际纠纷的常用途径,仲裁员的司法角色的正当性不容置疑。因为仲裁被广泛接受是来自国家之间的共识而不是任何主权国家对这种私人的争端解决方式的偏爱。

41. 和前面讨论的国际仲裁的表现形式相比,这种表现形式实质上体现了仲裁员的视角。认为仲裁的法律属性来自愿意在某个条

---

 [89] 对将这个观点适用于强行性规则(*lois de police*)的情况,例见,*e. g.*,*infra*,§111.

 [90] 就此问题,参见后文§73对仲裁协议的讨论和,后文§117对争议实体法的讨论。

件下承认裁决的效力的所有法律秩序的观点是陈旧落伍的。这种观点认为仲裁地,理解为仲裁管辖地,是仲裁法律属性的唯一渊源;它的最现代的版本以当事人明示或者默示的意愿为基础。[91] 可是仲裁地和仲裁的联系是如此不紧密,以至于它不适合成为国际仲裁的唯一基础。单个或多个执行地国的法律秩序有同样正当的原因来决定什么样的仲裁值得法律保护。[92] 在一个国际交易日益普遍的世界中,当事人可能会在许多国家中要求承认和执行仲裁裁决,所以认为某个法律制度,因为它是仲裁地,就可以决定国际仲裁法律约束力的观点日益落伍。即使通过以当事人主观意志为基础的法律虚拟,仲裁员也不等同于仲裁地的国内法官。[93] 意识到这一点必然会认为仲裁的法律属性扎根于多个国家。从国家的角度而言,这个观点是不证自明的。若当事人不顾仲裁协议而将争议提交法院,或者当法院被要求采取某种措施协助仲裁,或者由于当事人请求法院执行裁决,这时每个国家确实能够自由地根据本国法作出决定。然而,从仲裁员的角度出发,这个观点是不充分的,因为威斯特伐利亚模式是不稳定的。如果多个法律秩序对某个仲裁的观点不同——一个认为仲裁协议有效,另一个认为无效,或者,一个认为仲裁员们不公正,然而另一个认为程序正当——仲裁员不能简单地局限于这些观点。相反,他们必须作出自己的决定。他们可以根据冲突法在诸多不同的观点中进行选择,冲突法途径的缺点是将本质上国际的问题降格为国内问题。仲裁员也可以直接适用实体法,这个方法更有可能考虑到案件的国际性和法律秩序的多重性,并且这些法律秩序认为什么样的仲裁值得法律保护。当仲裁员面临多种观点时,他们总是致力于找到在某个时候被国际社会广泛接受的规则,并且认为这些规则的适用需要优先于某个国家的个体观点。在实践中,这种情况引发仲裁员裁决权力的跨国渊源和仲裁法律秩序存在的问题。这里,"跨

---

[91]　See *supra*, § 14.
[92]　See *supra*, § 36.
[93]　See *supra*, § 15.

国"(transnational)比"非国内的"(a-national)更恰当,因为后者并不表示这种规则根植于国内法。

所以,国际仲裁的表现形式全部展示出来了。它从以仲裁地为中心的单一地区主义的模式,发展为多地区主义(或者,威斯特伐利亚)的模式,再进一步演化为跨国的表现形式,这种表现形式不再考虑每个国家的个体,它关注的是从国家群体的规范活动中产生的趋势。多地区主义和跨国主义的主要区别是前者考虑到多个国家(plurality),而后者侧重于多个国家的集体(collectivity)。

42. 提出存在仲裁法律秩序的问题不等于重演20世纪80年代或者90年代对商人习惯法的辩论[94],尽管与此主题有关的著作,特别是那些尝试建立一个"商人习惯法法律秩序"的著作[95],有助于激发对法律秩序的思考。对商人习惯法的分歧主要集中体现在选择争议的实体法和仲裁程序法两方面。问题包括仲裁员是否可以通过仲裁地的法律选择方法之外的方法来决定准据法;是否可以适用非某个特定国家的规则来解决争议的实体问题;和是否可以背离仲裁地所在国规定的程序法。讨论这些问题非常有益,因为它推动现代仲裁法来解决仲裁国际化发展过程中可能遇到的障碍。这就是为什么现代仲裁法,在不同程度上,允许仲裁员不适用仲裁地的法律选择规则,这里的仲裁地被理解为仲裁管辖地,而适用"法律的规则"(rules of law)而非"法律"(a law)来解决争议的实体问题——法律的规则包括那些并非来自单个国家法律秩序的规则——并且现代仲裁法还认可仲裁员可以在符合当事人平等和程序正当等基本原则的条件下自由设定仲裁程序。但是若仅仅关注这些因素,我们会忽视仲裁员裁决权力的渊源这个基本问题,遗憾的是只有将仲裁地等同于

---

[94] See references *supra*, footnote 10.

[95] See esp. F. Osman, *Les principes généraux de la* lex mercatoria. *Contribution à l'étude d'un ordre juridique anational*, 1992, *op. cit.* footnote 10, and, E. Loquin, L'application de règles anationales dans l'arbitrage commercial international, *L'apport de la jurisprudence arbitrale*, ICC Publication No. 440/1, 1986, p.67, at p.119 *et seq.*,作者讨论"非国内规则"(a-national rules)和"非国家法律秩序的概念"(concept of an a-national legal order)。

仲裁管辖地的支持者们才详细讨论过这个基本问题。[96] 当事人自治或者仲裁的合同属性的观点不能解决渊源这个仲裁最基本的问题。如前述[97]，这些观点不过偷换了问题，因为它们没有解决一个更加基本的问题：当事人意思自治原则的基础是什么。对存在仲裁法律秩序的研究可以解决这些问题。

43. "仲裁法律秩序"的表述首先零星出现于 20 世纪 90 年代法国仲裁学术文献中。早在 1986 年，Loquin 教授讨论如何建立一个理论模式以承认法律秩序可以独立于国家而存在，并且仲裁员可以据其解决纠纷的时候，他使用了"非国家法律秩序"(a-national legal order)来指代这个理论模式。[98] 随后，Daniel Cohen 教授在他 1993 年出版的《仲裁和社会》一书中首次使用了"仲裁法律秩序"(arbitral legal order)的概念。[99] 那时，"法律秩序"仅仅表示"内在连贯的规则的总和"，以区别于 Santi Romano 的制度主义(institutionalist)理论所定义的"法律秩序"。再后来，Thomas Clay 教授在他的以《仲裁员》为题的博士论文中花了整整一章专门讨论"仲裁法律秩序"[100]，他强调仲裁的自治性和跨国性。最后，Jean-Baptiste Racine 教授在一篇关于国际仲裁的自治性的文章中[101]，尝试将仲裁法律秩序的概念系统化，他比较了此概念与 Santi Romano，François Ost 和 Michel van de Kerchove 提出的各种法律秩序的设想，以及规范法学派(normativist)和凯尔森式的(Kelsenian)法律制度的设想。[102] 在现实中，"仲裁法

---

[96] See *e. g.*, the authors quoted above, *supra*, § 18, footnotes 61 and 62, and § 28, footnote 77.

[97] See *supra*, § 9 and footnote 43.

[98] E. Loquin, L'application de règles anationales dans l'arbitrage commercial international, *op. cit.* footnote 95.

[99] D. Cohen, *Arbitrage et société*, Paris, LGDJ, 1993, at p. 21.

[100] Th. Clay, *L'arbitre*, Paris, Dalloz, 2001, at pp. 211—228. See also the critique by C. Reymond in *Rev. arb.*, 2001, p. 967.

[101] J.-B. Racine, Réflexions sur l'autonomie de l'arbitrage commercial international, *op. cit.* footnote 26, at p. 335 *et seq*.

[102] 对选择哲学模式的讨论，参见后文, see *supra*, § 5.

律秩序"的概念指的是一个能够独立的解释国际仲裁的法律属性的渊源的系统。如果缺乏一个拥有自己渊源的系统创造出的连贯性，法律秩序就不存在。如果不具有独立于各个国家法律秩序的自治性，仲裁法律秩序也不存在。

44．和前面论述的表现形式一样，我们将首先讨论这种表现形式的哲学前提。然后我们讨论，仲裁案例法和国内法律制度是如何认可存在一个真正的仲裁法律秩序的。

A. 哲学前提

45．如果人们接受自然法的观点，便不难理解仲裁法律秩序的概念。然而，无需成为一个自然法学家，人们就可以将国际法看成一个自治的法律秩序，同样，无需成为自然法学家，人们也可以接受仲裁法律秩序的观点。

（1）自然法学（jusnaturalist）派

46．如果人们愿意从自然法的角度看问题，就非常容易接受仲裁法律秩序的存在。来自事物或者社会本质的更高的价值，有时证明并强化了实证主义的解决方式，其他时候审查这些解决方式从而改善它们，这些价值很容易被当做存在一个法律秩序的证明，其高于主权国家建立的法律制度。

47．精确地分析自然法与国际仲裁有关的思想流派有两大困难。

第一，与自然法有关的哲学传统中有数不清的流派，其中存在不可计数的细微差别。有些流派保守，有些进步。有些崇尚永恒的价值，但是有些已经接受自然法可以随着社会的变化而变化。自然法有的推崇个人主义，有的强调社会价值。它有时候基于宗教价值，有时候却以俗世价值为基础。自然法学种种不同观点的唯一共性是都接受更高的价值在人或者社会固有本质中的存在，无论这些价值是否随后在技术上融入一个实证的法律制度。[103]

第二,在一个以技术方法(technical approach)探究法律占主导地位的世界中,自然法学的思想,虽有不同的形式,但是鲜有耳闻。Bruno Oppetit 表示"蓬勃日上的实证主义"看起来"在很早以前已经宣告了自然法的终结",但是

> 即使自然法的名称很少被提到……非常令人惊讶的是自然法十分频繁的成为律师所关切的现实问题。[104]

自然法的影响在本质上即便不是无从觉察,也是潜在和隐含的[105],这导致分析特别艰难。

48. 在所有仲裁法专家中,只有 René David 和 Bruno Oppetit 公开接受自然法学的方法。[106]

René David 认为在友好仲裁和在严格适用法律裁决之间进行区分是虚伪的,因为在任何情况下,仲裁员都应当在公平的基础上进行裁决。根据 David 的观点,仲裁员创造的"新商法"和自然法紧密相连:

> 新商法因企业专家组成的仲裁庭的推导而深受自然法的影

---

[103] 就自然法的各种表述, see, e. g. , G. Gurvitch, *L'expérience juridique et la philosophie pluraliste du droit*, op. cit. footnote 7, pp. 103 et seq.; Ch. Atias, *Philosophie du droit*, op. cit. footnote 35, pp. 183 et seq. ,其相信自然法是多样的而非零散的。

[104] B. Oppetit, *Philosophie du droit*, Paris, Dalloz, 1999, § 94, author's translation; compare with A. Sériaux, *Le droit naturel*, Paris, Coll. Que sais-je?, PUF, 2nd ed., 1993, p. 119,他认为"实证主义是占主导地位的哲学"和"[看起来]唯一仍然正式的发展自然法学思想的机构是天主教会"。

[105] 公平是保持谨慎而不是高调自夸的结果,后者与商人习惯法相联系,就此观点参见 P. Mayer, L'Arbitre et la loi, *Etudes offertes à Pierre Catala. Le droit privé français à la fin du XXe siècle*, 2001, Paris, Litec, p. 225, at p. 237:"公平……应该尽可能地保持谨慎,从这个角度而言,求助于商人习惯法是有害无益的", author's translation.

[106] 又见,有细微的差别, H. Motulsky, *Ecrits*, volume II, *Etudes et notes sur l'arbitrage*, op. cit. footnote 40, p. 14:"仲裁机构的持久存在和不断发展证明,私人主导的司法模式是有必要的观点已经得到社会的认可。所以,人们更倾向于探讨自然法", author's translation.

响。不论是否被国家法典化,新商法在本质上就像自然法和古代商法一样是国际性的。所以,它与国家实体法相离并与之区别。并且,与许多国家的实体法不同的是,它的特点是仲裁员愿意考虑当事人的商业利益,即使这意味着牺牲他们严格的权利。和客户或者供应商保持良好关系和在某个纠纷中当事人可以追回欠款同等重要。[107]

上述观点的全部基础是:当事人选择仲裁是因为他们希望能够以与法院诉讼不同的方式解决纠纷[108]。这在20世纪中叶仍然是一些律师所接受的主流观点[109]。Clay教授将之作为假设,在探讨仲裁法律秩序是否是自然法的新表述的时候,对其进行了详尽的阐述。[110]

Bruno Oppetit 在"援用自然法"(The Invocation of Natural Law)一章中表达了类似的观点,他认为国际商法

> 基于国际商界共同的需要和利益,有清楚的往统一化和普遍化方向发展的趋势。因此,国际商法不赞成分裂国际法律架构,相反它鼓励使用统一的法律概念,例如商人习惯法、法律的一般原则、或者真正的国际公共政策。[111]

49. 其他有影响力的学者,虽然没有明示地提到自然法,但是探讨了道德价值(moral values)在国际仲裁中的作用。Pierre Mayer

---

[107] R. David, Droit naturel et arbitrage, *Natural Law and World Law*: *Essays to Commemorate the Sixtieth Birthday of Kotaro Tanaka*, Tokyo, Yuhikaku, 1954, p. 19, at p. 24, author's translation。

[108] R. David, *L'arbitrage dans le commerce international*, op. cit. footnote 42, p. 80.

[109] 当仲裁逐渐朝着法院的方向发展的时候,把仲裁概括为解决国际商事争端的常用途径的观点已经逐渐没有说服力了。这就是为什么,当当事人寻找比国内法院和仲裁院更加灵活的争端解决方式的时候,他们日益倾向于使用和解、调停或者"简易审判"(mini-trials)等"选择性争端解决方式"。只有根据过时的概念把所有以非国家的争端解决途径都定义为选择性的时候,仲裁,这个解决国际商事争端的常用途径,才能算作"选择性"的。

[110] Th. Clay, *L'arbitre*, op. cit. footnote 100, p. 222 *et seq.*, author's translation.

[111] B. Oppetit, Philosophie du droit, op. cit. footnote 104, p. 119, author's translation.

教授在一篇引起广泛关注的文章中,先探讨了国家立法也考虑道德价值——这样做在理论上没有任何不妥——然后他提到,即使当事人没有授权仲裁员担任友好调停人(amiable compositeurs),在仲裁案件中仲裁员仍然可以直接应用道德规范[112]。他从以下观点开始叙述:

> 非常重要的是仲裁员能够排除"不道德的法律,例如基于种族或者宗教歧视的法律",并用其他规则取而代之,从而裁决不会违反他们遵循的道德价值。[113]

然后,假定准据法不能因为商人习惯法而被忽略,原因是当事人自治(party autonomy)是商人习惯法的基本要求之一,接着他强调:

> 如果不是法律秩序中包含的公共政策规则,就是[被当事人]所选择的法律所忽视的**具有内在优越性的原则**,可以排除适用当事人选择的法律。在仲裁员可以依赖的法律秩序之间不存在位阶高下的情况下,他们除了进行价值判断之外没有其他选择,并且根据价值判断的结果排除某个国家规则的适用。
>
> 所以这种排除机制是基于仲裁员自己的意志。[114]

Mayer 教授进一步观察到:

> 仲裁员甚至没有任何义务来主张,更不用证明,他们适用的道德规范已经被任何法律秩序所认可。没有什么可以阻止他们**这样**适用它。
>
> ……
>
> 因此,这个道德规范不需要存在于任何法律秩序中。它是由仲裁员们的良心决定的。因为没有裁判地法从外界强加于仲裁员,他们从自己心中找到对应的规则。他们的意志允许适用

---

[112] P. Mayer, La règle morale dans l'arbitrage international, op. cit. footnote 18.
[113] *Ibid.*, p.390, author's translation。
[114] *Ibid.*, p.392, author's translation。

这个规则并且他们的良心决定了规则的内容。[115]

十年之后,Mayer 教授在一篇关于"仲裁员和法律"的文章中,采用以下逻辑进一步证明当仲裁员的道德观念要求的时候,他们可以自由忽视当事人选择的法律,并代之以来自一个不同的法律秩序的强行规则。

> 没有人要求仲裁员做公共政策的监护人。当事人,而不是国家,要求仲裁员裁断案件是非。但是,仲裁员在断案时有很大的自由。例如,一方当事人要求他们适用合同准据法(lex contractus);另一方要求适用可以合理适用于此案的强行规则。无论仲裁员采用了哪方观点,他们都伸张了正义。但是有一种利益,它毫无疑问超越双方当事人的利益,并且它的正当性对每一个人而言都是显而易见的,那么为什么当决定采用哪方观点的时候,仲裁员不能考虑这种利益呢?例如,腐败这个瘟疫;它足以让仲裁员宣布适用饱受腐败之苦并且采取措施反对腐败的国家的法律。[116]

如果当事人选择的法律"严重违反仲裁员的道德观念"[117],仲裁员可以使用自由裁量权,根据自己的道德观忽视当事人选择的法律,这个观点与自然法学的界线非常模糊。因为如果将自然法定义为"必须以显而易见的要素作为其适用的依据的原则"[118]或者"明显的以合理要素作为被认可适用的法则"[119],允许仲裁员可以考虑当事人利益之外的其他利益并且"它的正当性对每一个人而言都是显而

---

[115] *Ibid.*, p. 393, author's translation.

[116] P. Mayer, L'arbitre et la loi, *op. cit.* footnote 105, at pp. 239—240, author's translation.

[117] P. Mayer, La règle morale dans l'arbitrage international, *op. cit.* footnote 18, p. 397, author's translation.

[118] P. Jestaz, L'avenir du droit naturel ou le droit de seconde nature, *RTD civ.*, 1983, p. 233, at p. 237, author's translation.

[119] J.-B. Robinet, *Dictionnaire universel des sciences morale, économique, politique et diplomatique, ou Bibliothèque de l'homme-d'Etat et du citoyen.* volume 16, *Droit naturel*, London, Libraires associés, 1780, p. 462, author's translation.

易见的"[120]，这种观点就和自然法看起来令人惊讶地相似。

虽然 Mayer 教授认为更高的价值标准授予仲裁员不采纳合同准据法的权力，但是他不认为这些价值是有系统的。他的思想的中心是有更高的价值存在。然而，他忽视了这些价值是否连贯并组织成一个系统。他认为，仲裁员们可以参考客观建立的"普遍承认的道德规范"或者"国内法几乎一致的趋同化"，但是它们只有"一个佐证的功能"并且不会成为"仲裁员适用的法律规则的渊源"[121]。根据他对仲裁的观点，道德价值不过是无体系的互相孤立的规范，它们完全依赖于仲裁员的主观意志。

与此截然不同的是，有观点认为规范体系存在的基础不是仲裁员的道德观念而是国家的实在法。

（2）跨国实证（Transnational Positivist）派

50. 实证派不认为仲裁法律秩序是一系列事先存在的规则，其渊源完全与国内法无关。相反，该派认为仲裁法律秩序完全基于国家的规范性活动，该秩序存在于国内法之中，并非与国内法并列，而且通过法律选择规则决定适用哪个法律。就仲裁而言，正是这个冲突法的渊源在任何情况下都可能带来严重的概念上的难题。一旦人们意识到多个国家法律秩序都有平等的资格管理某案件，所以来自某个法律秩序的规则——无论是否是冲突法规则——在以上假设没有被否定的情况下，没有理由可以优于其他法律秩序的规则被适用。由于我们无法否定对某个案件，可能多个国家法律秩序都有资格管理的假设，所以我们需要考虑其他方法。仲裁法律秩序的概念的依据是，在实践中，各国对什么样的仲裁才是有约束力的并且什么样的裁决才能得到承认和执行已经达成了广泛的共识。由于仲裁员的裁决权以他们的裁决最终得到国家的承认为基础，这个方法符合实证派的观点。由于没有国家能够垄断裁决的承认，这个国际仲裁的表

---

[120] P. Mayer, L'arbitre et la loi, *op. cit.* footnote 105, at p. 240, author's translation.

[121] P. Mayer, La règle morale dans l'arbitrage international, *op. cit.* footnote 18, p. 394, author's translation. 关于跨国规则方法的不同意见，参见后文，§ 55。

现形式认为各国法律的趋同可以孕育一个超越各个单独的国内法律制度的体系。

51. 第一种仲裁的表现形式可以被称为单独地区的,第二种表现形式为多地区的,第三种表现形式是仲裁法律秩序,自然法学派将其看成"非国家的",相对而言,"跨国的"称谓最确切地描述了这种表现形式。它的三大特点值得强调。

i) 超越国家法律秩序不足的主题

52. 在19世纪80年代,商人习惯法的学说立足的依据是国家立法提供的解决方法不足的观点。许多法律制度被认为不能提供满足国际商事交易需要的法律,从而仲裁员被认为应当可以舍弃法律选择方法以避免选择这些不适合国际商事交易的法律来解决纠纷,相反(若当事人如此约定,或者若当事人没有合意,当仲裁员认为恰当时)直接适用适合国际商事交易的实体规则。Eric Loquin 教授阐明,这些规则,有时被称为贸易惯例[122],总是围绕着国际商事交易息息相关的主题,例如交易安全、合同的调整(contract adaptation)、当事人之间的合作和商业忠诚。[123] 1982年 *Dow Chemical* 一案的裁决以宣言的形式解释了这一做法:

> (仲裁员作出的)裁决逐渐组成必须被考虑的案例法体系,因为它反映了经济现实的影响并且符合国际贸易的需要,国际贸易要求逐渐发展出国际仲裁的特殊规则。[124]

Loquin 教授认为,这个方法是一种"法律达尔文主义"(legal Dar-

---

〔122〕 就惯例和跨国规则之间更加严格的区别,参见 E. Gaillard, La distinction des principes généraux du droit et des usages du commerce international, *Etudes offertes à Pierre Bellet*, Paris, Litec, 1991, p. 203.

〔123〕 E. Loquin, La réalité des usages du commerce international, *Revue internationale de droit économique*, 1989, p. 163, at p. 168 *et seq*.

〔124〕 在ICC第4131号案件中,仲裁庭由 P. Sanders 担任主席, B. Goldman 和 M. Vasseur 组成,并于1982年9月23日作出裁决, *JDI*, 1983, p. 899, note by Y. Derains, author's translation。

winism），即"在所有的法律渊源，和那些最能够满足国际商事交易需要的规则的基础上进行选择"[125]。为了证明这个方法是正确的，存在一个商人社会其能够自发地发展出特别适合国际交易的法律的观点被提了出来。

53. 认可存在仲裁法律秩序的表现形式代表了截然不同的意识形态。它不再指责国内法的不足，它的基础是各个国家的法律，当作为整体考虑的时候，这些法律组成了仲裁法的共同规则，正是这些共同规则成为仲裁员裁决权的渊源。就像作为国际法渊源之一的法律的一般原则一样，这种表现形式不是国内法的对立面。相反，它完全以国家的规范性活动为基础。

ii）服从多数原则

54. 仲裁法律秩序以国家法律秩序为基础的事实并不意味着它所包含的全部规则必须被所有国家承认。识别一般原则的方法，也叫做"跨国规则方法"，是保持不变的，无论识别的对象是实体性的跨国规则，还是当事人不能减损的基本原则，或者是奠定仲裁员裁决权力基础的原则。它和《国际法院规约》(*Statute of the International Court of Justice*) 第 38 条规定的识别法律基本原则的方法没有区别[126]。它的目标是识别国内法中的主流，显然它不要求该主流已经得到各国一致认可。要求一致认可会使识别一般原则的方法失去意义，因为该方法只要求将广泛接受的规则和违反主流

---

[125] E. Loquin, Où en est la *lex mercatoria?*, *Souveraineté étatique et marchés internationaux à la fin du 20ème siècle. A propos de 30 ans de recherches du CREDIMI. Mélanges en l'honneur de Philippe Kahn*, Paris, Litec, 2000, p. 23, at p. 26, author's translation; E. Loquin, Les règles matérielles internationales, *Collected Courses*, volume 322 (2006), § 503.

[126] 关于国际商法或者国际公法的一般规则通常是如何形成的，参见 A. Pellet, La *lex mercatoria*, "tiers ordre juridique"? Remarques ingénues d'un internationaliste de droit public, *Souveraineté étatique et marchés internationaux à la fin du 20ème siècle. A propos de 30 ans de recherches du CREDIMI. Mélanges en l'honneur de Philippe Kahn*, op. cit. footnote 125, at p. 66 *et seq.*

或者过时的规则区别开来。[127]

55. 过去,各国的一致接受是一个规则要具有跨国性质或者成为法律的基本原则的必备条件,这一点被仲裁员用来证明不采用跨国规则而直接适用道德规范是正确的。其逻辑如下:

> 仲裁员希望采用客观存在的共识而不是他们的主观想法,但是他们无法总是实现这个正当的愿望。尽管声称具有普遍性,某些[国际]公约包含的原则并非得到一致赞同。对种族歧视的谴责并未阻止一些国家公开进行种族歧视;对化学武器的禁止被一些没有核武器的国家反对;目前国家们对消费和销售什么类型的药物应该被认定为非法还存在分歧,等等。然而,难道这就意味着我们要放弃提倡道德规范吗?[128]

这位作者接着提到 1855 年 1 月 15 日在伦敦由一个混合委员会(Mixed Commission)就 Le Créole 奴隶船一案作出的决定。在 Le Créole 案中,仲裁员已接受了船东的主张,作出了不利于英国政府的裁决,原因是在航行途中叛变的奴隶在到达拿骚(Nassau)时已经获得自由:

> 如果仲裁员已经考虑的是商人习惯法,而不是"万国公法"(law of nations),他们也会得出一样的结论(结论是,即便奴隶制度可鄙,该制度没有违背万国公法,因为它在有些地方是合法的):贩卖奴隶是国际贸易的热门分支。仲裁员怎么能够否认它的存在呢?所有他们能够做的——并且,我们认为,他们应当做的——是对奴隶贸易进行道德判断并且拒绝适用将自然人等同于物品的法律。[129]

---

[127] 就此问题的总体观点,参见 E. Gaillard, Thirty Years of *Lex Mercatoria*: Towards the Selective Application of Transnational Rules, *ICSID Review*, 1995, p. 208; E. Gaillard, Transnational Law: A Legal System or a Method of Decision Making?, *Arbitration International*, 2001, p. 59, at p. 61 *et seq.*

[128] P. Mayer, La règle morale dans l'arbitrage international, *op. cit.* footnote 18, at p. 395, author's translation. 关于直接援引道德规范的方法,参见前文, § 49。

[129] *Ibid.*, p. 396, author's translation.

从上述分析中我们能够看出,要求各国一致认可会导致以下谬论:尽管某行为违反一般接受的价值观念,但是仅仅由于一个国家或者少部分国家继续认为该行为合法,"万国公法"或者跨国法——这两个概念共用同一个方法论——就不能谴责该行为。

56. 同样的错误也导致拒绝承认仲裁协议的可分割原则(severability)是跨国规则,虽然相对而言,可分割原则只是一个较不引人注目的仲裁法问题。原因如下,这些原因在当时是正确的:

> 即使英国法拒绝[承认仲裁协议的可分割原则],使得该法处于孤立地位,由于英国拥有最发达的法律制度之一,再加上(至少在某些领域)它是重要的国际仲裁地,这些事实表明各国一致接受对建立一个一般法律原则而言是不必要的。[130]

相反,没有完全基于比较法得出的解决方法不能优于那些被国际社会更为广泛接受的方法而适用,这就是跨国规则的全部哲学[131]。这个例子进一步证明了跨国规则方法的动态本质,它与冲突法方法论的静态本质截然不同。

iii) 认识跨国规则方法的动态本质

57. 跨国规则是动态的,因为它考虑(或者,在实践中,促进了)国内法的演化。奴隶制度在 20 世纪受到比 19 世纪更加严厉的批评。在 1997 年经济合作和发展组织达成了《禁止在国际商业交易活动中贿赂外国公职人员公约》(1997 OECD *Convention on Combating Bribery of Foreign Public Officials in International Business Transactions*)后,以获得合同为目的而进行的贿赂行为受到更为猛烈的抨击。[132] 今天环境保护得到前所未有的重视[133]。所有国家的法律不以同一

---

[130] P. Mayer, L'autonomie de l'arbitre international dans l'appréciation de sa propre compétence, 217 *Collected Courses* 319 (1989), p.432, author's translation.

[131] E. Gaillard, Thirty Years of *Lex Mercatoria*: Towards the Selective Application of Transnational Rules, *op. cit.* footnote 127, p.229.

[132] 关于此 OECD 公约,参见后文,§ 120。

[133] 关于和环境保护有关的跨国公共政策,参见后文,§ 122。

个步伐革新,这个事实并不意味着我们不能以一个动态的视角来识别国际社会中的主流。当数目可观的国内法都采用了某个方法,在其他法律制度加入这个主流之前,与这个方法相对应的规则已经成为一般原则。法律选择方法仅仅考虑在某个时间点各种法律之间的冲突,但是跨国规则方法考虑法律演化的总方向以识别将代表主流的法律。较之孤立的规则,它更喜欢符合主流的规则。

58. 具有重大意义的是数个曾经用来否定某些原则具有跨国规则属性的例子,到后来反而证明了,虽然有些国家在历史上曾经制定不符合主流的法律,但是最终这些国家废除了这些法律。例如,认可奴隶制的法律最终被废除了。英国最终在 1996 年的《仲裁法》中承认了仲裁协议的可分割性原则。[134] 1991 年 2 月 13 日阿尔及利亚颁布的法律宣告该国加入了法律制度的主流,因为该法不再一概禁止使用中介人(intermediaries)的介入,而仅仅是管理中介人并且防止其腐败。这与阿尔及利亚 1978 年的立法和曾经根据此法作出的臭名昭著的裁决大相径庭。[135] 葡萄牙法院最终舍弃了对《葡萄牙民法典》第 809 条的僵化解释,该解释曾经导致每个限制责任的条款都无效。[136] 这些例子反映出,在这些革新发生之前,认为所有国家没有一致接受就不存在一般原则的观点代表了静止地看待法律的态度。相反,若当事人没有就准据法达成一致,识别这些规则的违反主流的本质会允许仲裁员,使用跨国规则

---

[134] 就英国法对仲裁协议的可分割性原则的传统的敌视态度反弹的例子,参见 2006 年 10 月 20 日英格兰和威尔士高院(商事法庭)(High Court (Commercial Court) of England and Wales) 在 Fiona Trust and Holding Corporation and Others v. Yuri Privalov and Others,[2006] EWHC 2583(Comm)的决定。2007 年 1 月 24 日该决定被上诉法院(Court of Appeal)撤销,[2007] EWCA Civ 20;2007 年 10 月 17 日英国上院(House of Lords)维持了上诉法院的决定,Fiona Trust & Holding Corporation & 20 Others v. Yuri Privalov & 17 Others sub nom Premium Nafta Products Ltd(20th Defendant) & Others v. Shipping Co Ltd (14th Claimant) & others,[2007] UKHL 40.

[135] 因为在 Hilmarton 一案中仲裁员适用违反主流的 1978 年法律而非合同准据法,所以瑞士法院撤销该裁决是正确的。参见后文,§ 113。

[136] 就此问题葡萄牙案例法的演变,参见后文,footnote 290.

方法,当这些反主流的规则和更广为接受的规则相冲突的时候避免适用前者,从而加快法律的演变。上述例子表明过去曾经推崇反主流规则的国家也最终舍弃了这些规则,所以它们最好地证明了跨国规则方法是有道理的。[137]

B. 对仲裁法律秩序存在的认可

59. 今天,仲裁案例法和国家法律秩序的变革都反映出仲裁法律秩序的观点已经被日益接受,特别是前者还代表了仲裁员对自身作用的认识正在不断深化。

(1) 承认在仲裁案例法中存在仲裁法律秩序

60. 仲裁员们使用跨国规则方法的行为反映出国际仲裁制度具有一个真正法律秩序的所有特点。

就构成而言,跨国规则和《国际法院规约》[138]第 38 条所包含的国际法的一般原则一样,具有系统化地使用比较法资源的特点。无论当事人是否就法律选择达成合意,仲裁员都可以援引这些跨国规则,并借助它们解决各种问题,例如作为管辖权的基础的仲裁协议的有效性、仲裁程序、或者案件的实体问题。[139] 这并不奇怪,当适用跨

---

[137] 美国法律选择理论中有类似的观点。与传统的法律选择方法不同,我们需要考虑备选法律的内容以便从中选择,哪个备选法律符合可预见的总趋势是该法是否被选中的一个决定因素(在就此问题的许多研究中,例见 M. Hancock, Three Approaches to the Choice-of-Law Problem: the Classificatory, the Functional and the Result-Selective, *XXth Century Comparative and Conflicts Law. Legal Essays in Honor of Hessel E. Yntema*, Leiden, A. W. Sythoff, 1961, p. 365)。因此从长远看,法律选择方法成为一个以前瞻性的方式解决时际冲突(*ratione temporis* conflicts)的方法。

[138] See A. Pellet, *Recherche sur les principes généraux de droit en droit international public*, Doctoral Thesis, Paris II University, 1974, p. 240 *et seq*.

[139] See E. Gaillard, The Use of Comparative Law in International Commercial Arbitration, *ICCA Congress Series No. 4. Arbitration in Settlement of International Commercial Disputes Involving the Far East and Arbitration in Combined Transportation* (P. Sanders ed.), Deventer, Kluwer, 1989, p. 283; E. Gaillard, Du bon usage du droit comparé dans l'arbitrage international, *Rev. arb.*, 2005, p. 375; E. Loquin, Où en est la *lex mercatoria*?, *op. cit.* footnote 125, at p. 34 *et seq*.

国规则方法的时候，仲裁员的首要渊源是比较法，以及仲裁案例法、国际公约和其他所有的可以用来建立一个广泛接受的规则的因素；归根结底，这个方法的目的是证明某个当事人主张适用的规则是否被国家们广泛接受还是孤立或过时的。

从仲裁员适用跨国规则过渡到对仲裁法律秩序的承认更加复杂。我们是否面临着彼此独立的规则，当仲裁员愿意适用法律的规则而不是某个国家的法律的时候[140]，他或者她是偶然从中选择适用呢？还是这些规则成系统并组成了一个名副其实的法律秩序，仲裁员不过是该秩序的代言人呢？要想从接受仲裁员适用跨国规则的观点，跨越到存在一个名副其实的仲裁法律秩序，需要两大质的飞跃。第一是从承认适用孤立的规则飞跃到承认存在一个有组织的规范体系；第二是认识到这个体系实际上满足法律秩序的更严格的标准。

61. 为了让一系列规则能够成系统，这些规则必须以相互联系的方式运作，并且具有法律逻辑的特殊条理[141]，其中首先也是最重要的是一般—特别和原则—例外的逻辑区分。

事实上，就像任何国家法律秩序的规则一样，在不同的概括性上跨国规则们互相联系。高度概括的一般规则，例如合同诚信，会产生更加具体的规则——例如合同订立时的诚信，合同解释问题上的诚信和合同履行诚信——从这些具体规则中甚至可以引出更加细化的规则，例如如果一份文件有多种解释，则需要采纳不利于单方面起草这份文件的当事人的解释。不能否认在仲裁案例法中对法律的一般规则日益细化的现象出现已久。[142]"原则"（principle）这个词不应当仅仅指代高度概括的规则，因为这些规则在现实中的唯一作用是让

---

[140] 就仲裁员决定哪个法律成为案件实体的准据法时，法律（law）和法律的规则（rules of law）的区别，参见后文，§104。

[141] 就此问题，特别参见，Ch. Perelman, *Logique juridique. Nouvelle rhétorique*, Paris, Dalloz, 2nd ed., 1999; G. Kalinowski, *Introduction à la logique juridique. Eléments de sémiotique juridique, logique des normes et logique juridique*, Paris, LGDJ, 1965.

[142] Regarding this specialization, see E. Gaillard, *La Jurisprudence du CIRDI*, volume I, Paris, Pedone, 2004, at p.157.

合同不受到法律的任何限制。谴责跨国规则的观点认为跨国规则只包括高度概括的规则,它们的内容是如此广泛(例如,合同诚信、契约即允诺)以致它们实际上成为自由放任原则(laissez-faire)的意识先锋[143],或者换句话说它们"没有任何实质内容"[144]。如果我们接受跨国规则强调的是一个方法而不是一个规则清单的话,我们就会意识到这种谴责无法令人信服。"方法"指的是优先采用被广泛接受的而不是违反主流的规则;使用这个方法确实能够解决每一个,无论多么具体,的问题[145]。因此跨国规则方法允许强行性和非强行性规则,以及和国际公法的强行规则(jus cogens)对应的真正的国际公共政策规则的发展。通过适用这些规则,仲裁员可以裁断出当事人的所谓合意实际是通过欺诈获得,一方当事人没有尽到忠诚履行合同的义务,或者合同义务因为违反国际社会采取的禁运而不能被履行。[146] "法律的一般原则"是"一般的"仅仅针对它们被广泛接受的程度而言,并不是因为它们不够具体。因此,相对而言,"跨国规则"的名称比"法律的一般原则"更为恰当,因为它没有模棱两可的问题。

跨国规则也满足原则—例外的逻辑。但是有时它们却遭到讽刺,被比作一团混杂[147]互相矛盾的原则,比如契约即允诺(pacta sunt servanda)和情势变更(rebus sic stantibus)两原则看起来互相矛盾[148]。实际上,这正体现了规则之间根据原则—例外的逻辑互相补充的特点。所有的法律制度都承认,情势变更原则(the doctrine of change in circumstances, imprévision)是契约即允诺原则的例外,它只在非常特殊的情况下适用。同样的,契约即允诺原则在特定情况下可能需要

---

[143] See, e. g., M. Mustill, The New Lex Mercatoria: The First Twenty Five Years, Liber Amicorum for the Rt. Hon. Lord Wilberforce, Oxford, Clarendon Press 149 (1987), p.181.

[144] P. Mayer, L'arbitre et la loi, op. cit. footnote 105, at p.236, author's translation.

[145] See E. Gaillard, Transnational Law: A Legal System or a Method of Decision Making?, op. cit. footnote 127.

[146] 就这些例子的讨论,参见后文, § 121。

[147] 对国际法受到的类似批评的反思, see J. Combacau, Le droit international: bric-à-brac ou système?, Archives de philosophie du droit. No.31, Le système juridique, 1986, p.85.

[148] See A. Kassis, Théorie générale des usages du commerce, Paris, LGDJ, 1984, p.349 et seq.

让位给不可抗力（force majeure）原则，它们之间不存在任何矛盾。在无法预见的情形破坏了合同的经济平衡的情况下，当事人或者仲裁员可能需要考虑这个情形从而重新平衡合同，这样做并不意味着全盘否定了契约即允诺原则。和合同有关的跨国规则法典化的成果也接受了这个观点。例如，《国际统一私法协会国际商事合同通则》（UNIDROIT principles）中的第6条第2款第2项和第3项——规定了艰难情形的定义和后果，若该情形发生，当事人可以要求为恢复合同均衡而重新谈判并修改合同，或者要求仲裁庭承认存在这种情形从而终止合同——这两个条款绝对没有与第6条第2款第1项规定的原则相矛盾，后者规定如果合同的履行使一方当事人负担加重，该方当事人仍应履行其义务。所以，如果人们认识到这些规则在不同的概括程度上相互联系，就会明白它们虽然表面上看似乎相互矛盾，但是实际上并非如此。

62. 即使"法律制度"（legal system）和"法律秩序"（legal order）经常被认为是同义词[149]，有组织的规范，或者体系，只有在能够解决它调整的对象之间的所有问题、说明它自己的渊源和它与其他法律秩序的关系的时候，才能称为法律秩序。

这里需要再次强调的是，比较法方法能够回答在国际商业关系中可能发生的所有问题，这是由于跨国规则是一个方法，而不是一个从仲裁案例法中得来的一劳永逸的规则清单，也不是某委员会将商业惯例法典化后的成果。当仲裁员面临着当事双方截然相反的主张的时候，他们需要决定哪个主张符合一般接受的规则，哪个代表违反主流的观点，从而决定支持哪个主张。所有的法律制度都包含违反主流的规则。例如法国法中过时的不承认减小损失义务的规则[150]，英国

---

[149] See, e. g., Ch. Leben, De quelques doctrines de l'ordre juridique, 33 *Droits* 19 (2001), p. 20, footnote 2.

[150] See, on tort liability, *Cour de cassation*, 2ème *civ.*, June 19,2003, *Bull. civ.* II, no. 203. 在合同案件中适用这条规则仍然是有争议的。

法中同意签约的意向书(agreement to agree)无效的规则[151],或者在1991年之前阿尔及利亚法中一概禁止使用中介人的规定[152],这些法律都不应当被适用,除非当事人明确表示这些法律需要适用。相反,仲裁员需要适用被更加广泛接受的规则,例如减小损失的义务,认定要求当事人诚信谈判的合同有效,或者惩罚实际发生的腐败的规则。另一个例子是法国法中的关于在长期买卖合同中确定价格的规定。如果当事人没有选择法国法,仲裁庭决定适用跨国规则而不是通过法律选择规则决定准据法[153],这是因为法国法规定没有清楚确定价格的合同无效,这种规定是违反主流的,所以不应当被适用,而不是因为跨国规则"默认"没有规定价格的合同有效。[154] 相反,承认参考市场价格的合同有约束力这个做法,符合通过比较法揭示的主流。[155] 值得注意的是法国法本身在这方面已经革新了[156],这体现了跨国规则的动态本质

---

[151]　See *e. g. Walford v. Miles* [1992] 2 AC 128, 138 (Lord Ackner):"为什么同意进一步协商的协议(an agreement to negotiate),就像同意签约的意向书一样,是不能强制执行的,原因很简单因为它不具有必要的确定性。"对这个原则的细致解释,参见 *e. g. Chitty on Contracts*, volume I, London, Sweet & Maxwell, 30th ed., 2008, § § 2-134 *et seq.*; G. Treitel, *The Law of Contract*, London, Sweet & Maxwell, 12th ed. (by E. Peel), 2007, p. 61.

[152]　See *supra*, § 58.

[153]　Award rendered in ICC Case No. 5953, September 1, 1988, *Primary Coal Inc. v. Compania Valenciana de Cementos Portland*, *Rev. arb.*, 1990, p. 701. 在此案中,仲裁庭认为要求当事人每6个月就煤炭的价格进行协商再达成协议的合同条款有效。

[154]　On this issue, see P. Mayer, L'arbitre et la loi, *op. cit.* footnote 105, at p. 236, author's translation.

[155]　例见,2004年《国际统一私法协会国际商事合同通则》第5条第1款第7(1)项(如果合同未规定价格,也无如何确定价格的规定,在没有任何相反表示的情况下,应视为当事人各方引用在订立合同时相关贸易中类似的情况下进行此类履行时通常收取的价格,或者,若无此价格,应为一个合理的价格)。

[156]　特别参见 *Cour de Cassation*, *Assemblée plénière*, December 1 1995 (4 cases), *Bull. civ.* I, no. 7, 并且,就此问题的更广泛的意见,La détermination du prix:nouveaux enjeux un an après les arrêts de l'Assemblée plénière, CEDIP Symposium of December 17, 1996, published in *RTD com.*, 1997, p. 1. 就如一位作者注意到的,最高法院(*Cour de Cassation*)[在1995年]的判决反映了被欧洲诸国法律广泛接受的观点,即合同是否有效并非以价格是否能够确定为基础。Ph. Malinvaud, *Droit des obligations*, Paris, Litec, 10th ed., 2007, § 241, author's translation.

以及这个规则预见法律变革的功能。[157] 这个例子也表明,尽管通说认为跨国规则方法过于抽象,但是相反的是适用这个方法比传统的法律选择方法,对结果的可预见性更强。所以,对没有选择合同准据法的当事人而言,仲裁员适用一个符合被广泛支持的立法运动的规则,比一个通常不被比较法接受的规则,更合情合理。[158]

评价存在仲裁法律秩序的事实,需要考察它是否能够回答它的渊源和与其他法律秩序的关系等基本问题,而不是仅仅判断它是否由一系列的规则组成,也不是评价它是否能够解决仲裁员可能遇到的所有争议。无论某规则体系是多么连续和完善,如果它不能回答自己的渊源和与其他法律秩序的关系,这个体系仍然称不上法律秩序。所有被称为法律秩序的理论,无论内容差别多大,都解决了渊源和与其他法律秩序的关系问题。追随 Kelsen 或者 Hart 的规范法学家认为"基本规范"或者"承认规则"扮演了每个法律秩序的"统一"(unification)和"确认"(validation)的角色。[159] 对 Santi Romano 而言,"相关性"(relevance)处于法律秩序之间的关系的中心。Ost 和 de Kerchove 认为这个中心是由"网络"(network)这个概念扮演的。

认可存在仲裁法律秩序的表现形式认为这个法律秩序源自国家,这和在国际法的国家实证主义设想中,国际法律秩序来自国家的意志是相同的。但是,这并不影响这个法律秩序的自治性。在国际商事关系领域,国家法律秩序的趋同,并通过它们广泛的接受仲裁,才使得仲裁的存在合法化。国际社会已经接受仲裁员在当事人同意的情况下有权力解决国际商事争端,并且要求各国在不进行实体审查的情况下就应当承认仲裁裁决,这表明国际社会已经认可仲裁享

---

[157] See *supra*, § 57.

[158] 就跨国规则的可预见性,参见 E. Gaillard, Du bon usage du droit comparé dans l'arbitrage international, *op. cit.* footnote 139, at p. 384; E. Gaillard, General Principles of Law—More Predictable After All?, *New York Law Journal*, December 6, 2001.

[159] 从国际法和国内法的关系的角度看待这些例子,参见 Ch. Leben, De quelques doctrines de l'ordre juridique, *op. cit.* footnote 149, at p. 30 *et seq.*

有真正的自治。一些最具有革新思想的法院将仲裁员誉为"国际法官"[160]，这最好的证明了今天仲裁员被认为是一个与众不同的法律秩序的代言人。作为"国际法官"，国际仲裁员们制定规范，这些规范虽然以国家规范性活动为基础，但是它们是跨国规则，并不完全属于某个特定的国家。只有国家能够强制执行仲裁裁决的事实绝对不否认仲裁员的司法功能和仲裁法律秩序的自治性。国家允许仲裁成为解决国际争议的通常方式，国家的功能仅仅在于保证执行仲裁过程的最终结果。仲裁自治性的最具有说服力的例子是国家本身，在签订仲裁协议后，也和合同当事人一样需要服从仲裁员的权威并且愿意执行对己不利的裁决。

（2）国家法律秩序接受仲裁法律秩序的存在

63. 国内法律制度本身并非对仲裁法律秩序和国家法律秩序并存的事实一无所知。越来越多国家的案例法和立法证明了这一点。

64. 首先，某些法院作出的有关国际公共政策的决定体现了对仲裁法律秩序的承认。在一个 1990 年作出的决定中，巴黎上诉法院（Paris Court of Appeal）提到存在一个"真正国际的和普遍适用的"公共政策，法院的结论是这种政策不允许仲裁员接受一个被当事人所选择的程序法专门排除的救济方式。[161] 在 1993 年，这个法院又参考了"构成国际社会的绝大多数的国家理解的国际商业道德"[162]。瑞士法院在判案中也赞同"跨国公共政策"的观点。1994 年在著名的 *Westland* 判决中，联邦法院（Federal Tribunal）认为，在瑞士对裁决

---

[160] See *infra*, §127. 就"仲裁法律秩序"的概念和内涵，进一步参见 E. Gaillard, L'ordre juridique arbitral: réalité, utilité et spécificité, 55 *McGill Law Journal* (2010).

[161] Paris Court of Appeal, May 25, 1990, *Fougerolle v. Procofrance*, *Rev. crit. DIP*, 1990, p. 753, author's translation.

[162] Paris Court of Appeal, September 30, 1993, *European Gas Turbines SA v. Westman International Ltd.*, author's translation, *Rev. arb.*, 1994, p. 359, note by D. Bureau; *Rev. crit. DIP*, 1994, p. 349, note by V. Heuzé; *RTD com.*, 1994, p. 703, obs. by E. Loquin; *Yearbook Commercial Arbitration*, 1995, p. 198.

的审查应当基于

> 跨国或者普遍的公共政策,包括"不论争议和某个国家的联系如何,都必须遵循的法律的基本原则"。[163]

不可否认的是,在国家法院可以审查仲裁裁决的背景下,上述判决的观点有些模棱两可。与仲裁不同,法院有一个管辖地,无论法院的灵感来自何处,它所必须执行的公共政策只能反映当地法院对国际公共政策的理解。即使我们可能希望这种公共政策反映普遍的价值,它的渊源说明它必定是国家的,因为它的范围是由每个审查裁决的国家法院所决定的。这就是为什么,当被国内法官使用的时候,"跨国公共秩序"的术语可能被认为是不贴切的[164],或者仅仅是形式上承认存在超越法官本国国家法律秩序的跨国法律秩序。因此,毫不令人惊讶的是,在最新的案例法中,瑞士联邦法院已经回到传统做法,即国家法院应当根据公共政策审查仲裁裁决。如今它的观点是:

> 一个裁决会被认为不符合公共政策,如果它不尊重必不可少的和被广泛接受的价值,根据瑞士的主流观点,这些价值应当成为所有法律秩序的基础。[165]

65. 其次,一些案例法认为裁决没有与仲裁地的国家法律秩序相"结合"(integrated),这是对仲裁法律秩序更加意义深远的认可。自从 1994 年,法国的案例法就连贯地使用了"与……结合"这个表述。法国最高法院(Cour de Cassation)在 *Hilmarton* 一案中首次表示:

> 在瑞士作出的裁决是国际裁决,所以它没有与瑞士的法律

---

[163] Swiss Federal Supreme Court, April 19, 1994, *Westland Helicopters Ltd.*, ATF 120 II 155, author's translation.

[164] See E. Gaillard and J. Savage (eds.), *Fouchard Gaillard Goldman On International Commercial Arbitration*, op. cit. footnote 37, at § 1648. Contra J.-B. Racine, *L'arbitrage commercial international et l'ordre public*, Paris, LGDJ, 1999, p.473.

[165] Swiss Federal Tribunal, March 8, 2006, *Bull. ASA*, 2006, p. 521, at p. 529, author's translation.

制度"结合",因此,即使该裁决在瑞士被撤销,它仍然存在,所以法国认可这个裁决没有违反国际公共秩序。[166]

巴黎上诉法院在 *Chromalloy*[167] 和 *Bargues Agro Industries*[168] 案件中采纳了同样的观点。在 2007 年 1 月 18 日,该院再一次认为:

> 确实,在法国执行外国裁决的最基本的原则是,裁决被仲裁地的法官撤销,不会影响该裁决的存在,也不会阻止该裁决在其他法律秩序中被承认和执行,因为仲裁员不是仲裁地的法律机构的不可或缺的一部分,在本案中仲裁地是比利时。[169]

法国案例法采用的方法直接来自 Berthold Goldman 对国际仲裁的观点,他是认为裁决不与仲裁地的法律秩序相"结合"的第一人。[170] 即便 Goldman 没有直接承认仲裁法律秩序的存在,但是他至少明确地谴责了相反的观点,那些观点认为在国际案件中仲裁的有效性的渊源是仲裁地的法律秩序。

在 2007 年 6 月 29 日作出的 *Putrabali* 决定中,法国最高法院更加明确地认可仲裁法律秩序存在的国际仲裁的表现形式。该案涉及一个

---

[166] Cour de cassation, 1re civ., March 23, 1994, *Hilmarton Ltd. v. Sté Omnium de traitement et de valorisation (OTV)*, author's translation, *JDI*, 1994, p. 701, at p. 702, note by E. Gaillard; *Rev. arb.*, 1994, p. 327, note by Ch. Jarrosson; *Rev. crit. DIP*, 1995, p. 356, note by B. Oppetit; *RTD com.*, 1994, p. 702, commentary by J.-C. Dubarry and E. Loquin; *Yearbook Commercial Arbitration*, 1995, p. 663.

[167] Paris Court of Appeal, January 14, 1997, *Arab Republic of Egypt v. Chromalloy Aero Services*, author's translation, *Rev. arb.*, 1997, p. 395, note by Ph. Fouchard; *JDI*, 1998, p. 750, note by E. Gaillard; *Yearbook Commercial Arbitration*, 1997, p. 691.

[168] Paris Court of Appeal, June 10, 2004, *Bargues Agro Industries v. Young Pecan Company*, author's translation, *Rev. arb.*, 2006, p. 154; *Yearbook Commercial Arbitration*, 2005, p. 499.

[169] Paris Court of Appeal, January 18, 2007, *La Société S. A. Lesbats et fils v. Monsieur Volker Le Docteur Grub*, unpublished; for an English translation, see *Yearbook Commercial Arbitration*, 2007, p. 297.

[170] B. Goldman, Une bataille judiciaire autour de la *lex mercatoria*. L'affaire Norsolor, *Rev. arb.*, 1983, p. 379, at p. 389. 对裁决没有与仲裁地的法律秩序相结合的观点的发展,参见 D. Hascher, L'influence de la doctrine sur la jurisprudence française en matière d'arbitrage, *Rev. arb.*, 2005, p. 391, at p. 412.

被仲裁地法院撤销的裁决,最高法院在它的决定中特别有力地强调:

> 一个国际仲裁裁决,不根植于任何国家法律秩序,是**一个国际司法裁断**(*a decision of international justice*),它的有效性必须取决于裁决的承认和执行国适用的规则……[171]

法国上诉法院仅仅认识到裁决没有与仲裁地的法律秩序结合,最高法院的决定更进了一步,认为裁决不根植于**任何**国家法律秩序。所以,法国最高法院清楚明确地承认仲裁法律秩序的存在。裁决被认为是一个"国际司法裁断",就像国际社会建立的常设国际法院作出的决定一样。

66. 最后,对仲裁法律秩序的承认也体现在最新的仲裁成文法中。这些法律允许当事人在某些条件下放弃要求仲裁地撤销裁决的权利。比利时法首先承认了这个可能性。该法规定如果比利时是仲裁地,并且没有一个当事人是比利时国民或者居民时,比利时法院不能撤销裁决。

这就是 1985 年 3 月 27 日比利时制定的一部法规的内容[172],其立法理由是,一个国家没有资格,或者确实也没有好处,在当事人不要求它执行裁决的情况下,去审查在它的国土上作出的裁决。这个观点曾经在短时间内出现在法国案例法中。早在 1980 年的 *Götaverken* 一案中巴黎上诉法院就采纳了相同的观点。在那个案件中,法院认为一个涉及某利比亚公司和某瑞典公司的在法国作出的 ICC 裁决

---

[171] *Cour de cassation*, *1ère civ.*, June 29, 2007, *PT Putrabali Adyamulia v. Rena Holding*, rendered following a report from President Jean-Pierre Ancel, emphasis added, *Yearbook Commercial Arbitration*, 2007, p.299, at p.301. The decision is also referred to *infra*, footnote 348. For a similar holding, see Paris Court of Appeal, January 31, 2008, *Société ivoirienne de raffinage c. Société Teekay Shipping Norway et autres*, *Rev. arb.*, 2008, p.163. See also D. Hascher, The Review of Arbitral Awards by Domestic Courts—France, *IAI Series on International Arbitration No. 6. The Review of Arbitral Awards* (E. Gaillard ed.), Huntington, Juris Publishing, 2010.

[172] 1985 年 3 月 27 日起草的《司法法典》(*Judicial Code*)的第 1717 条第 4 款规定:"只有在以下情况下比利时法院会考虑接受撤销裁决的申请:当至少裁决所解决的争议的一方当事人是具有比利时国籍或者居住在比利时的自然人,或者是一个在比利时成立的或者分支机构或者任何形式的商业运营存在于比利时的法人。"

并非根植于法国法律制度之中,因为双方当事人都是外国人并且合同是在国外签订和履行的。

所以,法院的结论是法国法院不能审查该裁决。法院也注意到,和仲裁员没有仲裁管辖地的观点相吻合:

> 若完全因为某地的中立性,它才被选定为仲裁进行地,这个地点没有意义,并且不能以选择此地推断出当事人默示地接受,即使是辅助性质的,法国程序法的管辖。[173]

在第二个阶段,许多国家的法律允许当事人放弃要求仲裁地撤销裁决的权利,许可的前提是,除了作为仲裁地外,这个国家和当事人没有其他任何联系。瑞士是第一个作出这种规定的国家。自从1987年颁布《国际私法法》(*Private International Law Statute*, PILS)之后,瑞士法允许住所、经常居住地或者商业存在不在瑞士的当事人能够,部分或者全部地,放弃要求仲裁地撤销裁决的权利。[174] 1993年突尼斯法也采纳了同样的观点。[175] 在1998年,比利时法进行修订从而和瑞士法保持一致。[176] 自从1989年瑞典案例法采纳这个观点后[177],瑞典的1999年仲裁法正式接受了这个观点。[178] 随着1996年

---

[173] Paris Court of Appeal, February 21, 1980, *Götaverken*, author's translation, *Rev. arb.*, 1980, p.524, note by F.-Ch. Jeantet, at p.533; *Yearbook Commercial Arbitration*, 1981, p.221. 1981年5月12日改革国际仲裁的法令没有接受这个观点,反之,在这个问题上接受了更为传统的观点。

[174] 1987年12月18日制定的瑞士《国际私法法》的第192条规定:"如果当事人的住所、经常居住地或者营业所在地都不在瑞士,他们可以在仲裁协议中明确表示或者通过一个书面补充合同,放弃所有撤销裁决的诉讼,或者他们可以把诉讼理由局限为第190条第2段所规定的理由中的一个或者多个。"

[175] Article 78(6) of the Tunisian Arbitration Code of 1993.

[176] Article 1717(4), of the Belgian Judicial Code, as drafted on May 19, 1998.

[177] Swedish Supreme Court, April 18, 1989, *Solel Boneh International v. Uganda*, *JDI*, 1990, p.597, commentary by J. Paulsson, p.589, at p.596; *Yearbook Commercial Arbitration*, 1991, p.606.

[178] Article 51 of the Swedish Arbitration Act of April 1, 1999.

对仲裁的改革,秘鲁也加入这一阵营。[179] 更值得称颂的是,自从 1999 年开始,巴拿马允许当事人在国际仲裁中,不论其国籍和住所,可以直接或者参考仲裁规则,放弃通过诉讼撤销裁决的权利。[180] 然而,这个规定不适用于需要在巴拿马执行的裁决,因为这种裁决属于规范在巴拿马以外作出的裁决的法律的调整范围。[181]

有理论认为,不能在仲裁地被审查的裁决无法在其他国家内得到《纽约公约》的保护,因为这个裁决没有充分地根植于一个国家法律秩序从而不能被认为是"外国的"[182]。今天,这个理论已经遭到法学著作的广泛批评。[183]

67. 所以,各个国家法律秩序逐渐摒弃了把仲裁地看做仲裁管辖地,认为仲裁裁决的有效性的渊源必须来自仲裁地的法律秩序的观点,也否定了仲裁裁决的有效性的渊源来自任何国家法律秩序的观点,最终各国逐渐倾向于认可仲裁法律秩序的存在。

---

[179] Article 126 of Peru's General Law on Arbitration of January 3, 1996, published in *Rev. arb.*, 2005, p. 861.

[180] Article 36 of the Government Decree of July 8, 1999, which established the general regime for arbitration, conciliation and mediation, published in *Rev. arb.*, 2005, p. 823.

[181] Article 38(4).

[182] See P. Sanders, *Quo Vadis Arbitration? Sixty Years of Arbitration Practice*, The Hague, Kluwer, 1999, p. 248. 在承认《纽约公约》没有定义仲裁的概念之后,作者根据自己对仲裁的设想分析到

> 只有以某个法律为基础时,仲裁才能存在并且被认可,这个法律调整并且控制这种私人的争端解决方式,因为,在仲裁中,法院的管辖权被排除了……所以,我认为将仲裁程序和国家脱离的观点和仲裁的概念相矛盾。

这个观点所代表的仲裁的表现形式得到 F. A. Mann 的拥护,F. A. Mann 的观点参见前文 supra § 13,但是,这种仲裁的表现形式不代表《纽约公约》的观点,因为公约在这方面完全是中立的。

[183] See especially H. Van Houtte, La loi belge du 27 mars 1985 sur l'arbitrage international, *Rev. arb.*, 1986, p. 29, at p. 39; A. Vanderelst, Increasing the Appeal of Belgium as an International Arbitration Forum? —The Belgian Law of March 27, 1985 Concerning the Annulment of Arbitral Awards, 2 *Journal of International Arbitration* 77 (1986); G. Keutgen and G. -A. Dal, *L'arbitrage en droit belge et international*, volume I. Le droit belge, Brussels, Bruylant, 2nd ed., 2006, § 602.

第二章

国际仲裁表现形式的后果

（一）国际仲裁表现形式对仲裁员裁决权的影响
（二）国际仲裁表现形式对仲裁员裁决的影响
（三）国际仲裁表现形式对裁决效力的影响

68. 对仲裁员和国家法院而言,接受三种中任何一种国际仲裁表现形式都会产生重大的实践影响。仲裁员裁决权力的渊源、国家法律秩序和仲裁的关系、或者存在仲裁法律秩序这些问题,虽然看上去很抽象,但是直接影响许多争议的解决。这些法律理论的基本问题极大地影响了一整个系列的国际仲裁问题,例如仲裁员的裁判权、他们作出的决定,或者在各个国家法律秩序中最终裁决的效力等。以下将对这些国际仲裁问题逐一分析。

(一) 国际仲裁表现形式对仲裁员裁决权的影响

69. 国际仲裁相互竞争的各种表现形式直接导致了对仲裁员裁决权的激烈分歧,还产生了相互竞争的方法论。分歧包括如何决定提交仲裁的标的,可以使用仲裁这种私人争端解决方式的当事人类别,有效的仲裁协议,仲裁员资格(包括资历、国籍,有时候甚至宗教信仰),或者什么机构可以组织仲裁程序。对接受让渡法院的部分裁判权力给仲裁员的国家而言,所有这些问题都是至关重要的。有些国家限制可以仲裁的事项或者可以选择仲裁的当事人的类别,有些国家还规定什么样的机构能够组织仲裁程序,或者要求仲裁协议必须满足特别的条件才有效,还有些国家设定仲裁员需要具备的条件;但是,有些国家却愿意把这一切留给当事人决定,只要当事人达成有效的合意,他们就可以决定如何解决争议。

在涉及是否允许当事人适用仲裁这个私人争端解决方式和仲裁程序应当如何展开时,分歧是难免的。而且,国家对这些问题的态度还可能随着时间变化。在 19 世纪仲裁被认为实质上是和国家法院竞争,这种对仲裁不信任的观点被广泛接受仲裁这种争端解决方式所取代。在很大程度上这个变化并不是为了减少国家法院过多的案件量,而是给当事人提供选择性的争端解决方式,这个方式和当事人各方的国家法院相比是中立的,并且当事人可以参与指定仲裁员和决定仲裁程序等工作。

70. 从方法论的角度出发,这些问题中最基本的是使用严格的法律选择方法在当事人的对立观点中进行选择,还是通过比较法识别并适用跨国规则。对此问题的回答直接取决于我们采纳的仲裁的表现形式。将仲裁员等同于仲裁地的国家法院的表现形式,不需要进一步的分析就直接根据仲裁地的法律来规范仲裁程序。如果仲裁地的冲突规则指向其他国内法,这些法中的限制规定也会被适用。相反,威斯特伐利亚模式允许各个国家决定自己的观点,而不考虑其他国家会怎么做。例如,在其他国家已经承认仲裁可以在仲裁机构之外进行的今天,一国仍然可以认定临时仲裁(*ad hoc* arbitration)协议无效,例如根据中国法临时仲裁协议就是无效的。[184] 然而,如果一方当事人认为必须适用中国法所以临时仲裁协议无效,原因是当事人之一来自中国或者裁决可能要在中国执行,所以中国法和争议有最密切的联系。在这种情况下,仲裁员很可能会意识到威斯特伐利亚模式的缺陷。因为这个模式局限在于许可其他国家可以自由决定是否承认和执行在中国作出的临时仲裁裁决,并不管这些裁决在中国的命运如何,原因是中国法对于临时仲裁的规定远远没有被他国广泛接受。

但是,当面临中国法和其他国家的法律对临时仲裁协议的有效性所持的立场相反时,威斯特伐利亚模式没有给仲裁员提供充足的指南。从仲裁员的角度看,威斯特伐利亚模式实质上是不稳定的。[185] 以下两种方法中的任意一个都可以解决这个问题:使用法律选择方式,从而适用仲裁地法或者当事人选择的法律等;或者采用被国际广泛承认的而非国际认可度不高的法律(这是就临时仲裁条款

---

[184] 根据1994年8月31日第31号主席令(即1994年《中华人民共和国仲裁法》)的第16条,中国法只承认机构仲裁。该条款规定仲裁协议必须包含当事人请求仲裁的意思表示、仲裁事项和选定的仲裁委员会。最高人民法院审判委员会于2005年12月26日就此颁布司法解释。这些法律规定和司法解释导致临时仲裁协议以及要求在非中国的仲裁机构中进行仲裁的仲裁协议的有效性令人怀疑,特别参见 J. Tao and C. von Wunschheim, Articles 16 and 18 of the PRC Arbitration Law: the Great Wall of China for Foreign Arbitration Institutions, *Arbitration International* 309 (2007).

[185] See *supra*, §§ 41 et seq.

的有效性而言）。若仲裁没有在中国进行，仅仅由于争议和中国的偶然联系，或者歪曲理解仲裁员有义务作出可以被执行的裁决[186]，就适用与国际主流不同的中国法，要求仲裁员认定临时仲裁协议无效。这样做是荒唐的。无论在裁决中是否承认这一点，在中国外进行仲裁的仲裁员可能非常不愿意由于中国法的规定而认定临时仲裁协议无效。若仲裁在中国进行，仲裁员的任务就更微妙了。但是，原则上说，仲裁员应当得出同样的结论，即根据国际社会对临时仲裁的广泛接受，裁定当事人愿意将争议提交这种仲裁的意愿是有效的。无论这种仲裁作出的裁决在中国命运如何，在其他国家法律秩序中愿意承认这种裁决的大量事实足以说明认可临时仲裁协议有效的做法是正确的。[187]

71. 仲裁员必须在接受截然不同的国际仲裁表现形式的国内法中进行选择，他们采用的方法，尽管微妙，但是却远远不如以下两种情况复杂：当与仲裁有关的司法决定已经在一个国家中作出，并且该国法律可能被仲裁员用于解决案件的实体问题，或者该国国家法院和仲裁员同时对案件的实体争议行使管辖权（这时的问题是仲裁员是否必须中止仲裁程序以待国家法院作出决定）。这两种情况最好地展现了国际仲裁的不同表现形式之间的区别。第一种情况关于对禁诉令（anti-suit injunctions）的态度，第二个是平行程序理论是否可以适用于在国家法院和仲裁员就某一争议都行使管辖权的情况。

A. 禁 诉 令

72. 近年来，国家法院为了终止或者暂停仲裁程序而针对当事人，或者甚至针对仲裁员，颁布禁诉令的现象急剧增加。

禁诉令最初是法官使用的一个普通法工具，当法官认为自己对某个问题有管辖权或者想要保护另一个法院或者仲裁庭的管辖权的

---

[186] See *supra*, § § 37 *et seq.*
[187] See *supra*, § § 124 *et seq.*

时候,他们会使用禁诉令来阻止当事人到外国法院诉讼或者继续进行外国的诉讼程序。但是今天,无论是位于印度或者巴基斯坦的普通法法院,还是巴西、委内瑞拉或者印度尼西亚的民法法院,都常常使用禁诉令来限制仲裁。[188]

不同的仲裁表现形式,对一个法院能否通过禁诉令来要求其他法律制度接受它对管辖权条款或者仲裁协议有效性的决定,有不同的看法。禁诉令往往是在当事人极度好讼的情况下采取的,所以它是测试国际仲裁表现形式的特别有意义的例子。在以下两种情况中更是如此,即当仲裁地之外的国家法院采取对仲裁不友好的措施,或者当仲裁地的法院根据自己对仲裁协议有效性或者仲裁进行条件的判断要求结束仲裁程序的情况。

(1) 位于仲裁地国之外的法院发布禁诉令

73. 禁诉令特别频繁地在涉及国家的争议中使用。国家或者国有单位常常撕毁自己自愿签署的仲裁协议,而在本国法院起诉,并要求法院禁止争议的另一方提起仲裁或者,若仲裁程序已经展开了,则禁止该方继续进行仲裁。*Hubco*, *COPEL* 和 *National Grid* 案件正是这种做法的典型代表。[189]

Hubco 案件涉及部分由外国股东持股的项目公司 Hubco,和巴基斯坦水电发展部门(Water and Power Development Authority of Pakistan, WAPDA)。案件与在巴基斯坦境内建造和开发一座价值 18 亿

---

[188] On this issue, see *IAI Series on International Arbitration No. 2. Anti-Suit Injunctions in International Arbitration*, op. cit. footnote 83; E. Gaillard, Il est interdit d'interdire: Réflexions sur l'utilisation des *anti-suit injunctions* dans l'arbitrage commercial international, *Rev. arb.*, 2004, p.47, and the reports of J. Lew and E. Gaillard on anti-suit injunctions at the ICCA Congress in Montreal, May 31—June 3, 2006, *ICCA Congress Series No. 13. International Arbitration 2006: Back to Basics?* (A. J. van den Berg ed.), Alphen aan den Rijn, Kluwer, 2007, p.185 and p.235.

[189] 就其他拉丁美洲国家的例子,see H. A. Grigera Naón, Competing Orders Between Courts of Law and Arbitral Tribunals: Latin American Experiences, *Global Reflections on International Law, Commerce and Dispute Resolution. Liber Amicorum in honour of Robert Briner*, op. cit. footnote 38, p.335.

美元的电站有关。相关合同规定了 ICC 伦敦仲裁。1998 年,一场对电站生产的电征税的争议被提交仲裁。WAPDA 提出某些合同是由于官员腐败而签订的,它申请巴基斯坦法院就这些问题行使管辖权,并且要求法院命令仲裁申请人暂缓仲裁程序。巴基斯坦法院批准了这个申请,随后,巴基斯坦最高法院(Supreme Court of Pakistan)在 2000 年 6 月 14 日维持下级法院的决定,原因是腐败使得争议不属于可以仲裁的事项。[190] 后来,双方达成和解协议。[191]

COPEL 一案涉及一家名为 Companhia Paranaense de Energia(COPEL)的巴西国有公司和一个叫做 UEG Araucária Ltda 的项目公司。COPEL 要求巴西法院下达禁诉令,禁止项目公司根据包含 ICC 巴黎仲裁条款的仲裁协议提起仲裁。根据巴西法律,国有公司能否通过仲裁解决争议尚无定论。[192] 这个国有公司以自己不能有效地签订仲裁协议为由,要求巴西法院宣布仲裁条款无效并要求仲裁申请人暂停仲裁程序。在 2003 年 6 月 3 日,位于库里提巴市(在巴西巴拉那州)的某法院同意了国有公司的请求,并且规定如果当事人违反禁令,要每日支付争议金额 0.5% 的罚款。这个决定也表明禁令的内容需要通知 ICC。[193] 就实体问题,在 2004 年 3 月 15 日库里提巴市第一审法院(Curitiba Court of First Instance)宣布仲裁协议无效。然而,在 2004 年 6 月 15 日,库里提巴市上诉法院(Curitiba Court of Appeal)允许仲裁申请人继续仲裁程序,因为第一审法官无视仲裁庭自裁管辖的原则(principle of competence-competence)。但是在 2004 年 7 月 5 日库里提巴市上诉法院的决定被巴西巴拉那州上诉法院

---

[190] Decision published in *Arbitration International*, 2000, p. 439.

[191] See the account of the case in L. Barrington, *Hubco v. WAPDA*: Pakistan Top Court Rejects Modern Arbitration, *American Review of International Arbitration* 385 (2000).

[192] 在 2005 年 10 月 25 日和 2006 年 8 月 14 日,巴西最高法院(Brazilian Superior Court of Justice)的公法庭的两个不同的分庭在两个已经下达禁诉令的案件中,均认可一个混合经济体的公司(a mixed economy company)有能力提起仲裁。就此问题,参见 A. Wald, La résolution, par l'arbitrage, des conflits entre l'administration publique et les entreprises privées en droit brésilien, *Les Cahiers de l'Arbitrage*, volume IV, Paris, Pedone, 2008, p. 175.

[193] 该决定可在巴西仲裁协会的网站上查询。

(Paraná Court of Appeal)的院长撤销。这些法院程序都没能阻止由 Karl-Heinz Böckstiegel 担任主席，Martin Hunter 和 Jorge Fontoura Nogueira 组成的仲裁庭进行裁决。在 2004 年 12 月 6 日，仲裁庭宣布了一项 Nogueira 先生持异议的多数裁决，认为仲裁庭对巴西国有公司能否签署仲裁协议的问题具有管辖权。[194] 在 2006 年初双方当事人最终达成和解。

在 National Grid 一案中，仲裁涉及一家根据英国法成立的名为 National Grid Plc 的公司，和阿根廷共和国。英国公司根据英国和阿根廷于 1990 年 12 月 11 日签订的双边投资条约提起仲裁。仲裁在华盛顿根据《联合国国际贸易法委员会仲裁规则》(UNCITRAL Arbitration Rules) 进行。[195] 当阿根廷在作为任命机构的国际商会仲裁院(ICC International Court of Arbitration)反对 Rigo Sureda 博士担任仲裁庭主席失败后，它在本国法院取得了禁令，希望阻止仲裁进一步进行。2007 年 7 月 3 日，联邦行政上诉法院(Federal Administrative Appellate Court)命令暂停仲裁，还针对 National Grid Plc 发出禁令要求它停止仲裁程序。但是仲裁庭无视该法院的决定，继续进行仲裁。

74. 禁诉令也被用于反对仲裁裁决的执行。在 Pertamina 一案中就是如此。该案涉及了一家印度尼西亚的国有公司(Pertamina)和一个项目公司(KBC)，关于在印度尼西亚建造和运作一家地热电站。当这个项目被印度尼西亚政府暂停之后，KBC 根据相关合同中的仲裁条款在瑞士根据《联合国国际贸易法委员会仲裁规则》提起仲裁。在 2000 年 12 月，仲裁庭要求 Pertamina 支付给 KBC 高达 2.6 亿美元的赔偿金。[196] Pertamina 要求仲裁地的法院撤销裁决，但是 2001 年 4

---

[194] 在 ICC 第 12656 号案件中，2004 年 12 月 6 日关于管辖权的部分裁决，*UEG Araucária v. Copel, Revista de Arbitragem e Mediação*, no. 11, October-December 2006, p. 257.

[195] 就案情介绍，参见 2006 年 6 月 20 日作出的裁决，在该裁决中，仲裁庭认为自己有管辖权，available on the *Investment Claims* and *ITA—Investment Treaty Arbitration* websites.

[196] *Karaha Bodas Company LLC v. Perusahaan Pertambangan Minyak Dan Gas Bumi Negara and PT, PLN (Persero)*, award of December 18, 2000, *International Arbitration Report*, March 2001, p. C-2.

月瑞士联邦法院以 Pertamina 没有按时缴费为由驳回了它的起诉。于是在 2002 年 3 月,Pertamina 在印度尼西亚法院提起诉讼要求法院撤销裁决并且禁止 KBC 在其他国家申请执行该裁决。实际上在 2001 年 12 月,KBC 已经成功地在美国申请承认该裁决。[197] 2002 年 8 月 27 日,雅加达中心地区法院(Central Jakarta District Court)以违反公共秩序为由撤销了仲裁裁决,并且针对 KBC 发出了禁令,要求它停止执行裁决,否则处以一天 50 万美元的罚款。[198] KBC 迅速要求美国法院命令 Pertamina 停止执行禁令。在 2002 年 4 月 26 日,美国得克萨斯州南区地区法院(U. S. District Court for the Southern District of Texas)批准了 KBC 的申请,并且针对 Pertamina 发出了临时的限制令(restraining order)。因为 Pertamina 没有遵守,再加上印度尼西亚的法院发出了禁令,KBC 申请得克萨斯州南区地区法院认定 Pertamina 蔑视法庭。地区法院接受了申请,认定 Pertamina 蔑视法庭,联邦第五巡回上诉法院受理了上诉并在 2003 年 6 月 18 日作出决定。与地区法院不同,上诉法院的决定体现了非常折中的观点。为了判断国外进行的诉讼是否是"无理取闹或者不公平的",法院分析了印度尼西亚法院撤销裁决的决定在美国可能产生的影响。非常值得注意的是法院考虑到本案涉及的问题争议颇多[199],并引用了 *Chromalloy* 一案的决定,认为:

>……即使(对撤销裁决有管辖权的)法院已经撤销裁决在先,美国法院和其他国家的法院还是执行了裁决,或者批准裁决的执行。[200]

---

[197] US District Court for the Southern District of Texas, *In the matter of an arbitration between Karaha Bodas Company LLC v. Perusahaan Pertambangan Minyak Dan Gas Bumi Negara*, December 4, 2001, 190 F. Supp. 2d 936.

[198] Central Jakarta District Court decision of August 27, 2002, available on the *International Arbitration Report* website.

[199] See *infra*, § 128.

[200] US Court of Appeals for the Fifth Circuit, *Karaha Bodas Company LLC v. Perusahaan Pertambangan Minyak Dan Gas Bumi Negara*, Decision of June 18, 2003, 335 F. 3d 357. On *Chromalloy*, see *infra*, footnote 351.

美国联邦第五巡回上诉法院和香港法院在 Pertamina 一案中得出的结论一致。[201] 该结论是：

>……其他执行庭能够，并且有时确实独立判断对执行外国裁决的实体问题的质疑是否成立。简而言之，就同一个法律问题进行多个司法程序是根据《（纽约）公约》承认和执行国际仲裁裁决的特点。[202]

所以法院的结论是印度尼西亚法院的决定并未给 KBC 造成不公平的困难境地，KBC 在印度尼西亚没有任何资产因此它完全可以无视该决定的存在。法院从国际法的角度分析这些因素，最终撤销了下级法院的判决。法院注意到：

>礼让原则包含着"本地限制"（local restraint）规则，它指导法院合理的限制主权的域外适用。

因此，即使"……印度尼西亚的禁令和认为仲裁裁决无效的决定可能真的违反了礼让原则"，这并不意味着美国法院必须发出禁令。"维持地区法院的禁令可能只会，即便不在法律层面也会从外交角度上，使问题雪上加霜。"所以，上诉法院宣布它虽然"同情地区法院并且也对 Pertamina 和它的律师的行为感到失望"，法院还是撤销了针对 Pertamina 发出禁令的决定。[203]

75. 从研究涉及禁诉令的诉讼中可以得出两大经验。

第一个经验与国家法院有关。一个国家通过惩罚措施或者其他形式的报复威胁的方式，将自己对于仲裁协议和，更广泛地说，仲裁程序的看法强加于所有其他国家，研究表明这种现象即便没有违背

---

[201] High Court of the Hong Kong Special Administrative Region, *Karaha Bodas Co. LLC v. Perusahaan Pertambangan Minyak Dan Gas Bumi Negara*, March 27, 2003, 2003 HKCU Lexis 378.

[202] US Court of Appeals for the Fifth Circuit, *KBC v. Pertamina*, Decision of June 18, 2003, *op. cit.* footnote 200.

[203] *Ibid.*

国际法[204]，也仍然是不合适的。[205] 但是仲裁员有权利——至少首先——根据仲裁庭自裁管辖的原则决定仲裁协议是否有效和仲裁程序是否正当这些问题。2003 年 6 月 18 日，第五巡回上诉法院作出的决定是威斯特伐利亚模式应用于国际仲裁的最好的例子。因为，它认为每个国家可以自主决定裁决的命运，这与每个国家法院无休止地使用禁—禁诉令（anti-anti-suit）来报复禁诉令，并希望以此将自己的观点强加给其他所有的国家法院的做法相比，无疑是一个进步。

  第二个经验是当面临禁诉令申请威胁的时候，仲裁员能够采取什么措施。根据仲裁庭自裁管辖的原则，仲裁员有权力裁断当事人造成的所有阻碍仲裁程序的行为，国家法院可以在裁决的承认和执行阶段对仲裁员的决定进行最终审查。根据将仲裁员等同于仲裁地的法院的国际仲裁的表现形式，仲裁员很可能会，就像国家法院的法官通常做的那样，运用法律选择方法进行分析。这样做会产生的结果是，仲裁员可能会适用某个国有机构所在的国家的法律来决定该机构是否有能力签订仲裁协议。法律选择方法无视在同意仲裁之后，又要求本国法院宣布它不受到仲裁协议约束的国家或者国家机构的叵测居心，所以在实践中，这个方法相当于完全剥夺了仲裁员在这个问题上自由裁量的权力。因为如果仲裁员已经决定适用某个国家的法律，他或者她很难完全无视该国法院就同样的问题依据同样的事实作出的决定。所以，把仲裁员等同于仲裁地的法院的国际仲裁的表现形式可能会让禁诉令发挥最大的作用。但是采用比较法的方法可能得出截然相反的结论。一个已经自愿签订仲裁协议的国家或者国家机构不能利用自己的国内法来逃避仲裁，这个规则已经被

---

  [204] See S. Schwebel, Anti-Suit Injunctions in International Arbitration. An Overview, *IAI Series on International Arbitration No. 2. Anti-Suit Injunctions in International Arbitration*, op. cit. footnote 83, p. 5.

  [205] See Ph. Fouchard, Anti-Suit Injunctions in International Arbitration—What Remedies?, *IAI Series on International Arbitration No. 2. Anti-Suit Injunctions in International Arbitration*, op. cit. footnote 83, p. 153.

比较法和仲裁案例法广泛认可,以至于它可以成为法律的一般原则。[206] 如果仲裁员认为应当适用被最广泛接受的而不是违反主流的规则(即使在违反主流的规则已经被和争议相关的国家的法院适用的情况下),他或者她会和严格按照法律选择方法的仲裁员,得出相反的结论。不仅从方法论而且从结果的角度看,这个例子都证明了国际仲裁的每一种表现形式的区别有多大。它们的区别在仲裁地的法院发布禁诉令的情形中更为显著。

(2) 位于仲裁地的法院发布禁诉令

76. 将仲裁员看成仲裁地所在国的临时代言人的观点,认为若此国的法院发出禁令要求停止仲裁,仲裁员没有选择只能接受并且机械地服从法院的命令。[207] 根据威斯特伐利亚模式的国际仲裁表现形式,仲裁员认为其他法律秩序没有必要一定赞同仲裁地法院的观点,他们甚至还可能认为因为无关紧要的理由停止仲裁是不公平的。然而,只有根据认可存在仲裁法律秩序的表现形式,当面临禁令的仲裁员认为依据广泛接受的国际仲裁原则,禁令是没有根据的时候,他或者她可以继续履行使命作出裁决。[208] 只有在裁决作出后,仲裁地之外的法律秩序才能就禁令问题有效地表明立场。这里再次表明,国际仲裁的第二种表现形式实质上是不稳定的,这为不接受第

---

[206] 就对证明这个结论的渊源的讨论, see E. Gaillard and J. Savage (eds.), *Fouchard Gaillard Goldman On International Commercial Arbitration*, op. cit. footnote 37, §§534 et seq.; J.-F. Poudret and S. Besson, *Comparative Law of International Arbitration*, op. cit. footnote 36, §235. 尽管后两位作者倾向于法律选择方式,他们所分析的多种渊源在现实中已经证明了在法律制度中存在着一个强烈的趋同的趋势,即反对国家或者国有单位依赖本国法背弃仲裁协议。

[207] See, e.g., E. Schwartz, Do International Arbitrators Have a Duty to Obey the Orders of the Courts at the Place of the Arbitration? Reflections on the Role of the *Lex Loci Arbitri* in the Light of a Recent ICC Award, *Global Reflections on International Law, Commerce and Dispute Resolution. Liber Amicorum in honour of Robert Briner*, op. cit. footnote 38, p.795.

[208] See E. Gaillard, L'interférence des juridictions du siège dans le déroulement de l'arbitrage, op. cit. footnote 74, at p.90 et seq.; J. Paulsson, Interference by National Courts, *The Leading Arbitrators' Guide to International Arbitration* (L.W. Newman & R.D. Hill eds.), Huntington, Juris Publishing, 2nd ed., 2008, p.119.

一种仲裁表现形式的人们接受第三种表现形式创造了条件。[209]

77. 许多案件证明,即使禁诉令由仲裁地的法院发出,仲裁员也会毫不迟疑地视其不存在,只要他们认为这样做是有道理的。

78. *Petrobangla* 一案就是例证。该案涉及一家名为 Saipem SpA 的意大利公司和一家名为 Petrobangla 的孟加拉国有公司关于修建管道的无谓的诉讼(trivial claims)。[210] 在 1993 年 6 月,Saipem 根据合同中的仲裁条款提起仲裁,合同规定在孟加拉首都达卡进行 ICC 仲裁。1995 年 11 月 27 日,由 Werner Melis 担任主席,Riccardo Luzzatto 和 Ian Brownlie 组成的仲裁庭裁定本庭有管辖权。于是,国有公司要求仲裁庭命令另一方提供某些文件。当仲裁庭拒绝这个请求后,Petrobangla 在达卡一审法院(court of first instance)提起诉讼,要求制裁仲裁庭,原因是它侵犯了当事人的权利,所以它的使命到此结束。略去程序的细节不谈,1997 年 11 月 24 日,孟加拉最高法院(Supreme Court of Bangladesh)发出禁令,禁止意大利公司继续仲裁,并且在 2002 年 4 月 5 日,达卡一审法院以仲裁庭不当拒绝国有公司的要求为由撤销了仲裁庭的裁决权。[211]

但是,在 2001 年 4 月 30 日仲裁庭还是就程序问题作出决定,认为仲裁程序可以继续进行。仲裁庭的决定是基于它所持的在什么情况下

---

[209] See *supra*, § 41.

[210] ICC Case No. 7934, unpublished, described in the Decision on jurisdiction and provisional measures rendered on March 21, 2007 in ICSID Case No. ARB/05/07, *Saipem SpA v. Bangladesh*, *International Arbitration Report*, April 2007, p. B-1. See also the Award rendered on June 30, 2009 in ICSID Case No. ARB/05/07, *Saipem SpA v. Bangladesh*, available on the *Investment Claims* and *ITA—Investment Treaty Arbitration* websites.

[211] 参见 *ASA Bull.*, 2000, p. 821 的决定,并且评论员建议转移仲裁地是保持仲裁程序完整性和使当事人的仲裁协议有效的唯一方法,*ibid.*, p. 829. 参见,同理——单独地区的仲裁表现形式的主观主义观点的特点(*supra*, § 14)—Scherer's commentary, quoted *infra*, footnote 223. 从跨国观点的角度,比较 P. Lalive, On the Transfer of Seat in International Arbitration, *Law and Justice in a Multistate World. Essays in Honor of Arthur T. von Mehren* (J. A. R. Nafziger & S. C. Symeonides eds.), Ardsley, New York, Transnational Publishers, Inc., 2002, p. 515.

仲裁员可以被解散的观点,它认为只有国际商会仲裁院,而不是国家法院,有权力根据当事人已经同意的仲裁规则解散仲裁员。这个决定导致孟加拉法院的进一步命令,其禁止 Saipem 继续仲裁程序。这一切都没能阻止仲裁庭于 2003 年 5 月 9 日就案件的实体问题作出裁决,该庭认为 Petrobangla 需要为违反合同义务支付各项赔偿。国有公司要求孟加拉最高法院撤销裁决,法院认为,由于仲裁庭的裁决权已经被取消了,没有所谓的裁决存在以供撤销,用法院的话来说:"一个不存在的裁决既不能被撤销也不能被执行"[212]。孟加拉法院拒绝承认国有公司自愿签署的仲裁协议的法律效力,这最终迫使 Saipem 依据这个仲裁协议,向解决投资争端国际中心(International Center for Settlement of Investment Disputes, ICSID)提出仲裁请求,要求根据孟加拉和意大利签订的双边投资条约追究孟加拉的国际责任。2009 年 6 月 30 日,由 Gabrielle Kaufmann-Kohler 担任主席,Christoph Schreuer 和 Philip Otton 组成的 ICSID 仲裁庭认为,取消 ICC 仲裁员的权力不但违背了国际法,而且相当于剥夺了当事人在孟加拉根据《ICC 仲裁规则》仲裁解决纠纷的权利,所以作为赔偿,仲裁庭要求 ICC 裁决中规定的金额必须被支付给 Saipem。[213]

79. 另一个例子是在一家名为 Himpurna California Energy Ltd. (Himpurna)的在百慕大群岛建立的公司和印度尼西亚共和国之间关于发展和开发地热资源的合同纠纷。本案中,1999 年 5 月 4 日作出的第一个裁决要求 PLN(印度尼西亚国家电力公司)支付 3.9 亿美元本金给 Himpurna。由于 PLN 没有履行裁决,Himpurna 提起了第二个仲裁,被申请人是印度尼西亚共和国,申请仲裁的依据是印度尼西亚财政部(Ministry of Finance)签署的担保书,该担保书规定争议应当根据《联合国国际贸易法委员会仲裁规则》在雅加达进行。仲裁庭由 Jan Paulsson 担任主席,Antonino de Fina 和 Priyatna Abdurrasyid 组

---

[212] Cited in *Saipem SpA v. Bangladesh*, 在 2007 年 3 月 21 日,就管辖权和临时措施作出的决定, *op. cit.* footnote 210, § 36.

[213] *Saipem SpA v. Bangladesh*, *op. cit.*, footnote 210.

成。尽管国有公司 Pertamina 仅仅是签订产生争议的合同的一方而不是第二个仲裁程序的当事人,它请求印度尼西亚法院暂停仲裁,原因是仲裁程序可能损害该公司。1999 年 7 月 22 日,雅加达中央地区法院(Central District Court of Jakarta)批准了 Pertamina 的请求,命令暂停仲裁程序,还规定不遵守禁令的后果是每天 100 万美元的罚款。1999 年 9 月 7 日仲裁庭作出程序决定,认为尽管雅加达始终作为仲裁地,但是审讯可以在海牙进行。这个决定的根据是《联合国国际贸易法委员会仲裁规则》的第 16 条,该条允许仲裁庭根据仲裁的实际情况,在它认为合适的地方进行审讯。于是印度尼西亚共和国请求荷兰法院发布禁令,禁止仲裁的进一步进行。1999 年 9 月 20 日,海牙第一审法院驳回了这个请求。[214] 由印度尼西亚指定的仲裁员是该国国民,没有参加仲裁审讯。所以程序在另外两位仲裁员主持下进行,被申请人(印度尼西亚财政部)在审讯中缺席。1999 年 9 月 7 日仲裁庭就程序问题作出决定,认为印度尼西亚法院的决定不能阻碍它继续仲裁。仲裁庭认为,根据国际法国家需要对本国法院的行为负责,仲裁庭将契约即允诺和拒绝司法(denial of justice)的原则作为决定继续仲裁程序的基础:

> 考虑到合同神圣是国际法的基本规则,禁令违背了印度尼西亚共和国在任命规则(Terms of Appointment)之下的承诺,正是根据该规则国际仲裁庭才被建立起来的;
> 考虑到阻止仲裁庭根据印度尼西亚事先正式同意的程序完成它的使命会导致拒绝司法。[215]

被申请人的律师对仲裁庭的决定表示异议:

> 我们对决定的内容表示极度愤怒,因为一个处理由印度尼西

---

[214] *Yearbook Commercial Arbitration*, 2000, p. 469. For a description of the case, see also J. Paulsson, *Denial of Justice in International Law*, London, Cambridge University Press, 2005, pp. 150—153.

[215] Order issued on September 7, 1999, cited in the Award of September 26, 1999, *Yearbook Commercial Arbitration*, 2000, p. 109, at p. 144.

亚法律调整的案件的仲裁庭不但无视该法的规定,还认为可以不尊重该国法院的命令,并公开藐视该国法院的管辖权。[216]

被申请人还把对仲裁庭的异议提交到作为仲裁员的委任机构的 ICSID 的秘书长处,被申请人认为:

> 在仲裁界众所周知的是,(该仲裁庭的主席)一直致力于提高国际仲裁的地位和他自己在内的国际仲裁员的权力,以望不受到世界上任何法院的管辖。[217]

在 1999 年 9 月 26 日作出的关于管辖权的裁决中,仲裁庭重申它不认为自己受到印度尼西亚法院发出的禁令约束,因为本仲裁不是印度尼西亚国内仲裁而是一个国际仲裁。[218] 仲裁庭还认为虽然没有证据表明禁令是针对仲裁庭作出的[219],但是,在任何情况中,该禁令都导致拒绝司法,因此违反了国际法:

> 本庭认为,若一个国家已经同意了某仲裁庭的权力,而且明确知道外国当事人考虑到可以通过仲裁解决争议才投资于该国的,但是事后该国法院阻止该外国当事人到此仲裁庭前请求救济,这构成了拒绝司法。本庭已经提醒双方当事人了,一个国家需要对自己法院的行为承担责任,国家与此相关的责任之一正是拒绝司法产生的责任。[220]

在这个背景下,在第三位仲裁员缺席的情况下[221],仲裁庭裁定它对本案有管辖权,并且随后就实体问题作出裁决,认为根据政府提

---

[216] Ibid., p. 146.

[217] Ibid., p. 151. 委任机构驳回了该项异议,从而仲裁庭在 1999 年 10 月 16 日就实体问题作出裁决,ibid., p. 109 et seq.

[218] Ibid., p. 178.

[219] Ibid., pp. 183—185.

[220] Ibid., pp. 182—183.

[221] 就"缺员仲裁庭"仲裁的可能性,特别参见 S. Schwebel, *International Arbitration: Three Salient Problems*, Cambridge Publications, 1987, p. 177 et seq.

供的担保书,印度尼西亚共和国应当承担责任,所以需要支付给 Himpurna 在第一份裁决中确定的金额。[222]

80. 第三个国际仲裁庭不认为自己受到仲裁地发出的禁诉令约束的例子是 ICC 第 10623 号案件的裁决。该案涉及一家叫 Salini Costruttori SpA 的意大利公司和埃塞俄比亚联邦民主共和国。[223] 争议的焦点是一个为亚的斯亚贝巴建造污水处理池的 FIDIC 合同。合同包含一个仲裁条款,其规定在亚的斯亚贝巴进行 ICC 仲裁。意大利公司向由 Emmanuel Gaillard 担任主席以及 Piero Bernardini 和 Nael Bunni 组成的仲裁庭提出多项仲裁请求。

根据本案所适用的《ICC 仲裁规则》中的受托事项(Terms of Reference)的明确规定,仲裁庭可以在它认为合适的任何地方开庭审理案件,所以仲裁庭决定在巴黎开庭听取某些证人的证词,但是亚的斯亚贝巴仍然作为仲裁地。被申请人认为这是一个非法的程序决定,它向国际商会仲裁院对仲裁员提出回避要求,但是最终失败。接下来,被申请人向埃塞俄比亚联邦最高法院(Federal Supreme Court of Ethiopia)申请——并且获得了——禁令,命令仲裁庭立即暂停程序,直到法院就 ICC 驳回对仲裁员的回避申请一案作出决定。被申请人也向第一审法院(First Instance Tribunal)对仲裁庭的管辖权提出异议。该院命令申请人停止仲裁直到它对仲裁庭的管辖权作出决定为止。但是就在这种情况下,2001 年 12 月 7 日,仲裁庭仍然就管辖权问题和就被申请人要求暂停仲裁程序问题作出裁决。

---

[222] 1999 年 10 月 16 日就实体问题的裁决, *International Arbitration Report*, 2000, volume 15, no. 2, p. A-1, and excerpts in *Yearbook Commercial Arbitration*, 2000, p. 186.

[223] *Salini Costruttori SpA v. The Federal Democratic Republic of Ethiopia, Addis Ababa Water and Sewerage Authority*, Award of December 7, 2001, ICC Case No. 10623, in *IAI Series on International Arbitration No. 2. Anti-Suit Injunctions in International Arbitration*, op. cit. note 83, p. 227; excerpts in *ASA Bull.*, 2003, p. 82. 就对于该裁决的介绍和评价,参见 A. Crivellaro, International Arbitrators and Courts of the Seat—Who Defers to Whom?, *ASA Bull.*, 2003, p. 60, and M. Scherer, The Place or "Seat" of Arbitration (Possibility, and/or Sometimes Necessity of its Transfer?)—Some Remarks on the Award in ICC Arbitration No. 10623, *ASA Bull.*, 2003, p. 112.

仲裁庭认为它的首要职责是为当事人解决提交的争议：

> 由于下述原因，本庭就此问题认为，在这种情况下组建的仲裁庭可以行使自由裁量权决定是否服从法院的命令。
>
> 国际仲裁庭和仲裁地的国家法院不同，它不是该国的一个国家机关。本庭权力的首要来源是当事人同意仲裁的协议。这产生的重要结果之一是本庭对当事人负有职责来保证他们达成的仲裁协议不会落空。在某些情况下，有必要拒绝服从仲裁地法院的命令，目的是让本庭履行对当事人负有的更大的职责。
>
> 当然，这不是说合同，包括仲裁协议的有效性是独立于任何法律秩序的。诚然，合同的约束力来自它被一个或者多个法律秩序认可。但是，将争议提交国际仲裁的协议并不完全基于仲裁地的法律秩序。这种合同的有效性来自一系列在仲裁地之外的国际渊源和规范。[224]

仲裁庭的裁决参考了各种渊源，其中不但有1958年《纽约公约》还有埃塞俄比亚的法律：

> 需要注意的是虽然埃塞俄比亚尚未批准或者加入《纽约公约》，《埃塞俄比亚民法典》认可仲裁协议的有效性，该法典是国际仲裁现代立法的典型代表。这在许多方面使得埃塞俄比亚没有批准《纽约公约》的问题不存在了。实际上，《埃塞俄比亚民法典》的某些条款比略显陈旧的《纽约公约》更加自由。[225]

仲裁庭先强调它有充分的自信认为，埃塞俄比亚法院在审理支持仲裁的当事人提起的上诉后，会最终认可当事人的仲裁协议有效；接着仲裁庭指出：

---

[224] *Ibid.*, §§ 127—129.
[225] *Ibid.*, § 132.

本庭有职责保障当事人同意提交国际仲裁解决争议的协议被有效执行,**即使这样做会和仲裁地的法院产生矛盾**。[226]

仲裁庭为支持自己的决定,也参考了仲裁员有义务作出可以执行的裁决的观点,以及法律的一般原则,后者要求国家或者国有单位不能利用本国法来否定自愿达成的仲裁协议。仲裁庭的结论再次肯定了自己具有管辖权,而且宣布它会发出程序命令以决定解决案件的实体问题的步骤。在这个裁决作出后,当事人达成了和解协议。

81. 上述三个例子说明,当仲裁员面临着旨在废除当事人自愿达成的仲裁协议的诉讼时,他们不但不会认为自己受到仲裁地的法院约束,相反会毫不迟疑地决定当事人争议的实体问题。这证明了,对于仲裁员而言,仲裁地的法律秩序不是国际仲裁的法律属性的渊源,至少不是排他性的渊源。这个观点的基础正是认可存在仲裁法律秩序的国际仲裁的表现形式。

B. 在国家法院和仲裁庭之间的平行程序问题

82. 平行程序的概念是否可以决定,某国的法院还是仲裁庭可以优先审理案件的问题,最终取决于我们依据的国际仲裁的表现形式。当一个当事人认为就争议事项存在有效的仲裁协议,并且向某仲裁庭提出解决该争议的申请;同时,另一当事人认为仲裁协议是无效的或者是不适用的,所以将争议诉诸国家法院。在这个情况下,我们是否要适用平行程序的概念,就像我们正在处理两个国家法院之间的诉讼一样,或者我们需要使用特别的规则来决定是仲裁庭还是国家法院有管辖权呢?

83. 如果我们采用第一种国际仲裁的表现形式,就会认为仲裁庭已经和仲裁地的国家法律秩序结合了,仲裁庭的地位就像当地法院一样,所以平行程序的规则是完全适用的,这就像涉及同样当事人

---

[226] *Ibid.*, § 138, emphasis added.

的同样的案件被两个国家法院同时审理一样。

然而,如果我们采用威斯特伐利亚的国际仲裁的表现形式,就会认为,若一个当事人依据仲裁协议提起仲裁,另一个当事人对仲裁协议有异议所以将争议诉诸法院的时候,每个法律秩序都可以自由决定仲裁协议的有效性,所以适用平行程序的规则是不合适的。根据定义,每个国家不受到其他国家对仲裁协议和裁决的有效性的看法的约束,所以没有理由暂停仲裁程序以等待受理同样问题的法院作出决定。根据这个国际仲裁的表现形式,平行程序的观点是站不住脚的。认可存在仲裁法律秩序的表现形式会依据不同的理由得出同样的结论。

根据认可存在仲裁法律秩序的仲裁的表现形式,仲裁庭和国家法院之间的冲突是通过这个法律秩序特殊的机制解决的,而不是通过借用国际私法平行程序的概念,来识别在同样有权力审理争议的机构中的哪一个将受理纠纷。这个机制的基础是仲裁庭自裁管辖权原则,当仲裁员的管辖权被质疑的时候,它授予仲裁员决定他们自己的管辖权的权力——仲裁员的管辖权还没有被确定的事实并不会使自裁管辖权原则在逻辑上有问题。这个原则并不意味着国家法院没有权力决定作为仲裁员管辖权基础的仲裁协议的有效性和范围。这个原则仅仅允许,在存在表面上(*prima facie*)有效的仲裁协议的时候,仲裁员可以优先决定他们的管辖权,但是仲裁员随后需要服从被申请决定裁决是否在本国法律秩序中有效的国家法院的审查。对仲裁员而言,仲裁庭自裁管辖权原则有一个积极影响(positive effect),即它让仲裁员们能够继续完成使命。对国家法院来说,该原则有一个消极影响(negative effect),即它请求法院不要审理被表面上有效的仲裁协议包含的事项,这样仲裁员才能够首先有针对性地决定产生争议的仲裁协议的有效性和范围。[227]

---

〔227〕 关于仲裁庭自裁管辖权原则的积极和消极影响,参见 E. Gaillard and J. Savage (eds.), *Fouchard Gaillard Goldman On International Commercial Arbitration*, *op. cit.* footnote 37, at § § 650 *et seq.* See also E. Gaillard and Y. Banifatemi, Negative Effect of Competence-Competence: The Rule of Priority in Favour of the Arbitrators, *Enforcement of Arbitration Agreements and International Arbitral Awards* (E. Gaillard & D. di Pietro eds.), London, Cameron May, 2008, p. 257.

84. 所以,仲裁庭自裁管辖权原则和平行程序原则有清楚的区别。后者仅仅考虑哪一个法院先受理案件。如果将后者适用于仲裁,它甚至不要求对一方当事人认为有效但是另一方认为无效的仲裁协议进行表面审查。在对同一个争议有平等的管辖权的法院之间进行选择的时候,纯粹的时间先后测试才是合理的。例如,在欧盟内部,案件是由被告的住所地还是争议的义务履行地的法院管辖没有区别。因为根据和管辖权有关的规则,两地的法院都可以同样正当地审理案件。[228] 在这个背景下,将处理争议的优先权授予在时间上首先受理案件的法院的规则是完全中立的,因为它仅仅取决于诉讼当事人先向哪个法院起诉。这个规则仅仅为了避免同样的争议被提交多个法院,防止浪费司法资源,并且避免产生使司法系统失信的矛盾决定。它的目的不是针对其他法院,来保护某个法院的管辖权。

仲裁庭自裁管辖权原则和平行程序原则有完全不同的逻辑。它不是中立的,因为保护仲裁是它的特别目的。当现代立法者推广仲裁这种私人的争议解决方式,并常常将之誉为解决国际纠纷的常用途径的时候,他们非常清楚仲裁的弱点。这是因为仲裁员的管辖权完全基于当事人的意愿。和质疑国家法院的管辖权相比,故意破坏仲裁就容易多了——只要提出纯粹的形式理由即可,例如主张如果仲裁员的管辖权还不明确,他们就没有权力决定包括他们自己的管辖权在内的任何问题。所以,为了对付在许多情况下纯粹属于诉讼策略的抗辩,仲裁法认为有必要授予仲裁员首先决定自己管辖权的可能性。国家对仲裁员管辖权的复查绝对不能,就像有时候有人建议的那样,否定这个优先规则。国家的复查应当推迟到仲裁程序结束之后。这就是仲裁庭自裁管辖权原则有消极影响的根本原因。仲裁优先是这个原则的核心,它和以中立

---

[228] See Articles 2(1) and 5(1) of the Council Regulation (EC) No. 44/2001 of December 22, 2000 on jurisdiction and the recognition and enforcement of judgments in civil and commercial matters, known as "Brussels I", *OJEC*, January 16, 2001, p. L 12/1.

精神为特点的平行程序概念截然相反。[229]

85. 瑞士法——尽管被认为是对仲裁最友好的法律之一——也经历了一小段不确定时期。

2001年5月14日,瑞士联邦法院就 Fomento 一案作出决定,法院认为当在瑞士进行某仲裁之前,一个在其他国家就同样问题进行的诉讼已经展开的时候,仲裁员需要暂停仲裁程序以待外国法院就同样的争议作出决定为止。瑞士法院引用了《国际私法法》第9条作为依据,该条授予出现平行程序的时候受理案件在先的法院优先权[230]。在此案中,一家名为 Fomento 的西班牙公司和一家名为 CTT 的巴拿马公司,签订了一份包含 ICC 瑞士仲裁条款的合同。当争议发生后,西班牙公司到巴拿马法院起诉,法院受理了案件。巴拿马公司对巴拿马法院的管辖权提出异议,因为当事双方签订有仲裁协议。但是,甚至在 CTT 还没来得及根据合同规定的争端解决条款申请仲裁之前,巴拿马法院已经决定自己具有管辖权,原因是 CTT 没有按时提出管辖权异议,并且法院还就争议的实体问题作出了决定。当上诉还在巴拿马法院进行的时候,仲裁庭被组建起来并随后裁定自己对案件有管辖权。瑞士联邦法院撤销仲裁裁决的原因是:

---

[229] See, on these issues, E. Gaillard, La reconnaissance, en droit suisse, de la seconde moitié du principe d'effet négatif de la compétence-compétence, *op. cit.* footnote 38. In the same vein, see A. Bucher, L'examen de la compétence internationale par le juge suisse, *La semaine judiciaire*, 2007, p. 153, at pp. 173 *et seq.*

[230] Swiss Federal Tribunal, May 14, 2001, *Fomento de Construcciones y Contratas S. A. v. Colon Container Terminal S. A.*, ATF 127 III 279; *Rev. arb.*, 2001, p. 835, note by J.-F. Poudret; *Yearbook Commercial Arbitration*, 2004, p. 809. See also A. Bucher's commentary, L'examen de la compétence internationale par le juge suisse, *op. cit.* footnote 229, at pp. 182 *et seq.*; M. Scherer, When Should an Arbitral Tribunal Sitting in Switzerland Confronted with Parallel Litigation Abroad Stay the Arbitration?, *ASA Bull.*, 2001, p. 451; C. Oetiker, The Principle of *Lis Pendens* in International Arbitration: The Swiss Decision in *Fomento v. Colon*, *Arbitration International*, 2002, p. 137; C. Söderlund, *Lis Pendens*, *Res Judicata* and the Issue of Parallel Judicial Proceedings, *Journal of International Arbitration*, 2005, p. 301.

当仲裁地在瑞士的仲裁庭受理了一件正在被瑞士法院或外国法院审理的案件的时候,该庭必须适用《国际私法法》的第9条。[231]

从实践的角度看,这个结论是特别不幸的。如果我们跟着这个分析往下走,它等于允许,一个想阻止仲裁进行的当事人只要先在某国法院(可能是它本国的法院)发起诉讼,然后要求已经受理该案的仲裁员暂停仲裁程序。如果诉讼成功,这个当事人会要求仲裁庭接受国家法院的决定,因为法院受理纠纷在先。

从理论角度而言,这个结论也站不住脚。它忽视了《国际私法法》的第9条——和该法第19条关于强行规则的规定一样[232]——不能适用于国际仲裁,因为它们没有包含在该法第12章专门适用国际仲裁的条款中。所以,瑞士联邦法院在程序问题上将仲裁地位于瑞士的仲裁员等同于瑞士法官的做法没有理论根据。

因此,令人欣喜的是,瑞士立法机构迅速在2006年10月6日制定了一个2007年3月1日生效的法规,目的是推翻 Fomento 案的判决。这项法规在《国际私法法》的第186条关于仲裁庭可以自裁管辖权的规定中增加了一段话。新的第1款之二如下:

> 除非存在重大理由需要暂停仲裁程序,(仲裁庭)应当决定自己的管辖权,即使在相同当事人之间就同样问题的诉讼已经被国家法院或者其他仲裁庭受理。[233]

---

[231] Swiss Federal Tribunal, May 14, 2001, *Fomento de Construcciones y Contratas S. A. v. Colon Container Terminal S. A.*, Recital 2c. cc, author's translation.

[232] 就瑞士的法律选择规则,包括瑞士《国际私法法》的第19条,不能适用于仲裁的问题,参见后文 § 109。

[233] New Article 186 (1 bis). For a commentary, see Ch. Poncet, Swiss Parliament Removes *Lis Pendens* as an Obstacle to International Arbitrations in Switzerland, *World Arbitration & Mediation Report*, 2006, volume 17, no. 12, pp. 395—397; D. Baizeau, Modification de l'article 186 de la LDIP suisse: procédures parallèles et litispendance, clarification du législateur après la jurisprudence Fomento, *Les Cahiers de l'Arbitrage*, volume IV, Paris, Pedone, 2008, p. 226; E. Gaillard, Switzerland Says *Lis Pendens* Not Applicable to Arbitration, *New York Law Journal*, August 7, 2006; A. Bucher, L'examen de la compétence internationale par le juge suisse, *op. cit.* footnote 229, at p. 188 *et seq.*

因为适用于瑞士法官的规则不一定适用于在瑞士仲裁的仲裁员,所以通过撤销 *Fomento* 案的决定,瑞士的立法机构恢复了瑞士法的承认国际仲裁完全自治的传统。

(二) 国际仲裁表现形式对仲裁员裁决的影响

86. 从国家的角度出发,仲裁员裁决权力的渊源集中反映了各种不同的国际仲裁表现形式对仲裁这种私人的争议解决方式[234]的态度,它比仲裁员决定每个争议的实体问题所用的方式要重要得多——甚至在国家享有排他的执行司法决定的权力的限度内[235],裁决在国家法律秩序中的命运也比仲裁员决定每个争议的实体问题所用的方式更加重要。一旦国家认可了仲裁员这个私人的法官能够胜任主持正义的职责,并且一旦国家确定了什么争议能够通过仲裁这个争议解决机制解决,除非国家改变认可仲裁的态度,它们只能授予仲裁员很大的自由来进行仲裁程序以及识别和适用解决争议的实体问题的规则。由于裁决和国家法律秩序相结合,仲裁员需要保证仲裁程序满足程序正义的基本原则,并保证裁决的实体内容符合国家法律秩序的根本要求。所以,根据定义,仲裁程序进行的方式和仲裁员决定争议的分析方法,是仲裁员可以行使最广泛的自由裁量权的两大领域。然而,这两大领域中仍然残余着国际仲裁的各种表现的形式的影响。

仲裁员对国际仲裁的表现形式有不同理解,这会更加直接地影响他们如何界定当事人在选择决定解决争议的实体规则方面意思自治的范围。就支持或者拒绝适用各个国家法律秩序中不同甚至矛盾的强行规则的问题,不同的仲裁表现形式会得出不同的结论。这种分歧,就如不同的仲裁表现形式对仲裁员裁决权的看法的分歧一样鲜明。

在这一个章节中,首先分析的是,在仲裁员进行仲裁程序和识别

---

[234] See *supra*, § 69.
[235] See *infra*, § 124.

并适用解决争议的实体规则方面,各种国际仲裁的表现形式会如何影响他们行使自由裁量权。然后,讨论每种表现形式如何看待限制当事人自由选择解决争议的实体规则的问题。

A. 国际仲裁表现形式对仲裁员自由进行仲裁程序和识别解决争议的实体规则的影响

87. 就历史而言,值得注意的是,相对于国家法律秩序,在仲裁程序适用的法律和解决实体问题的法律两方面,仲裁自治的首次表现是在 20 世纪上半叶。一方面,仲裁程序从仲裁地的法律秩序中解放出来,另一方面,仲裁员能够自由决定是否采用仲裁地——仲裁地被认为是仲裁管辖地——的冲突法规范以确定解决争议的实体法,正是这两个方面导致了第一场揭示了存在不同的国际仲裁的表现形式的论战。本书在尝试将这些表现形式系统化的同时,还会讨论仲裁员的裁决权这个重大问题。

这两个方面都经历了一场清晰的演变过程。在每个方面的演变中,认为仲裁员等同于仲裁地的国内法官的观点逐渐让位于认为仲裁员可以自由背离仲裁地的国家法院采纳的规则的观点,演变的途径代表着日益形成一个认可存在自治的仲裁法律秩序的国际仲裁的表现形式。

(1) 仲裁程序

88. 就仲裁程序而言,几乎所有国际仲裁法的渊源都向着给予仲裁员更多自由的方向演变(i),这个演变提出了是否有必要持久地将一个国际仲裁的表现形式置于另一个之上的问题(ii)。对上述问题的回答是肯定的,所以非常有必要分析仲裁领域的发展趋势(iii)。

i) 演变进化中的渊源

89. 就仲裁程序而言,1923 年 9 月 24 日的《日内瓦仲裁条款议定书》(*Geneva Protocol on Arbitration Clauses*)采纳了第一种国际仲裁表现形式。它的第 2 条规定:

>仲裁程序,包括仲裁庭的建立,必须受到当事人的意志和仲裁进行地所在国的法律的调整。

对这种表现形式最清晰的表述是在 1952 年锡耶纳(Siena)会议上讨论和 1957 年的阿姆斯特丹会议上接受的《国际法研究所决议》(Resolutions of the Institute of International Law)中。因为它的起草者们,包括最早也是最重要的委员会报告起草者 Georges Sauser-Hall 在内,完全接受了将仲裁员等同于仲裁地的国内法官的观点,所以该决议授予仲裁地的法律在调整程序问题上的决定性地位。该决议允许当事人只有在仲裁地法律许可的情况下才可以无视该法中的禁止性规定。1957年《阿姆斯特丹决议》(Amsterdam Resolution)的第 9 条规定:

>仲裁地的法律必须决定当事人是否可以自由制定仲裁程序。[236]

所以并不奇怪,F. A. Mann 等学者会无条件地接受了这个决议。[237]

90. 后来《国际法研究所决议》被法学著作严厉批评。许多学者强调了仲裁程序和仲裁地之间的联系根本无关紧要,而且允许当事人选择调整程序的法律更加符合仲裁的本质,所以当事人的合意应当胜过仲裁地法律的禁止性规定。[238] 因此,1962 年在 Clive Schmitthoff 教授组织的关于国际贸易法渊源的讨论会上,Lagergren 法官就程序法问题作出如下评论:

>过去(仲裁)的一个显著特点……是某些法律制度要求仲裁员将仲裁进行地的法律作为仲裁程序法。在现代国际商事交易

---

[236] Institute of International Law, *Yearbook*, 1957, volume 47, part II, p. 394, at p. 419;《阿姆斯特丹决议》的英文翻译可以在国际法研究所的网站上找到。See Institute of International Law, *Yearbook*, 1952, volume 44, part I, p. 469, at p. 597.

[237] F. A. Mann, *Lex Facit Arbitrum*, *op. cit.* footnote 44, at pp. 164 *et seq.*

[238] On this issue, see Ph. Fouchard, *L'arbitrage commercial international*, *op. cit.* footnote 48, § § 495 *et seq.*

中……这常常不过意味着在某个对所有当事人和证人都便利并且易于抵达的城市的旅馆中进行审讯,因此那个地方的法律和仲裁实在关联甚微。[239]

就决定调整仲裁程序的规则而言,只将仲裁和当事人的意愿相联系从许多方面看起来都更加合适。[240]

91. 1958 年的《纽约公约》摒弃了《国际法研究所决议》的观点。在决定仲裁程序法方面,它明确了当事人的意愿要优先于仲裁地的法律适用。[241] 1961 年《国际商事仲裁欧洲公约》(*European Convention on International Commercial Arbitration*)从先前的认可当事人的意愿在决定仲裁程序法方面的优先性,进一步过渡到在当事人没有意思表示的时候,仲裁员可以在不考虑仲裁地法律的情况下决定仲裁程序法。[242] 即使当事人没有明示排除仲裁地法律的适用,仲裁员也没有义务适用该法。今天,大多数现代仲裁法都接受:

> 认为在当事人没有达成程序协议的情况下仲裁地采用的……民事程序法对仲裁员有约束力的老学说,已经不再被遵循了……[243]

92. 1989 年,国际法研究所也表示 1957 年阿姆斯特丹会议上采纳的决议已经不再反映主流观点了。在关于"在各个国家、国有企业或者国家机构,和外国企业之间的仲裁"的著作中,该研究所重新

---

[239] Judge Lagergren, *in The Sources of the Law of International Trade* (C. Schmitthoff, ed.), *op. cit.* footnote 10, p. 271.

[240] See esp. F.-E. Klein, *Considérations sur l'arbitrage en droit international privé*, Basel, Helbing & Lichtenhahn, 1955, §§ 127 *et seq.* and, by the same author, Autonomie de la volonté et arbitrage, *Rev. crit. DIP*, 1958, p. 255, at p. 280 *et seq.*

[241] See *supra*, § 33.

[242] For a commentary, see, *e. g.*, L. Kopelmanas, La place de la Convention européenne sur l'arbitrage commercial international du 21 avril 1961 dans l'évolution du droit international de l'arbitrage, *Annuaire français de droit international*, 1961, p. 331.

[243] J.-F. Poudret and S. Besson, *Comparative Law of International Arbitration*, *op. cit.* footnote 36, at § 532.

审查了1957年决议中以仲裁必须,与(由于各种原因)恰巧成为仲裁地的国家的法律相联系为前提的条款。研究所接受了大会报告起草人 Arthur von Mehren 的观点,他在分析了1957年决议中包含的原则后,指出:

> 这些观点已经丧失一致的支持。许多人现在认为仲裁程序没有必要和任何国内法相联系;当事人可以建立以合意为特点的程序,其空白将会被当事人进一步合意或者仲裁员所填补。[244]

1989年在圣地亚哥德孔波斯特拉(Santiago de Compostela)会议上国际法研究所采纳的决议反映了今天占统治地位的观点。与参考仲裁地的法律截然不同的是,甚至在当事人没有明示排除的情况下,决议认可:

> 当事人有完全的自治来决定适用于仲裁程序的……规则和原则。特别……这些规则和原则可以来自不同的国内法律制度以及非国家的渊源,例如国际法原则、法律的一般原则和国际商业惯例。[245]

所以,仲裁程序相对于国家法律秩序的自治性一目了然。

93. 绝大多数的主要仲裁规则都允许仲裁员自由决定仲裁程序。早在1975年,《ICC仲裁规则》认为仲裁员甚至不需要参考"当地程序法"(a municipal procedural law)以解决可能发生的仲裁程序

---

[244] Report by A. von Mehren, Institute of International Law, Santiago de Compostela session, *Yearbook*, 1989, volume 63, part 1, pp. 35 *et seq*., at § 27, p. 44.

[245] Institute of International Law, Session of Santiago de Compostela, 1989, Arbitration Between States, State Enterprises, or State Entities, and Foreign Enterprises, Article 6, *Yearbook*, 1989, volume 63, part I, p. 324, at p. 330. On the significance of the Resolution, see also A. T. von Mehren, Arbitration Between States and Foreign Enterprises: The Significance of the Institute of International Law's Santiago de Compostelle Resolution, *ICSID Review*, 1990, p. 54. A. von Mehren 这样总结演变过程:"在阿姆斯特丹,仲裁地法占控制地位。在圣地亚哥,仲裁地被当事人自治所取代;仲裁协议代替了仲裁地法", at p. 57.

问题。[246] 其他所有现代仲裁规则都持有类似的开明观点[247]。在此背景下,实践表明,在大多数案件中,仲裁员不再抽象地在开始仲裁的时候选择一个规范整个程序的法律;相反,他们在仲裁过程中出现程序问题的时候才具体问题具体分析。这显然不阻止仲裁员在开始仲裁程序的时候,根据当事人的意见,决定时间表、递交书面材料、提供文证、审问证人等仲裁程序应当进行的方式。因此解决和仲裁程序相关的问题越来越少地参考某个法律。[248]

因此,选择适用于仲裁程序的法律已经被在个案中具体问题具体分析所取代,唯一的规则是承认当事人自由,并且在当事人没有达成合意的情况下,承认仲裁员可以自由决定案件中具体的仲裁程序问题。

ii) 持续存在的风险

94. 在国际仲裁中广泛的自由化运动暗示接受任何一种仲裁的表现形式对解决仲裁程序问题根本毫无影响。真的有必要了解为什么仲裁员可以自由决定仲裁程序吗?无论仲裁员的自由来自仲裁员是一个自治的仲裁法律秩序的代言人的事实;或者完全来自仲裁地的法律秩序;再或者来自可能不需要审查仲裁员是如何行使这种自由就承认裁决的各种法律(它们对仲裁程序的唯一限制是要求仲

---

[246] 1998 年 1 月 1 日生效的《ICC 仲裁规则》第 15 条第 1 款从 1975 年至今本质上没有变化,该款规定:"仲裁庭审理案件的程序适用本规则。本规则没有规定的,适用当事人约定的规则,若当事人没有约定,则适用仲裁庭确定的规则,**无论仲裁庭是否援用仲裁适用的国内法的程序规则**。"(黑体强调为作者所加)。1975 年版本(第 11 条)"当地程序法"(a municipal procedural law)的用语被 1998 年的"**国内法的程序规则**"(rules of procedure of a national law)所取代,目的是更加清楚的强调 ICC 仲裁程序独立于仲裁地的法律。

[247] See, *e. g.*, Article 15(1) of the 1976 UNCITRAL Arbitration Rules, Article 16 of the 1997 ICDR (AAA) International Arbitration Rules, or Article 14 of the 1998 LCIA Arbitration Rules,都赋予仲裁员在进行仲裁程序方面的很大的自由裁量权。

[248] On this issue, see esp. D. Hascher, Principes et pratique de procédure dans l'arbitrage commercial international, *Collected Courses*, volume 279 (1999), p. 51; J. Lew, Achieving the Dream: Autonomous Arbitration, *Arbitration International*, 2006, p. 179, at p. 202; A. Baum, International Arbitration: The Path Toward Uniform Procedures, *Global Reflections on International Law, Commerce and Dispute Resolution. Liber Amicorum in honour of Robert Briner*, *op. cit.* footnote 38, p. 51.

裁员遵从当事人平等和正当程序原则,因为这些原则已经被广泛地接受从而成为跨国法律秩序的一部分)。对于在一个非常支持仲裁的国家中进行仲裁的仲裁员而言,他或者她不仅仅会自然地,而且可能倾向于参考仲裁法——实践中是仲裁地法[249]——而不是依赖对仲裁员自由的跨国理解。因为当应用跨国规则方法不产生直接的法律后果的时候,这个方法往往难以应用。实际上,在某些有经验的仲裁员中出现了一个趋势,若他们常常在非常支持仲裁的国家中进行仲裁,他们会认可仲裁程序和仲裁地法的联系[250];与此相反的是他们的前辈们利用每个机会倡导,在仲裁程序方面,仲裁员需要与所有法律秩序保持独立。Gabrielle Kaufmann-Kohler 教授是一位富有经验的仲裁员和学者,她在 1998 年进行了一项研究,内容涉及仲裁地法在决定和适用调整仲裁程序的规则方面的作用,她表示如果仲裁地——该地的选择完全取决于当事人的意愿——的法律确实调整仲裁程序的话,也不会给仲裁带来任何真正的不利因素,因为全世界对仲裁程序自由的广泛接受足以使得仲裁和谐发展:

> 如果我们已经认可(法律的)地点可能是虚构的,那么非内国化(delocalization)的问题就不存在了,因为非内国化的目的实际上已经实现了,虽然方式是间接的。就像曾经讨论的那样,非内国化的主要目的之一是避免碰巧成为仲裁地的地点的法律意外影响仲裁。选择一个对仲裁友好的虚构的仲裁地点完全实现了这个目的。
>
> ……如果通过对地点的选择,我们可以避免实际审理争议

---

[249] 就支持这个概念的作者在仲裁法(*lex arbitri*,或者 *lex arbitrii*)和仲裁地法之间建立的联系,see *supra*, § 14. 持不同意见者认为将仲裁法等同于仲裁地法不是不能避免的,see J. Gentinetta, *Die lex fori internationaler Handelsschiedsgerichte* (The *Lex Fori* International Commercial Arbitration Tribunals), Bern, Verlag Stämpfli et al., 1973, and F. Eisemann, La *lex fori* de l'arbitrage commercial international, *Travaux du Comité français de droit international privé*, Paris, Dalloz, 1977, p. 189 (March 19, 1975 session).

[250] See, *e. g*., G. Kaufmann-Kohler, Globalization of Arbitral Procedure, *Vanderbilt Journal of Transnational Law*, 2003, volume 36, no. 4, p. 1313, at p. 1315.

的地点的法律中不友好的因素,那么非内国化就丧失了它在实践中的许多好处。更不要说各地的仲裁法日益统一已经使得不太必要去专门寻找友好的裁判地点了。[251]

这个对仲裁程序的理想化的观点[252]和在 ICC 第 1512 号案件中作为独任仲裁员的 Pierre Lalive 作出的更加激烈的言论截然相反:

> 然而,被告没有意识到或者没有考虑到——由于问题是如此复杂,被告的表现可以理解——存在一个国际惯例,这个惯例现在已经得到广泛的认可,并且对这个惯例的表述存在于包括印度和巴基斯坦在内的多数文明国家们签订的国际条约中。根据这个惯例,国际商事仲裁可能完全与当事人的国家的法律分离:仲裁必须只受到当事人选择的或者在当事人协议中提到的仲裁规则(例如本案中的 ICC 规则)的约束。[253]

95. 上述言论仍然只是为了促进仲裁法的渊源向着更加自由的体系演化吗?若使用哲学术语,这里的对立体现在争取的自由(freedom gained)和获准的自由(freedom granted)之间。就像一个有开明的主人的奴隶,他能自由行动是因为他或者她根据存在一个适用于所有人的更高的价值有权利这样做,还是因为他或者她得到主人的许可呢?从方法论的角度看,奴隶的问题和仲裁员的问题如出一辙:仲裁员的自由是来自他们隶属的一个自治的法律秩序,还是这

---

[251] G. Kaufmann-Kohler, Identifying and Applying the Law Governing the Arbitration Procedure—The Role of the Law of the Place of Arbitration, *ICCA Congress Series No. 9. Improving the Efficiency of Arbitration Agreements and Awards—40 Years of Application of the New York Convention*, (A. J. van den Berg ed.), Deventer, Kluwer Law International, 1999, p. 336, at p. 354.

[252] 假设国家法律秩序已经统一的采取了对仲裁的友好态度,所以不太有必要保持仲裁和国家法律秩序的距离,从而试图复兴将仲裁员和仲裁地的国内法官等同的观点——人们可能觉得这种想法过分乐观——的例子之一,参见 see, e. g., R. Goode, *op. cit.* footnote 43, § 22, footnote 69.

[253] Award rendered by Pierre Lalive in ICC Case No. 1512 on January 14, 1970, *Yearbook Commercial Arbitration*, 1980, p. 174, at p. 176.

种自由是被仲裁地所在国或其他国家法律秩序所授予的呢？在后一种情况中，从实质上说，仲裁员的自由是有条件的。某个国家先前的开明态度实际上可能和后来它采取的对仲裁更加保守的态度截然相反，或者一个国家的法律给仲裁员的自由会和另一个国家通过法律或者法院给仲裁员的自由有天壤之别。[254] 相反，仲裁员的自由可以来自一个自治的仲裁法律秩序并不意味着他们的自由不受限制。法律的融合要求仲裁员在进行仲裁程序的时候尊重当事人平等和正当程序的基本原则，因为没有这些原则就没有公平裁判；遵守这些原则毫无疑问地组成了仲裁法律秩序的一部分，该秩序的内容可以通过比较法的方法确定。

96. 在现实中，就程序问题而言，有观点认为只要仲裁员遵守程序平等和正当程序的基本原则，他们在进行仲裁程序时的自由源自何处的问题日益丧失重要性。这种观点有两大局限。

97. 第一，不是所有的法律制度都有效保证，只要仲裁员遵守程序平等和正当程序的基本原则，他们就有按照自己的观点进行仲裁程序的自由。这种自由若干年前就在法国、瑞士或者英国等法律制度中得到保证的事实并不否认，在其他法律制度中，对这种自由的承认尚未付诸仲裁实践，还仅仅是一种奢望。

例如，迪拜法院审理的涉及 2002 年 2 月 20 日在迪拜作出的临时仲裁裁决。该仲裁的一方当事人是一家美国公司 International Bechtel Company Limited，另一方是迪拜政府的民航局（Department of Civil Aviation of the Government of Dubai），仲裁根据《联合国国际贸易法委员会仲裁规则》进行。争议涉及在迪拜建立一个主题公园。在审理过程中，仲裁员听取了许多专家和事实证人的证词。当事人就规范听取证人证词的程序规则达成合意，并且随后该合意载入一份仲裁庭和当事人签署的程序决定中。仲裁庭遵循了这个程序决

---

[254] 就国内法的现代化和与此相反的支持背离主流的地方司法实践的现象，参见 see *supra*, §22.

定，并且在完成审讯后，确保了每个当事方对程序的进行没有反对意见。当事人也都确认了他们对程序没有异议。[255] 尽管作出了确认，在被申请人被要求按照仲裁裁决支付 2440 万美元之后，它在当地法院中对仲裁裁决提出异议。被申请人主张，证人没有按照当地法律的要求宣誓作证。一审和上诉法院分别在 2002 年 11 月 16 日和在 2003 年 6 月 8 日作出决定，它们都接受了该主张并决定撤销裁决。无论这些法院的决定是否应当在仲裁地之外的国家法律秩序中产生影响[256]，这个案件表明了，就程序问题而言，尽管 1958 年的《纽约公约》摒弃了 1923 年的《日内瓦公约》，并承认了当事人意志优先于仲裁地法律[257]，仲裁法向日益自由方向的规范化发展，并不像人们希望的那样已经达到了高级阶段。

这种局面引发如下哲学思考：是否仲裁要受制于仲裁地的违反主流的法律，而满足于通过避免某些不友好的仲裁地来实现当事人进行仲裁的意愿——这些例子在现实中体现为到传统上对仲裁友好的地方进行仲裁——或者，与仲裁的普遍性保持一致，我们是否可以继续沿着 20 世纪 70 年代某些仲裁员所开拓的将仲裁与仲裁地法律分离的道路[258]，倡导可以到所有的地方仲裁（包括那些刚刚接受仲裁这种争端解决方式的国家）。

98. 第二，在程序问题上，当仲裁员行使大多数仲裁法渊源授予的自由的时候，他们一定会受到自己接受的国际仲裁表现形式的影响。在当事人没有协议的情况下，若仲裁员认为自己的权力完全来自仲裁地所在国的法律，他或者她会自然地采用仲裁地法院适用的程序规则，特别是如果该仲裁员在此国家接受过法律培训并且经常在此国的法院中代理诉讼。相反的是，若仲裁员认为存在一个超国家的仲裁程序，或者常常和许多具有不同背景的仲裁员在许多仲

---

[255] Unpublished award rendered on February 20, 2002, §§ 58—61. 就在美国的申请执行行为，see *infra*, footnote 362.

[256] On this question, see *infra*, §§ 125 *et seq*.

[257] See *supra*, § 33.

[258] See *supra*, footnote 253.

裁地点共事,他们就会将自己理解的公平和有效率的仲裁程序的要求,置于某个国内法之上,而无论该国是否是仲裁地。

例如,在当事人没有达成协议的情况下,如果在德国进行仲裁的仲裁员认为仲裁和仲裁地的法律紧密联系,他或者她往往会和德国法院一样认为某方当事人的高级经理不可以作为证人。[259] 在另一方面,一个支持更加跨国方法的仲裁员会更愿意接受这位高级经理的证言——接受这种证言在国际仲裁程序中是惯常做法——同时这个仲裁员会考虑证人和一方当事人的关系以判断该证人证言的证明力。[260]

类似地,在一个争议中,一方当事人以取消银行担保来报复提起仲裁的另一方当事人,认为程序必须被某个国内法规范的仲裁员,只有在适用于这个问题的法律有明文或者判例规定,并满足该法的全部其他条件的时候,才会要求恢复担保。相反,接受存在跨国程序规则的仲裁员可能直接依据禁止一方当事人采用加剧争端的行为的原则作出决定,因为该原则是被仲裁案例法广泛认可的一般原则。[261]

推而广之,不用说,一个仲裁员"不相信"存在跨国规则"而且更不相信存在内容全然不由得知的程序商人习惯法"(a procedural *lex mercatoria*)[262],他或者她当然对依据被其他仲裁员重复采用的原则或者比较法方法得出的观点不感兴趣;然而,若一个仲裁员认为法律

---

〔259〕 See, *e. g.*, V. Fischer-Zernin and A. Junker, Between Scylla and Charybdis: Fact Gathering in German Arbitration, *Journal of International Arbitration*, 1987, no. 2, p. 9, at p. 24.

〔260〕 On this question, see esp. D. Hascher, *Collected Courses*, op. cit. footnote 248, at p. 93 *et seq.*

〔261〕 See, *e. g.*, the Award rendered in 1981 in ICC Case No. 3344, *JDI*, 1982, p. 978, the Award rendered in 1987 in ICC Case No. 4761, *JDI*, 1987, p. 1012, the Award rendered in 1988 in ICC Case No. 5910, *JDI*, 1988, p. 1216 and, for a general view on the matter, Y. Derains, L'obligation de minimiser le dommage dans la jurisprudence arbitrale, *IBLJ*, 1987, p. 375.

〔262〕 A. Kassis, *L'autonomie de l'arbitrage commercial international. Le droit français en question*, op. cit. footnote 15, p. 236, footnote 14, author's translation.

融合使得识别跨国规则成为可能,他或者她会更加愿意接受这个观点。[263] 从所有认为仲裁员可以自由进行仲裁程序并且只需要服从程序公平的基本原则的法律渊源看来,这两个方法都同样可以接受。

iii) 对发展趋势的不断关注

99. 如果我们撇开仲裁员在个案中的心态,而将目光集中于从仲裁实务中产生的趋势,我们会对适用国际仲裁的特别规则得到广泛支持这一现象感到震惊。

这些规则取自民法法系和普通法系国家法院所遵从的程序规则,但是它们被组合、改造——有时是"杂交"(bastardization)[264]——已经重生成为特别适用于国际仲裁程序的规则[265]。这个趋势不是新的[266]。它只是在过去的几年中强化了[267]并且从私人的法典化行为中受益,这些行为包括国际律师协会制定的《国际商事仲裁取证规则》(Rules on the Taking of Evidence in International Commercial Arbitration of the International Bar Association)[268] 以及联合国国际贸易法委

---

[263] See, e.g., E. Loquin, L'application de règles anationales dans l'arbitrage commercial international, 1986, op. cit. footnote 95.

[264] 这符合赞赏杂交而非保持纯粹种族的哲学观点,就此问题,参见,e.g., J. L. Nancy, Etre singulier pluriel, Paris, Galilée, 1996, esp. the chapter entitled "Eloge de la mêlée", p.171.

[265] 就仲裁员所识别的原则,区分法律传统的基础,和采信证据的关系,参见 see Y. Derains, La Pratique de l'administration de la preuve dans l'arbitrage commercial international, Rev. arb., 2004, p.781.

[266] See, e.g., Ph. Fouchard, L'arbitrage commercial international, 1965, op. cit. footnote 48, § § 471 et seq.; see also the systematization of general principles of procedure put forward by M. de Boisséson, Le droit français de l'arbitrage interne et international, Paris, GLN Joly, 2nd ed., 1990, § § 714 et seq.

[267] For the scale of the phenomenon, see, e.g., M.-C. Rigaud, La procédure arbitrale transnationale, Doctoral Thesis, Paris XII University, 2008; G. Petrochilos, Procedural Law in International Arbitration, Oxford, Oxford University Press, 2004, at the list of known principles p.218 et seq.

[268] 1999 年 6 月 1 日国际律师协会制定的《国际商事仲裁取证规则》(可以在国际律师协会的网站上找到)。参见处理国际仲裁中的利益冲突的规则(《国际律师协会国际仲裁中的利益冲突指引》,国际律师协会理事会于 2004 年 5 月 22 日批准,可以在国际律师协会的网站上找到)。

员会和美国法律学会就程序问题的共同成果。[269] 在这方面需要注意的是，早在 1950 年[270]，国际法委员会（International Law Commission），根据特别大会报告起草人 Georges Scelle 的报告，已经起草了《仲裁程序示范规则》（Model Rules on Arbitral Procedure），其所提倡的诸原则在今天仍被津津乐道。[271]

像所有的跨国规则一样[272]，在仲裁实践中形成的程序规则也会演变。引人瞩目的例子是，在过去的几年间，一个不再被认为是纯粹美国模式的证据开示规则被在大陆法系国家进行仲裁的仲裁员们日益接受，他们往往根据该规则要求当事人提供和解决纠纷有关的文证，但是与此同时，这种规则常常不存在于仲裁地的国家法院程序中。[273]

（2）识别解决实体争议的规则

100. 和仲裁程序一样，决定用于解决争议实体问题的规则也经历了一场广泛的自由化运动（i），这揭示了国际仲裁的各种表现形式之间存在持久分歧的问题。由于仍然存在这些分歧（ii），非常有必要在这里讨论这场自由化运动的典型特征（iii）。

i）演变进化中的渊源

101. 同样在 20 世纪 70 年代，当仲裁程序从仲裁地的法院适用的规则中解放出来的时候，认为仲裁员需要根据仲裁地的法律选

---

[269] 美国法律学会/罗马国际私法协会《跨国民事诉讼原理》（*The ALI/UNIDROIT Principles of Transnational Civil Procedure*），分别在 2004 年 5 月和 4 月被美国法律学会和罗马国际私法协会正式通过 *Unif. L. Rev.*，2004，no.4，p.758；ALI／UNIDROIT, *Principles of Transnational Civil Procedure*, London, Cambridge University Press, 2006.

[270] See Report by Georges Scelle on arbitral procedure by the International Law Commission, *Yearbook of the International Law Commission*, 1950, volume II, p. 114.

[271] See the Model Rules on Arbitral Procedure adopted by the International Law Commission in 1958, *Yearbook of the International Law Commission*, 1958, volume II, p. 83 *et seq.*

[272] See *supra*, § 57.

[273] See D. Hascher, *Collected Courses*, *op. cit.* footnote 248, p. 89 *et seq.*; and G. Kaufmann-Kohler and P. Bärtsch, Discovery in International Arbitration: How Much is Too Much?, *SchiedsVZ*, 2004, no. 1, p. 13.

择规则决定适用于解决争议实体问题的法律规则的观点,已经日益让位于承认当事人自由的观点,并且在当事人没有达成合意的情况下,仲裁员可以自由选择适用于争议实体问题的法律,而不需要和仲裁地的法院保持一致。

决定解决争议的实体法和程序法的演变是同步进行的。这里再次重复国际仲裁的第一种表现形式出现在以 Sauser-Hall Report 为基础的 1957 年《国际法研究所决议》中。该决议的第 11 条关于"适用于不同实体的法律"规定:

> 仲裁地所在国所采用的法律选择规则必须用于确定解决不同实体问题的法律。
>
> 在这个法律的限度内,仲裁员应当适用当事人选择的法律或者,在当事人没有明示表示的时候,应当考虑案件的所有情形以决定在这方面什么是当事人的意志。[274]

仲裁地被当做仲裁管辖地,它的法律选择规则必须被适用的原因是,决议采用了"必须"这个字眼,并且当事人自己选择的解决实体问题的法律需要"在这个法律的限度内",例如,在"仲裁地所在国所采用的法律选择规则"的限度内。这个概念清晰地表明,无论当事人的意愿如何,国际仲裁仅仅是仲裁地的法律秩序主持正义的渠道之一。

102. 这个决议中和程序问题有关的条款受到强烈质疑。回顾采纳 1957 年决议之前发生的讨论,我们发现因为当事人合意是仲裁这座大厦的精髓所在,所以委员会的一些成员已经对草案没有足够考虑到当事人的意愿表示担忧了。例如,Georges Ripert 非常有策略地表示,他理解"让争议的所有问题受到同一个法律约束和将所有问

---

[274] Resolution adopted in 1957, Article 11, paragraphs 1 and 2, Institute of International Law, *Yearbook*, 1957, volume 47, part II, p.420;该决议的英文翻译可以在国际法研究所的网站上找到。See also, in identical terms, Article 11 of the draft Resolution presented at the 1952 Siena Session, *op. cit.* footnote 2, p.476.

题归于单个仲裁地调整的好处",然后他沉思道:"在仲裁员使用自由裁量权决定仲裁地的案件中,采用这个规则是否合情合理"[275]。他对这个问题[276]的三次干涉对大会草案起草者的决定没有任何影响,决议最终被采纳了。然而,生效的决议几乎立即遭到猛烈抨击。特别是,1963 年 Berthold Goldman 将他在海牙国际法学院课程的绝大部分用于证明决定实体争议适用的法律的体系可以完全独立于仲裁地的法律。[277]

学者们,例如 Lazare Kopelmanas 在 1964 年[278], Philippe Fouchard 在 1965 年[279] 或者 Pierre Lalive 在 1967 年[280] 都抨击了 1957 年国际法研究所的决议。Pierre Lalive 讨论了在瑞士进行仲裁的国际仲裁员们如何决定解决争议实体问题的法律,在文中他表示:

> 很难说明瑞士,作为国际仲裁地所在国,有兴趣用它的实体法甚至冲突法来解决常常和它毫无关系的争议的实体问题。从国际私法的术语以及从具体的准据法的角度,提交仲裁的争议和瑞士之间没有任何结构性联系,这在绝大多数情况下,足以使仲裁地理论失去说服力。[281]

---

[275] Institute of International Law, *Yearbook*, 1957, volume 47, part II, p. 424, author's translation.

[276] *Ibid.*, pp. 423, 424 and 427.

[277] *Collected Courses*, op. cit. footnote 3, at p. 480.

[278] L. Kopelmanas, *The Sources of the Law of International Trade*, op. cit. footnote 10, p. 272. 这位作者,当时是联合国欧洲经济理事会(the United Nations Economic Commission for Europe)的法律顾问,表示"用仲裁地的法律决定应当适用哪个冲突法体系是荒谬的"。

[279] Ph. Fouchard, *L'arbitrage commercial international*, op. cit. footnote 48, at §§ 546 *et seq.*

[280] P. Lalive, Problèmes relatifs à l'arbitrage commercial international, *Collected Courses*, volume 120 (1967), p. 569, at p. 613 *et seq.* By the same author, see Les règles de conflit de lois appliquées au fond du litige par l'arbitre international siégeant en Suisse, *Rev. arb.*, 1976, p. 155, at p. 168 *et seq.*, and Le droit applicable au fond par l'arbitre international, *Droit international et droit communautaire*, Colloquium Proceedings, Paris, April 5—6, 1990, Fondation Calouste Gulbenkian, 1991, p. 33, at p. 41 *et seq.*

[281] P. Lalive, Les règles de conflit de lois appliquées au fond du litige par l'arbitre international siégeant en Suisse, op. cit. footnote 280, at pp. 170—171, author's translation.

103. 1989年圣地亚哥德孔波斯特拉会议上，国际法研究所不但接受了仲裁程序独立于国家法律秩序的观点，还摒弃了在1957年处于主导地位的单独地区主义的仲裁表现形式。在讨论确定适用于政府合同的法律的时候，国际法研究所注意到陈旧的单独地区主义的仲裁表现形式已经不再代表主流观点了[282]，该研究所赞成当事人完全自治，并且认为在缺乏当事人合意的情况下，仲裁员有完全的自由来决定解决争议实体的法律。

1989年决议的第6条，在采纳了以 Arthur T. von Mehren 的报告的基础上，规定：

> 当事人享有完全的自由来决定……在仲裁案件中适用的实体规则和原则。特别……这些规则和原则可以来自不同的国内法律制度以及非国家的渊源，例如国际法原则、法律的一般原则和国际商业惯例。
>
> 若当事人没有达成合意，仲裁庭应当从第4条规定的渊源（当事人选择的法律、当事人约定的国际私法体系中规定的法律、国际公法和国际私法的一般原则、国际仲裁的一般原则或者仲裁庭所在地的国家的法院会适用的法律）中寻找必要的规则和原则。[283]

尽管仲裁地的法律选择规则没有从分析中完全消失，但是它们，在这个方面，仅仅是仲裁员考虑的众多因素之一，仲裁员的首要职责是执行当事人的协议，如果当事人没有签订协议，仲裁员需要自己选择适用于争议实体的法律。这个决议所体现的仲裁表现形式和1957年阿姆斯特丹会议所采纳的截然相反。仲裁地已经成为诸多参考因素之一并且，从规范的位阶而言，仲裁地法已经退居第二位，第一位

---

[282] See *supra*, § 92.

[283] Resolution adopted on September 12, 1989, *op. cit.* footnote 245, Article 6 (with reference to Article 4). See also A. T. von Mehren's commentary, Arbitration between States and Foreign Enterprises: The Significance of the Institute of International Law's Santiago de Compostela Resolution, *op. cit.* footnote 245.

是当事人的意志或者,在当事人没有合意的情况下,是仲裁员的意志。

104. 这个观点已经被大多数现代仲裁法和主要的仲裁规则所接受。今天,所有现代仲裁法均认可,在国际仲裁中,在决定准据法方面仲裁员的首要职责是尊重当事人的意愿,并且在当事人保持沉默的时候,仲裁员享有很大的作决定的自由。《联合国国际贸易法委员会国际商事仲裁示范法》确认了这一点。虽然该法没有反映就此问题的最现代的观点[284],但是它请仲裁员尊重当事人的意愿并且,在当事人没有合意的情况下,适用"(他们)认为合适的冲突法规则决定的法律"[285]。和许多国内法相反[286],虽然示范法仍然通过冲突法规则间接地约束仲裁员,但是由于仲裁员有完全的自由裁量权来选择他们愿意采用的冲突法规则,因此示范法并没有真正地约束仲裁员。在实践中,承认仲裁员有完全的自由来选择可以适用的法律,和承认仲裁员可以自由选择他们认为合适的冲突法规则以便找到可以适用于实体问题的法律,没有显著区别。类似的,今天大多数仲裁规则认可仲裁员有完全的自由来决定适用于争议实体问题的法律规则。[287]

ii) 持续存在的风险

105. 形成悖论的是,作为国际仲裁首先从国家法律秩序中脱离出来的两个领域之一,国内法承认当事人和仲裁员可以自由决定

---

[284] On the question, see, e. g., Ph. Fouchard, La Loi-type de la CNUDCI sur l'arbitrage commercial international, *JDI*, 1987, p. 861.

[285] See Article 28(1) and (2) of the Model Law of June 21, 1985.

[286] 关于承认仲裁员可以自由采用"直接的法律途径"(*voie directe*)方法,即在当事人没有选择的情况下,仲裁员可以采用他们认为合适的任何规则来解决实体问题,例见,《法国民事诉讼法典》第 1496 条:"仲裁员必须根据当事人选择的法律规则解决争议;在当事人没有选择的时候,根据他们认为合适的法律规则"(作者的翻译),《荷兰民事诉讼法典》第 1054 条第 2 款也有非常类似的规定。

[287] 特别参见,1988 年《ICC 仲裁规则》的第 17 条第 1 款、1998 年《伦敦国际仲裁院仲裁规则》的第 22 条第 3 款和 1997 年《争端解决的国际中心仲裁规则》(*1997 ICDR Arbitration Rules*)第 28 条第 1 款。

准据法引发了如下思考：就程序问题而言[288]，认为某种国际仲裁的表现形式优于其他的表现形式的观点在今天是否还有意义？在法国进行仲裁的仲裁员可以自由无视法国法院通常适用的法律选择规则，这是因为这些仲裁员不是法国法律秩序的代言人，还是因为《法国民事诉讼法典》第1496条允许他们那样做？对于仲裁程序而言，当仲裁发生在一个国家，但是该国仲裁法还没有和其他大多数国家的仲裁法一样经历自由化革新，这时对这个问题的回答就有重大的实践意义。即使在发生过这种革新的地方，当仲裁员行使今天他们通常享有的自由裁量权决定程序问题的时候，他们会自然地被自己接受的仲裁表现形式所引导。若一位仲裁员认为自己的作用相当于仲裁地所在国的法官，他或者她将自然地采用那个国家的冲突法规则来选择适用于实体问题的法律。一位接受威斯特伐利亚仲裁观点的仲裁员将会对多样化的法律制度，和他或者她可以采用的各种冲突法规则极其敏感，结果，在当事人没有合意的情况下，该仲裁员将倾向于适用自己认为合适的冲突法规则。1976年《联合国国际贸易法委员会仲裁规则》就是一个例子。若一位仲裁员认为仲裁是和国家法律秩序分离的，他或者她将会更加倾向于通过比较法分析过程来识别跨国法律选择规则；在当事人没有选择准据法的时候，仲裁员秉承的存在跨国规则的坚定信念，可能会导致这位仲裁员不适用任何法律选择规则，而直接适用通过比较法分析和识别的实体规则，或者适用某个学术团体特别制定出来以适应国际商事交易需要的实体规则[289]。不适用法律选择规则是因为它将一个国际问题降格为国内问题，所以它是不合适的。

iii) 对发展趋势的不断关注

106. 认为仲裁员在决定准据法方面的自由会导致他们采用的方法完全无迹可寻是一个误解。实践证明当当事人没有选择处理实体争议的准据法时，仲裁员往往强烈倾向于，无论他们这样做的原因

---

[288] See *supra*, §§ 94—98.
[289] 就国际商事活动的特别需要的观点，参见 *supra*, § 52。

何在,忽略可能和当事人的合理预期相反的当地特殊规则。例如,一个法国当事人和一个葡萄牙当事人签订了一份合同,其中包含限制责任的条款,该条款在法国法中有效,但是依据葡萄牙最高法院(Portuguese Court of Cassation)对《葡萄牙民法典》第809条的解释是无效的。[290] 若当事人没有选择准据法,一般仲裁员不会忽视大多数国内法承认有经验的当事人之间签订的限制责任条款有效的事实,他们也不会不考虑如果他们适用一个包含在当事人很可能不知道并且没有明示选择的法律之中的案例法,会使签订限制责任条款的当事人合理的希望落空。取决于仲裁员如何看待法律选择规则的作用和他们是否愿意采用不属于某个特定国内法律制度的规则来解决争议的实体问题,对于准据法他们会作出如下两个选择:第一,他们不会采用一个使在国际商事交易中广泛使用的条款无效的国家的法律;或者,第二,他们会选择一个认可这种条款的跨国规则。但是,如果仲裁员认为这种条款根据一个广泛接受的根本价值标准是无效的,他们就会认定这种条款无效。在所有其他情况下,他们往往都尊重当事人的合理期望。

所以,对仲裁员而言,真正限制当事人自治原则的是国际强行规则。接下来,我们会从各种国际仲裁的表现形式如何影响一些仅仅从表面上看完全是技术性问题的角度,来讨论强行规则。

B. 国际仲裁表现形式对限制当事人自由选择解决争议的实体规则的影响

107. 对国家法院而言,限制当事人自由决定争议实体问题的

---

[290] See Supremo Triubnal de Justiça, July 9, 1991, *Boletim do Ministério da Justiça*, no. 409, October 1991, unpublished, pp. 759—763, quoted in the Award rendered on June 20, 2001 in ICC Case no. 10625, § 122. 有趣的是,在2002年,葡萄牙最高上诉法院采纳了对《葡萄牙民法典》第809条放宽限制的解释,将限制责任条款的无效情况局限为故意违约、严重过失或者违反某个强行法规。这使得葡萄牙法律和国际商事交易的通常作法保持一致(Supremo Tribunal de Justiça, March 19, 2002, Case No. 01A3321, available on the Court's website)。再一次,我们能够看到跨国规则的动态本质,它与传统法律选择方式看待法律的静态观点相反。关于这个问题,参见 *supra*, § 58 and footnote 136.

准据法不存在本体论性质上的困难。在国际案件中,每个法律秩序都可以决定何时以违反根本性价值标准为由,忽略当事人选择的法律规则。它可以决定哪个规则有强行规则的性质并且,即使争议有国际性质,该规则必须在法定的特别情况下适用。从国家间合作的利益出发,每个法律秩序也能够决定在什么情况下,它应当执行属于另一个法律制度的国际强行规则。公共政策或者裁判地以及其他司法辖区的高于一切的强行规则(overriding mandatory rules/lois de police)都可以导致适用国际强行规则,而不是一般情况下可以适用的外国法。

相反地,对于国际仲裁员而言,这些规范中的每一个都带来重要问题。仲裁员不过是从当事人意愿处获得权力的私人法官,凭什么能够无视当事人选择的法律呢?什么渊源赋予了这些规则强行规则的性质以至于它们可以排除通常适用的法律?若当事人自己已经选择,或者传统的法律选择规则指向一个国家的法律的时候,凭什么仲裁员要执行其他国家的强行政策呢?只有国际仲裁的表现形式可以回答这些问题。

(1) 单独地区(monolocal)方式

108. 国际仲裁的第一种表现形式将仲裁员等同于国内法官,通过要求仲裁员和仲裁地国的法官采取同样的方式解决上述问题。仲裁员应当支持的国际公共政策是那个特定国家的政策。他或者她也必须保证遵守那个国家的高于一切的强行规则。不属于仲裁地的法律秩序的强行规则被称为"外国"的,仲裁员只能在仲裁地的法律秩序许可的范围内承认这些强行规则。如果仲裁地的法律秩序中包含一个和 2008 年 6 月 17 日的《关于合同之债法律适用的欧盟罗马条例 I》(*European Union Rome I Regulation of June 17, 2008 on the Law*

Applicable to Contractual Obligations)第 9 条第 3 款类似的规范[291],或者类似 1987 年瑞士《国际私法法》第 19 条[292]的规定的话,仲裁员——就像国内法官一样——可以采用合同准据法(lex contractus)之外的其他法律,只要该法与争议有足够密切的联系并且可以适用于这个争议。

109. 有些法律不赞同国际仲裁的第一种表现形式。若把这种表现形式适用于这些法律,就可能产生重大误解。例如,1988 年 11 月 24 日 F. A. Mann 在《金融时报》(Financial Times)上发表的广受争议的文章。该文题为"在瑞士仲裁存在新危险",讨论的是瑞士当时新颁布的规范国际仲裁的法律。在文中,F. A. Mann 假设瑞士《国际私法法》的第 19 条适用于在瑞士仲裁的任何仲裁员,他谴责该条允许第三国的强行规则凌驾于当事人选择的适用于争议实体问题的法律之上。所以,假设一家英国公司和一家位于想象中的某王国的公司签订一份需要在该王国履行的建筑合同。当事人约定英国法应当适用于解决任何争议的实体问题,Mann 认为当事人的约定会因为在瑞士进行仲裁的仲裁员适用该想象中的王国的强行规则而落空。

---

[291] See Regulation (EC) No. 593/2008 of the European Parliament and of the Council of June 17, 2008 on the Law Applicable to Contractual Obligations (Rome I), Article 9(3):

当依据合同履行地所在国的高于一切的强行规则,已经履行或者尚未履行的合同义务是非法的时候,可以考虑这些强行规则的效力。在考虑是否要承认这些规则的效力的时候,需要考虑它们的性质和目的以及适用或者不适用它们的结果。

这个条款取代了《关于合同之债法律适用的欧盟罗马公约》第 7 条第 1 款。受到英国案例法的影响(see infra footnote 295),现在的第 9 条第 3 款通过引进两个必须同时满足的条件来限制法官自由适用外国强行规则:只能考虑合同履行地所在国的强行规则,并且只有在这些规则使得合同的履行成为非法的情况下它们才能适用。

[292] 1. 只有根据瑞士法律的概念,这些利益是合理的并且清楚的十分重要的时候,才能考虑本法之外的其他法规定的强行规则,条件是案件和被考虑的强行规则有密切联系。

2. 在考虑是否要适用这个强行规则的时候,必须考虑它的目的和适用的结果,以达到瑞士法认为合适的结论。(author's translation)。

又见《魁北克民法典》(Quebec Civil Code)的第 3079 条,或者以 1998 年 11 月 27 日的法律为基础的《突尼斯国际私法法典》(Tunisian Code of Private International Law)的第 38 条第 2 款。

这会导致"最严峻的"危险,所以英国公司必须要严肃考虑选择何处仲裁。这个批评在两方面有误。没有理由认为在瑞士仲裁的仲裁员会接受将仲裁等同于当地法官的国际仲裁的表现形式。瑞士仲裁员长久以来青睐国际仲裁自治的观点[293],而且瑞士《国际私法法》的第19条不包括在该法规范国际仲裁的第 12 章中[294],所以据此我们已经可以得出在瑞士仲裁的仲裁员有可能不接受将仲裁等同于当地法官的国际仲裁的表现形式。Mann 的批评最滑稽之处是,因为英国对当时适用的《罗马公约》第 7 条第 1 款的保留,所以英国的法官不承认外国强行规则的效力,但是,英国法一贯规定在履行地非法的合同也会被认为违反英国法。这等于说,如果英国法官和仲裁员要用英国法解决争议的实体问题,他们应当适用合同履行地的所有强行规则。[295] 在这个背景下,如果英国当事人希望他们选择的准据法不被该想象中的王国的强行规则的意外适用而影响,他们唯一的指望是在英国和其他欧盟国家里进行仲裁的仲裁员不接受国际仲裁的第一种表现形式。

---

[293] See P. Lalive, J.-F. Poudret, and C. Reymond, *Le droit de l'arbitrage interne et international en Suisse*, Lausanne, Payot, 1989, at p.398:

> 外国法律实务工作者应当小心避免以下错误观点,即认为瑞士《国际私法法》的第 19 条,在某些情况下,赋予瑞士**法院**有能力以任何方式约束在瑞士进行仲裁的国际**仲裁员**。

See also M. Blessing, *Introduction to Arbitration—Swiss and International Perspectives*, Basel, Helbing & Lichtenhahn, 1999, § 787.

[294] 但是 F. Knoepfler 认为仲裁员可以参照适用瑞士《国际私法法》的第 19 条,参见:F. Knoepfler, L'article 19 LDIP est-il adapté à l'arbitrage international?, *Etudes de droit international en l'honneur de Pierre Lalive*, Basel, Helbing & Lichtenhahn, 1993, p.531.

[295] 现在《罗马条例 I》(*Rome I Regulation*)第 9 条第 3 款采用了同样的解决方法,它在英国以及其他欧盟成员国是可以直接适用的。就在 2009 年 12 月 17 日《罗马条例 I》生效之前英国法院所采用的解决方法,参见 *supra*, footnote 291。在这之前,若合同根据履行地的强行规则是非法的,英国案例法和最有影响力的英国法律评论员都认为在这种情况下,履行地的强行规则成为英国实体法的一部分(与法律选择问题相对而言),以避免适用英国对《罗马公约》第 7 条第 1 款的保留,参见 Collins, L., Briggs, A., Harris, J., McClean, J. D., McLachlan, C., Morse, C. G. J. eds., *Dicey, Morris and Collins on the Conflict of Laws*, London, Sweet & Maxwell, 14th ed., 2006, volume 2, § § 32-148 *et seq*.

(2) 威斯特伐利亚方式

110. 威斯特伐利亚方式是国际仲裁的第二种表现形式,它强调许多国家——不仅仅是仲裁地所在国——都有平等的资格规范仲裁,这包括仲裁的进行和解决实体争议的方法。这种表现形式认为裁决执行国——或者执行国们——和仲裁进行地所在国有同等的资格来要求仲裁员在适用合同准据法之前,必须优先适用该国认为重要的必须适用的规则。[296]

这种国际仲裁的表现形式,根本上是从国家的角度看待仲裁,就在某个法律秩序中承认和执行裁决方面,这种表现形式是顺理成章的。根据这种表现形式,每个国家都有资格主张,裁决的执行不会违反该国高于一切的强行规则等基本价值,遵守这些价值是国际公共政策的要求。从仲裁员的角度出发,这种表现形式要求评价各国包括基本规范在内的价值取向之间的相互关系;在当事人对适用甲国的基本规则而非乙国的有争议的时候,它本身并没有给仲裁员提供足够的指引。只有同时考虑其他因素,这种表现形式才能够指引仲裁员是否适用某国的高于一切的强行规则。根据不同的考虑因素,指引的结果也不同。

111. 一些作者提倡,为了让一个裁决可以在尽可能多的国家里执行,裁决必须符合所有可能要执行裁决的国家中有强制属性的规范的总和——无论这些规范是否是高于一切的强行规则或者是国际公共秩序规则。裁决也应当符合仲裁地的强行规则,以避免裁决被撤销。因此,在一份关于国际商事交易的非法行为的研究中,作者表示:

> 仲裁员必须尊重仲裁地所在国的强行规则以及执行国可以适用于本案的强行规则。否则,他们的裁决可能被撤销且/或变得不能执行。[297]

---

[296] See *supra*, §§ 23 *et seq.*, esp. at § 32.

[297] A. Court de Fontmichel, *L'arbitre, le juge et les pratiques illicites du commerce international*, *op. cit.* footnote 19, p. 205, author's translation.

有些强行规则虽然既不属于仲裁地的法律秩序也不属于执行国的法律秩序,但是由于仲裁地或者执行国的法律可能要求适用这些规则,所以它们也应当被遵守:

> 这是因为仲裁地所在国和执行地所在国可能都认为不遵守这个强行规则的裁决违反了它们的国际公共政策,即使被违反的法律并非它们法律秩序正式的一分子。[298]

如果沿着这种逻辑推理下去,一个国家完全可以主张只要争议和这个国家的法律秩序有最轻微的联系,国际仲裁员就必须尊重这个国家所认可的具有普遍性的价值或者高于一切的强行规则。这个方法要求把所有强行规则累加起来适用,这会导致盲目地适用最严格的规则。例如,一个使交易无效的法律总是胜过使交易有效的法律,一个强加某些限制的法律总是优于认可合同自由的法律。

前文已经强调了,在国际仲裁法领域很难证明执行法主义是有道理的。[299] 特别是当高于一切的强行规则互相矛盾的时候——例如,一个法律允许联合抵制行为但是另一个不允许,或者一个法律允许经济数据的传播,但是另一个禁止——执行法主义根本行不通。例如,1999 年 8 月 8 日美国的《伊朗—利比亚制裁法》(US *Iran-Libya Sanctions Act of August 8, 1996*)——所谓的《达马托法》(*D' Amato Act*)[300],和 1996 年 11 月 22 日欧盟理事会制定的反对该美国法的域外效力和禁止欧洲公司服从该法的条例[301]针锋相对,所以如果一个仲裁员必须适用所有和争议有联系的高于一切的强行规则,他或者她要如何在这些矛盾的规则中进行选择呢?

---

[298] *Ibid*, author's translation. See, along the same lines, A. Kassis, *L'Autonomie de l'arbitrage commercial international*, *op. cit.* footnote 15, at § 600, p. 345.

[299] See *supra*, § 39.

[300] *Iran and Libya Sanctions Act of 1996*, Pub. L. 104-72, 104th Cong., 2d Session (August 5, 1996).

[301] Council Regulation (EC) No. 2271/96 of November 22, 1996 protecting against the effects of the extra-territorial application of legislation adopted by a third country, and actions based thereon or resulting therefrom, *OJEU*, No. L 309 of November 29, 1996, pp. 1—6.

即使在没有高于一切的强行规则的情况下,主张这些规则必须适用就意味着强行规则和合同准据法之间存在价值冲突。如果一个在日内瓦进行仲裁的仲裁员被要求判定一名马来西亚卖家违约。该卖家以货物可能会被销往以色列为由拒绝发运货物,因为发运货物可能会导致它违反马来西亚对以色列的联合抵制规定。仅仅因为马来西亚有强硬的政策要求适用这个强行规则,仲裁员就必须适用该规则吗?或者相反,必须按照契约即允诺和自由贸易的原则适用合同准据法吗?后者所崇尚的保护合同自由的价值和要求联合抵制的前者一样有资格适用于该案。适用一个规则而非另一个并不是仅仅因为前者在颁布它的国家中具有强行规则属性:就仲裁员而言,不存在一个法律先验性地比另一个有更正当的理由要优先适用。当国家间政策相反,无论这些政策是否体现在强行规则中,现实要求我们意识到,实现某些国家的要求就必然会使得另一些国家失望;由于不同的法律根据定义对裁决是否有效存在不同的观点,因此仲裁员不能仅仅考虑裁决的有效性问题来决定准据法。

112. 因为完全基于裁决的有效性的方法是不可行的,所以我们不得不考虑其他理论。

在一份关于高于一切的强行规则和仲裁公正(arbitral justice)的研究中,Christophe Seraglini 教授尝试证明为了满足国际社会的要求,当仲裁员认为强行规则的目标、对应的方法和适用这些规则是正当的时候,仲裁员应当适用和争议有联系的国家的强行规则,即使这些规则不是合同准据法的一部分[302]。仲裁员这样做可以满足国际社会的期望,即仲裁尊重组成国际社会的国家用强行规则保护的整体利益。Seraglini 教授认为这个方法优于要求仲裁员为了真正的国际公共秩序仅仅执行被国际社会广泛认可的规则的方法。国内法采用

---

[302] Ch. Seraglini, *Lois de police et justice arbitrale internationale*, Paris, Dalloz, 2001. For a similar reasoning, see L. G. Radicati di Brozolo, Arbitrage commercial international et lois de police. Considérations sur les conflits de juridictions dans le commerce international, *Collected Courses*, volume 315 (2005), p.265, at § § 168 *et seq.*

各种方法实现某些目标的事实并不必然导致这些方法是不正当的，若仲裁员完全尊重这些方法，国际正义会受益匪浅。[303]

当分析强行规则是如何制定的时候，Seraglini 教授的理论将跨国规则方法仅仅适用于国家所追求的目标，这样做的灵感来自国际法研究所于 1991 年采纳的《巴塞尔决议》(*Basel Resolution*)。该决议的主题是私人或私主体之间达成的国际合同所涉及的当事人自治问题 (Autonomy of the Parties in International Contracts between Private Persons or Entities)。决议的第 9 条规定了裁判地的法官如何适用强行规则，它警告道，就有关的外国强行规则而言：

> 这类条款能阻止适用被选择的法律，条件是在合同和制定这类条款的国家之间有紧密联系，并且这类条款能够帮助实现国际社会广泛接受的目标。[304]

有许多例子能够证明与采用具有真正的国际公共秩序性质的实体规则的方法相比，强行规则方式更有优势，其中，我特别以国际商事交易中的腐败问题为例。有观点认为，为了反对腐败，国际仲裁员不仅应当按照国际社会对腐败的广泛谴责反对腐败，而且应当适用和争议有密切联系的国家关于腐败的具体规定，即使该法不是合同准据法的一部分。阿尔及利亚 1978 年的规定和伊朗 1975 年的规定就是证明。[305]

---

[303] 就仲裁员可以根据他们自己的道德观念自由适用强行规则，参见 P. Mayer, L'Arbitre et la loi, *op. cit.* footnote 105, at pp. 239—240；Effect of International Public Policy in International Arbitration?, *Pervasive Problems in International Arbitration* (L. Mistelis and J. Lew, eds.), Kluwer, 2006, p. 61. 就对让仲裁员完全根据自由裁量权适用强行规则的谴责，参见 see supra, § 49. 毫无疑问 F. A. Mann——这一次应该——可能会认为这对国际仲裁构成一个"新的危险"(see *supra*, § 109)。

[304] Institute of International Law, Session of Basel, 1991, Resolution entitled "The Autonomy of the Parties in International Contracts Between Private Persons or Entities", Article 9, *Yearbook*, 1991, volume 64, part I, p. 79；决议的英文翻译可以在国际法研究所的网站上找到。

[305] See Ch. Seraglini, *Lois de police et justice arbitrale internationale*, *op. cit.* footnote 302, at § § 659 *et seq.*

113. 1978年,阿尔及利亚立法者决定,为了反对腐败,有必要全面禁止以获得某些采购合同为目的而使用中介人。[306] 在一桩涉及英国的Hilmarton公司和法国的Omnium de Traitement et de Valorisation(OTV)公司的案子中,一个在日内瓦作出的裁决认为一份"法律和财政"咨询协议无效。该协议涉及当事人之间在阿尔及尔城建立污水处理项目的"行政协助",尽管当事人选择瑞士法作为协议的准据法,仲裁员还是适用了阿尔及利亚1978年的规定,认为该协议违法。[307] 1989年11月17日日内瓦法院(Geneva Court of Justice)根据当时的瑞士仲裁法撤销了裁决,因为根据瑞士对国际公共政策的理解,合同准据法必须适用,但是裁决既没有适用合同准据法,也没有说明为什么不应当适用合同准据法是有道理的。[308] 联邦法院支持了这个决定,原因是:

> 即便没有发生贿赂、贩卖权力或者其他可能引起怀疑的行为,阿尔及利亚法律仍然禁止在签署合同的时候使用任何类型的中介人,该法不但设定了过于广泛的禁止措施,而且体现了过分的以实现政府垄断对外贸易为目的的保护主义倾向。除非涉及根据瑞士法可以定性为具有腐败嫌疑的行为,否则,从瑞士法的角度而言,阿尔及利亚法严重限制了当事人的订约自由,所以从道德的角度,它不能优先于合同自由这个一般和根本的法律原则而适用。[309]

---

[306] 就1978年阿尔及利亚立法的确切含义,参见 see A. Mebroukine, Le Choix de la Suisse comme siège de l'arbitrage dans les clauses d'arbitrage conclues entre entreprises algériennes et entreprises étrangères, *ASA Bull.*, 1994, p.4. 就阿尔及利亚在1991年废除了这部立法, see *supra*, § 58。

[307] Award of August 19, 1988, ICC Case No. 5622, *Rev. arb.*, 1993, p.327, with a commentary by V. Heuzé, p.179; *Yearbook Commercial Arbitration*, 1994, p.105, at p.112.

[308] Geneva Court of Justice, November 17, 1989, *Rev. arb.*, 1993, p.316, author's translation. For an English translation, see *Yearbook Commercial Arbitration*, 1994, p.214. 值得注意的是,在制定1987年的《国际私法法》之后,瑞士联邦法院获得了撤销程序的排他性管辖权。

[309] Swiss Federal Tribunal, Decision of April 17, 1990, author's translation, *Rev. arb.*, 1993, p.322; *Yearbook Commercial Arbitration*, 1994, p.214.

反对腐败的例子强调，除了参考国际社会的观点之外，Seraglini 教授的理论和执行法主义有一样的毛病。它本质上依赖于考察国家的强烈意愿，以按照国家的需要适用它们规定的强行规则。与执行法主义的唯一的细微差别是它没有机械性的本质，因为它认为仲裁员可以自由适用那些在他们看来追求的目的正当和采用的方式合理的强行规则，它不认为适用强行规则是为了保证裁决能够被普遍执行。但是，Seraglini 教授的理论仍然没有给仲裁员任何真正的标准来决定在各种候选政策中应当选择哪一个。强行规则的正当性，甚至它的目标，不是一个有效的标准，因为内容相反的强行规则根据这个标准也可能是正当的。瑞士联邦法院的决定表明，阿尔及利亚立法者通过在某些类型的交易中一概禁止使用中介人，他们的目的是消灭任何腐败的可能性，但是保护合同自由是瑞士立法者认同的"一般和根本的原则"，所以阿尔及利亚的政策和瑞士同样强硬的政策矛盾。阿尔及利亚和瑞士的法律制度同样认可反对腐败和自由贸易等价值。然而，当这些同样正当的价值之间必须有所取舍的时候，每个法律制度得出的答案不同。为什么一个国际仲裁员要将阿尔及利亚法置于瑞士法之上呢？需要适用合同准据法是因为这符合当事人可以自由选择准据法这个在国际实务中被广泛认可的原则。在另一方面，当其他人认为必须尽可能地捍卫贸易和产业自由的时候，置合同准据法于不顾而适用强行规则的原因必须和仲裁员反对腐败的主观态度或者同情心理无关——虽然这种主观性可能在其他情况下可以佐证适用强行规则是正确的。无论国际社会是否真的希望这些强行规则得到遵守，强行规则方法的基础是强硬的国家政策和需要执行它们的强烈意愿，这和美国的政府利益分析如出一辙。由于这些政策彼此不同，当它们没有正面冲突的时候，国际仲裁员不能以某些国家要求适用它们制定的规范的意愿或者仲裁员自己的主观意志，令人信服地置合同准据法于不顾。

114. 1975 年伊朗的规定也印证了这个结论。由于以往杜绝腐败的立法失败，伊朗权力机构要求所有和政府或者国有公司有业务往来的外国公司都签订一份声明,表示他们没有为了得到业务机会而支付任何佣金或者好处费。Seraglini 教授认为这种规定细节清晰是以有效地打击腐败为目标的强行规则的最好的例子。在他看来,较之于国际社会广泛接受的原则,执行单个国家制定的并且反映其对某个问题有强烈兴趣的法律更有助于保证国际交易的道德化。[310] Seraglini 教授的观点基于 1982 年国际商会作出的第 3916 号裁决。但是这个裁决却表明了无论仲裁员们如何无视合同准据法,他们仔细地将自己的裁决以国际社会广泛接受的规范为基础,而不是依据某个国家强烈的适用自己法律的意愿。[311] 在那个案子中,裁决认为一份在伊朗当事人和希腊当事人之间签订的适用法国法的代理合同无效,因为它的目的是保证获得伊朗政府的采购合同,所以这份代理合同无论根据法国法还是伊朗法都是违法的,此外还违背国际商事交易的道德要求。

这个裁决更确切地表现了适用以国际社会共识为基础的跨国公共政策,而非仅仅因为某强行规则反映了某国的强硬政策所以要适用该强行规则。

(3) 跨国方式

115. 国际仲裁的第三种表现形式,接受了存在仲裁法律秩序的观点,在选择实体法方面,通过跨国公共政策或者真正的国际公共政策的概念限制当事人自治。

作为国际公共政策的当地化解释,在每一个国家法律秩序中国际公共政策的概念允许法官无视通常应当适用的法律,包括当事人在合同中选择的法律。类似,在仲裁法律秩序中,当仲裁员认为当事人在合同中选择的法律违背国际社会的根本价值的时候,仲裁员有权无视该法。国际公共政策确保这些价值的实现并且反映了各国广泛的谴责某些行为的共识,这个共识并不意味着它必须被世界上所

---

[310] Ch. Seraglini, *Lois de police et justice arbitrale internationale*, op. cit. footnote 302, § 661.

[311] Award rendered in 1982, ICC case No. 3916, *JDI*, 1984, p.930.

有国家全体一致地接受[312]，例如腐败、毒品或者走私人体器官，保护某些弱势群体，或者甚至，在国际社会实行禁运的时候，以推进某些旨在维护国际和平和安全的政策。在当事人和法院都不可以减损的规则中，跨国规则方法论的基础是比较法方式和就特定问题而达成的反映了国际社会的广泛共识的国际协定。[313]

116. 法学文献坚定地支持存在一些规则，仲裁员必须采用它们以履行职责，原因是他们代表国际社会主持正义。Frédéric Eisemann[314]，Lambert Matray[315]，Pierre Lalive[316]，Philippe Kahn[317]，Eric Loquin[318]，或者晚近的，Jean-Baptiste Racine[319] 和 Lotfi Chedly[320] 的著作都支持了这种观点。在 1989 年，国际法研究所的决议也接受了

---

[312] See *supra*, § 54.

[313] On this methodology, see *supra*, § § 50 et seq.

[314] F. Eisemann, La *lex fori* de l'arbitrage commercial international, *op. cit.* footnote 249, at p. 198. 早在 1975 年，F. Eisemann 当时是 ICC 仲裁院的秘书长，并且他的观点代表了 ICC 主张的跨国仲裁概念，他认为仲裁员就实体问题的自由裁量权"只受到真正的国际公共政策的限制"（author's translation）。

[315] L. Matray, Arbitrage et ordre public transnational, *The Art of Arbitration. Essays on International Arbitration. Liber Amicorum Pieter Sanders* (J. C. Schultsz & A. J. van den Berg eds.), Deventer, Kluwer Law and Taxation Publishers, 1982, p. 241.

[316] P. Lalive, Transnational (or Truly International) Public Policy and International Arbitration, *ICCA Congress Series No. 3. Comparative Arbitration Practice and Public Policy in Arbitration* (P. Sanders ed.), Deventer, Kluwer, 1987, p. 257. See also, L'ordre public transnational et l'arbitre international, *New Instruments of Private International Law. Liber Fausto Pocar*, Milan, Giuffrè Editore, 2009, volume II, p. 599.

[317] Ph. Kahn, Les principes généraux du droit devant les arbitres du commerce international, *JDI*, 1989, p. 305 and, by the same author, A propos de l'ordre public transnational: quelques observations, *Mélanges Fritz Sturm offerts par ses collègues et ses amis à l'occasion de son soixante-dixième anniversaire*, Liège, Ed. Jur. Univ. Liège, 1999, p. 1539.

[318] E. Loquin, Les manifestations de l'illicite, *L'illicite dans le commerce international* (P. Kahn & C. Kessedjian eds.), Paris, Litec, 1996, p. 247, at p. 273 *et seq.*

[319] J.-B. Racine, *L'arbitrage commercial international et l'ordre public*, *op. cit.* footnote 164. 但是，作者确实接受仲裁员能够采用不符合跨国公共政策的要求的强行规则，see at § § 596—597.

[320] L. Chedly, *Arbitrage commercial international & ordre public transnational*, Tunis, Centre de Publication Universitaire, 2002.

类似的观点：

> 在任何情况下仲裁员都不可以违反国际公共政策的原则，因为这些原则代表了国际社会的广泛共识。[321]

117. 仲裁员一贯参考这个观点来撤销为掩盖腐败为目的的佣金合同。例如，1981 年作出的 ICC 第 3913 号案件的裁决认为这类合同不但不符合法国法也不符合"被大多数国家都认可的国际公共政策的概念"[322]。1998 年 ICC 第 8891 号案件的裁决也持有同样的观点：

> 仲裁案例法已经完全认可了涉及腐败的合同是非法的。尽管腐败在绝大多数的法律秩序中都是非法的，仲裁员通常不局限于按照某个国内法进行裁决，他们也参考法律的一般原则以及国际或者跨国公共政策。[323]

相反，仲裁庭往往不愿意无视当事人选择的法律而采用代表某国的强硬政策的强行规则，只要后者不符合被国际社会广泛接受的规则。例如，1990 年 ICC 第 6379 号案件的裁决中，仲裁庭拒绝适用 1961 年 7 月 27 日制定的比利时法律中包含的强行规则，该规则允许单方面撤销不限定期限的独家分销协议。仲裁庭采用了当事人选择的意大利法。在裁决中，仲裁庭列举了如下理由：

> 立即（或者强行）适用的法的概念是由 G. Sperduti 提出的。Sperduti 强调"必须适用的法律的**强制本质只存在于制定它的国家中**，但是这个本质不能成为阻止其他国家适用该法的唯一

---

[321] Institute of International Law, Arbitration Between States, State Enterprises, or State Entities, and Foreign Enterprises, Article 2, Session of Santiago de Compostela, *op. cit.* footnote 245, at p. 326.

[322] Award rendered in ICC Case No. 3913 in 1981, *Collection of ICC Arbitral Awards 1974—1985*, pp. 497—498, author's translation.

[323] Award rendered in ICC Case No. 8891 in 1998, *JDI*, 2000, p. 1076, author's translation.

原因"。

清楚的是根据 Gothot 和 Sperduti 的著作，Sperduti 理论在很多国家被许多学者长篇累牍地讨论，有些学者大力褒奖，有些学者强烈批评。

这个概念的确切内涵不明，并且如何确定某个法律是否包括在它的范畴中也不非常清晰。Gothot 将之称为"有点含糊的讨论"。

这是一个非常有趣的概念，但是不是本案中仲裁员应当适用的明确的意大利规则。

为支持自己的裁决，仲裁庭也提到"在国际仲裁中，仲裁庭不是国家体系中的一个机构"[324]。

该裁决在法律文献中找到如下依据：

> 无论比利时的法院会如何识别它，1961 年 7 月 27 日颁布的比利时法不能被认为具有国际公共政策的性质。[325]

类似地，在 1994 年涉及某国有公司和某外国当事人的 ICC 第 7047 号案件的裁决中，该案仲裁庭拒绝考察国有公司所属国的强行规则是否被违反了，原因是当事人没有选择该法并且违反该法"不能

---

[324] Award rendered in ICC Case No. 6379 in 1990, *Rev. dr. com. belge*, 1993, p. 1134, at p. 1140, author's translation; see also *Yearbook Commercial Arbitration*, 1992, p. 212. 简而言之，在裁决的脚注中，仲裁庭参考了 G. Sperduti 进行的一项研究，该研究题为 "Les lois d'application nécessaire en tant que lois d'ordre public", *Rev. crit. DIP*, 1977, p. 257, at p. 265. 又见 2004 年 ICC 第 12193 号裁决，该裁决无视黎巴嫩法律，即便该法是合同准据法并赋予分销商所在地的法院专有管辖权来解决和分销合同有关的争议，*JDI*, 2007, p. 1276, at p. 1284, E. Silva Romero 的评论。后面这个裁决参考并且支持了 1997 年 ICC 在第 8606 号案件中作出的裁决，对于仲裁协议的有效性的争议问题，其意见如下："因为仲裁员不属于任何国家法律秩序，他们能适用跨国规则而不是国家法律秩序的规则，因为后者对他们没有约束力"，*Revue libanaise de l'arbitrage*, § 9, p. 20, at p. 24, author's translation.

[325] B. Hanotiau, note on the Award rendered in 1990 in ICC Case No. 6379, *Rev. dr. com. belge*, 1993, pp. 1146—1152, author's translation; see also by the same author, *L'arbitrabilité*, *Collected Courses*, volume 296 (2002), p. 25, at p. 189 *et seq*.

被认为违反国际公共政策"[326]。

118. 无论强行规则方法要求适用执行法(lex executionist),还是允许仲裁员只适用他们认为"正当的"强行规则,它和跨国公共政策方法的主要区别在于:只有跨国公共政策方法给了仲裁员确切的指导。国际法中的强行规则(jus cogens)在国际商事交易中的对应体是跨国公共政策,这两个概念因其含糊的本质遭到谴责。在现实中,对跨国公共政策的谴责仅仅限于很难永久和彻底地列举出它包含的所有规则。一方面,这个列举由于两个原因是不可能实现的。第一,因为跨国公共政策的概念是由它的功能来定义的,其功能是排除适用违反国际社会根本价值的规则,所以尝试通过一个清单把跨国公共政策描述出来是不可行的;第二,还因为国际社会就什么是违反跨国公共政策的行为的认识是不断发展的。在另一方面,如果人们接受跨国公共政策是一个功能概念或者,换句话说,跨国规则不是由列清单的方法产生的[327],就应当认为与允许仲裁员不顾合同准据法而适用他们认为"正当的"任何强行规则相比,跨国规则方法给仲裁员提供更加具体的指导。因为"正当性"标准无法帮助仲裁员在就单独而言是正当的但是在某个具体情形中却可能产生冲突的各种价值之间,进行选择。

跨国公共政策方法却非如此。在当事人要求不顾合同准据法而适用某个强行规则的时候,这个方法给仲裁员提供了明确的指导。因为仲裁员不代表任何特定的国家主持正义,所以他们自然倾向于采纳国际社会对案件中涉及的问题的共识。该共识并不意味着要求

---

[326] See Award rendered on February 28, 1994 in ICC Case No. 7047 by an Arbitral Tribunal composed of Hilmar Raeschke-Kessler, President, Jean Patry and Dobrosav Mitrovic, *ASA Bull.*, 1995, p. 301, at p. 319.

[327] 就跨国规则方式的特点,参见, § 62。

国际社会的一致同意。[328] 通过分析国内法和国际法就此问题采用的解决方式，可以找到这个共识。此外，国际组织采纳的方法、非政府组织制定的法典和国际公约都可以反映国家之间对一个规则的内涵的共识。

119. 有许多例子可以说明这个方法是如何运作的，还可以揭示它为什么比强行规则方法更优越。

120. 今天为获得政府合同而进行贿赂或者从事类似行为受到国际社会的广泛谴责。值得注意的是，这些例子表明跨国公共政策方法不仅仅认可存在极其概括抽象的原理。1997年签订的经济合作与发展组织《禁止在国际商业交易中贿赂外国公职人员公约》表明国际社会已经发展出具体的规则，仲裁员可以根据跨国公共政策来适用它们。这些规则特别定义了应受到谴责的行为，驳斥了触犯者们经常提出的某些抗辩。例如，假设某公务员抗辩其接受的好处费微不足道或者接受好处费的行为在其所在国是广泛存在的，仲裁员可以强调，在国际社会看来：

> 贿赂外国公职人员以获得或者保持某项业务的行为都是违法的，无论贿赂的数额和结果如何，也无论当地风俗和当地政府部门是否姑息贿赂行为。[329]

121. 禁运或者联合抵制法的例子表明仲裁员可以运用跨国公共政策方法从国家以保护各种至关重要的利益为由而采取的禁运和联合抵制措施中识别，哪些措施是国际社会认为合理的，哪些代表某

---

[328] 要求国际社会的一致同意会使得问题没有意义，一致同意只意味着强行规则必然已经成为合同准据法的一部分。See, however, P. Mayer, La règle morale dans l'arbitrage international, *op. cit.* footnote 18, § 27, 他主张，如果国际社会不"一致同意"，禁止种族歧视和化学武器就不能被认为是跨国公共政策的一部分；对此观点的回应在 *supra*, § 54。

[329] Convention on Combating Bribery of Foreign Public Officials in International Business Transactions, November 21, 1997, Annex entitled "Agreed Common Elements of Criminal Legislation and Related Action", point 3.

个国家或者一部分国家的单边政策。例如,在一个案件中,仲裁员面临的问题是,是否可以根据古巴法律或者不对古巴采取禁运的国家的法律来审理往古巴运送货物的合同。假设卖方在合同履行过程中通过并购成为一家美国公司的子公司,它主张如果它继续履行合同就会受到严厉制裁。其依据是 1996 年的《古巴自由和民主联盟法》(*Cuban Liberty and Democratic Solidarity (Libertad) Act of 1996*),即所谓的《赫尔姆斯—伯顿法》(*Helms-Burton Law*)。该法禁止美国公司直接地或者通过它们的子公司和古巴做生意。毫无疑问该法属于强行规则,其目的是适用于类似本案的争议,并且该法的确与本案有密切的联系。强行规则总是可以应用的,即使是合同准据法也会把它当作不可抗力事件考虑进来,所以如果仲裁员不考虑它的实际(de facto)效果,就会使仲裁处于困境。执行法方式,盲目的依据裁决应当能够在所有地方执行,导致《赫尔姆斯—伯顿法》必须适用,因为美国的法律秩序不会承认无视它的强行规则的裁决。允许仲裁员评价强行规则的目的和方式的正当性会导致同样的结果。《赫尔姆斯—伯顿法》确实仔细地说明它的目的是协助

> 古巴人民重新获得自由和繁荣,并且加入在西半球蓬勃发展的民主国家社区。

并且鼓励

> 在国际公认的观察员的监督下,在古巴进行自由和公平的民主选举。[330]

仲裁员怎能对这些崇高的目的无动于衷呢?至于评价本案涉及的措施,仲裁员怎能不同意禁运是经济制裁的常用武器呢?但是,跨国公共政策方法导致相反的结果。上述案件涉及的措施毫无疑问是一个国家对另一个国家单方面的禁运,并没有得到国际社会的支持。把自己当做国际社会的代言人的仲裁员不会认可这种单方面的禁

---

[330] *Cuban Liberty and Democratic Solidarity (Libertad) Act* 1996, Section 3.

运,除非它是合同准据法的一部分(当合同准据法本身不违背跨国公共政策的时候)。在另一个例子中,货物需要根据合同规定运到伊朗,合同的准据法是伊朗法。卖方依据 1996 年的《伊朗—利比亚制裁法》(*Iran-Libya Sanctions Act*)拒绝履行合同。和上述例子一样,本案涉及单方禁运。但是由于针对伊朗的禁运是在其 1990 年入侵科威特之后采取的,所以处理这个禁运的方法和上述例子不同。这个禁运是联合国安理会的一系列决议之一。[331] 对于热衷于确保国际社会所倡导的价值得到尊重的仲裁员而言,具有这个性质的禁运毫无疑问是跨国公共政策的一部分,应当优先于合同准据法适用。在其他所有的情况中,国家的强行规则,无论其是否正当,对仲裁员而言仅仅是一个事实,而不是一个在国际社会看来不能减损的规则。

122. 第三个例子关于环境保护,它表明跨国公共政策的本质是不断演变的。在过去的几年中,许多保护环境的国际规则被发展起来。国际仲裁员们不能对这些规则无动于衷。例如,假设石油开采商根据一份产品分成合同开采石油,但是该合同比较陈旧,并没有要求在生产结束后石油开采商承担恢复自然环境的义务。后来该石油开采商就在什么条件下它可以撤离和东道国产生争议。仲裁员可以根据保护环境的国际法[332],裁定石油开采商需要在开采结束后重建该地区的生态环境;即使在产品分成合同中或者合同准据法中没有这个规定,该石油开采商仍然可以要求将重建环境的费用作为石油成本的一部分由合同双方共同承担。

123. 这些例子表明,跨国公共政策规则,并不宏观抽象,它就像其他任何通过比较法方式识别的跨国规则一样[333],给仲裁员提供了解决最复杂和敏感的争议的具体方式。

---

[331] See esp. Security Council Resolutions No. 660 and No. 661 of August 2 and 6, 1990.

[332] 特别参见,在与近海采油活动有关的海洋环境的保护和维持方面,1982 年 12 月 10 日在蒙特哥贝制定的《联合国海洋法公约》第 7 部分。

[333] See *supra*, § 62.

（三）国际仲裁表现形式对裁决效力的影响

124. 仲裁裁决,在本质上是私人性质的,在承认和执行的阶段或者当它们被撤销的时候都受到国家法律秩序的审查。毫不令人惊讶的,这些关键环节特别需要国际仲裁哲学表现形式的分析。国际仲裁的各表现形式直接决定实在法如何回答争议颇多的问题:例如是否仲裁地所在国作出的撤销裁决的决定可以在执行国的法律秩序中自动生效。就纯粹理论而言,各表现形式也应当回答一个相反的问题,即仲裁地所在国拒绝撤销裁决的决定在执行国的法律秩序中效力如何。

A. 被仲裁地的法律秩序撤销的裁决的效力

125. 认为国际仲裁的法律属性排他地来自仲裁地的法律秩序的观点,直接导致在仲裁地被撤销的裁决不可能在其他所有法律秩序中执行。根据这个国际仲裁的表现形式,问题很简单:一个被仲裁地撤销的裁决就不复存在了。因此,它不能在其他任何地方被承认。

威斯特伐利亚的表现形式导致一个相反的结论。因为每个国家可以根据自己的法律决定仲裁协议和裁决有效的条件,因此被一国撤销的裁决在另一国执行不存在理论上的障碍。和一个没有在仲裁地被撤销的裁决可以在一国执行但是不能在另一国执行相比,这个结论既不更陌生也不更令人惊讶。《纽约公约》明示认可这种可能性,因为它允许每个国家根据本国规定的可仲裁性标准以及本国理解的国际公共政策的要求来审查裁决。[334]

认可存在仲裁法律秩序的仲裁表现形式会得出相同的结论。确实,在某个国家承认和执行裁决的时候,裁决和仲裁地的法律秩序没有关系,即使该裁决被仲裁地的法律秩序撤销,它仍然能够在其他地方被承认。裁决被认为存在于仲裁法律秩序中,这成了执行地的法

---

[334] See *supra*, § 33.

院认可裁决是独立存在的依据：无论裁决是否被任何一个国家法律秩序认可，每个国家都能在满足其承担的国际义务的前提下，自由根据自己设定的条件承认裁决。

126. 在法国和美国，大量的案例法涉及被仲裁地撤销的裁决在其他国内法律制度中的命运问题。

在这两个国家中就此问题作出的大量持不同观点的司法决定，以及在法律著作中进行的激烈争论[335]，都无法掩盖这一事实，即在某些条件下，包括荷兰、比利时和奥地利在内的许多其他国家的法院都愿意承认和执行被仲裁地撤销的裁决。

1973 年 10 月 26 日荷兰最高法院承认了著名的 Ripert-Panchaud 裁决[336]，该裁决于 1956 年 7 月 2 日在瑞士作出，当事双方是 Société Européenne d'Etudes et d'Entreprises(*SEEE*)和南斯拉夫联邦人民共和国，该裁决在被荷兰法院承认之前，已经被仲裁地的法院撤销并被认定为不复存在。[337]

类似的，在 1988 年 12 月 6 日，布鲁塞尔一审法院根据比利时仲裁法的一般规则承认了在阿尔及利亚作出的一个裁决，该裁决对外

---

[335] 就此问题，特别参见，支持其他国家承认在仲裁地所在国被推翻的裁决：Ph. Fouchard, La portée internationale de l'annulation de la sentence arbitrale dans son pays d'origine, *Rev. arb.*, 1997, p.329; J. Paulsson, Enforcing Awards Notwithstanding a Local Standard Annulment (LSA), *ICC Bull.*, May 1998, p.14; E. Gaillard, L'exécution des sentences annulées dans leur pays d'origine, *op. cit.* footnote 85. 但见 J.-F. Poudret, Quelle solution pour en finir avec l'affaire *Hilmarton*? Réponse à Philippe Fouchard, *Rev. arb.*, 1998, p.7; A. J. van den Berg, Enforcement of Annulled Arbitral Awards?, *ICC Bull.*, Nov. 1998, p.15; H. Gharavi, *The International Effectiveness of the Annulment of an Arbitral Award*, The Hague, Kluwer, 2002.

[336] Supreme Court of the Netherlands (*Hoge Raad*), October 26, 1973, *Société européenne d'études et d'entreprises v. Socialist Federal Republic of Yugoslavia*, *Nederlandse Jurisprudentie*, 1974, no.361; *Netherlands Yearbook of International Law*, 1974, volume V, p.290; *Rev. arb.*, 1974, p.311, note by H. Batiffol. 最近，关于在俄罗斯撤销在该国作出的裁决违反了荷兰的国际公共政策的问题，参见 Amsterdam Court of Appeal (*Gerechtshof*), April 28, 2009, *Yukos Capital SARL v. OAO Rosneft*, *Rev. arb.*, 2009, p.559, note by S. Bollée; *Yearbook Commercial Arbitration*, 2009, p.703.

[337] See the Swiss Federal Tribunal's decision of September 18, 1957, *Rev. arb.*, 1957, p.136.

国当事方有利而对阿尔及利亚的某国有公司不利,并随后被阿尔及利亚法院撤销。[338] 1990 年 1 月 9 日布鲁塞尔上诉法院维持了承认裁决的决定。[339]

另一个例子是,奥地利法院承认了一个在斯洛文尼亚作出并被该国法院撤销的裁决[340],原因是 1961 年的《欧洲公约》废除了仲裁地可以撤销裁决的某些条件。[341]

127. 根据法国法,法院一贯承认满足《法国民事诉讼法典》要求的裁决,无论该裁决是否已经或者可能被仲裁地的法院撤销。这个做法,自从 1984 年 10 月 9 日法国最高法院在 *Norsolor* 一案中采纳后[342],就被无数的后续案例接受。例如巴黎上诉法院在 *Chromalloy*[343],*Bargues Agro Industrie*[344] 或者 *Bechtel*[345] 案中以及最高法院在

---

[338] *Sonatrach v. Ford, Bacon & Davis Inc.*; *Journal des tribunaux*, 1993, p. 685, obs. by G. Keutgen; *ASA Bull.*, 1989, p. 213; *Yearbook Commercial Arbitration*, 1990, p. 370. Adde G. Horsmans, Actualité et évolution du droit belge de l'arbitrage, *Rev. arb.*, 1992, p. 417, at p. 426.

[339] Brussels Court of Appeal, January 9, 1990, *Journal des tribunaux* 1990, p. 386. On this topic, see also W. W. Park, *International Forum Selection*, The Hague, Kluwer, 1995, p. 76 and 132.

[340] Supreme Court of Austria (*Oberster Gerichtshof*), October 20, 1993, *Radenska v. Kajo*, *Österreichische Juristen-Zeitung*, July 15, 1994, volume 49, § § 14—15, p. 513 and *Rev. arb.*, 1998, p. 419; I. Seidl-Hohenveldern, Chronique de jurisprudence autrichienne, *JDI*, 1998, p. 1003.

[341] Article IX of the European Convention on International Commercial Arbitration, signed in Geneva on April 21, 1961.

[342] *Cour de cassation, 1re civ.*, October 9, 1984, *Pabalk Ticaret Limited Sirketi v. Norsolor S. A.*, *Rev. arb.*, 1985, p. 431, note by B. Goldman; *JDI*, 1985, p. 679, note by Ph. Kahn; *Dalloz*, 1985, p. 101, note by J. Robert; for an English translation, see *Yearbook Commercial Arbitration*, 1986, p. 484.

[343] Paris Court of Appeal, January 14, 1997, *Arab Republic of Egypt v. Chromalloy Aero Services*, *op. cit.* footnote 167.

[344] Paris Court of Appeal, June 10, 2004, *Bargues Agro Industrie v. Young Pecan Company*, *op. cit.* footnote 168.

[345] Paris Court of Appeal, September 29, 2005, *Directorate General of Civil Aviation of the Emirate of Dubai v. International Bechtel Co. Limited*, *Rev. arb.*, 2006, p. 695, note by H. Muir Watt; *JCP*, 2006, p. 1174, commentary by Ch. Seraglini; *Rev. crit. DIP*, 2006, p. 387, note by A. Szekely. See also commentary by Ph. Pinsolle, *Stockholm International Arbitration Review*, 2005, p. 151, and A. Mourre, *ibid.*, p. 172. For an English translation, see *Yearbook Commercial Arbitration*, 2006, p. 629.

Polish Ocean Line[346],*Hilmarton*[347] 和 *Putrabali*[348] 案中维持了巴黎上诉法院的决定。

这些案例法的理论依据,以巴黎上诉法院在 *Bargues Agro Industrie* 中的话来说,是:

> (一个裁决)没有和(仲裁地所在国)的法律秩序相结合,所以裁决可能被仲裁地的法院撤销不影响它被其他国家的法律秩序承认和执行。

确切地说,因为仲裁相对于仲裁地的法律秩序而言是自治的,所以被仲裁地撤销的裁决能够在执行地被承认。2007 年 6 月 29 日,在 *Putrabali* 一案中,法国最高法院更加明确地承认:

> 国际裁决源自国际正义(international justice),不基于任何国家法律秩序,其有效性必须根据承认和执行国的有关规则确定。[349]

通过阐明这一原则,最高法院为这个被法国法长期接受的方法

---

[346] *Cour de cassation*, 1re *civ.*, March 10, 1993, *Polish Ocean Line v. Jolasry*, *Rev. arb.*, 1993, p. 276, 2nd case, note by D. Hascher; for an English translation, see *Yearbook Commercial Arbitration*, 1994, p. 662.

[347] *Cour de cassation*, 1re *civ.*, March 23, 1994, *Hilmarton Ltd v. OTV*, *op. cit.* footnote 166.

[348] *Cour de cassation*, 1re *civ.*, June 29, 2007, *PT Putrabali Adyamulia v. Rena Holding and Mnogutia Est Epices* (which upheld the Paris Court of Appeal's decision of March 31, 2005, *Rev. arb.*, 2006, p. 665, note by E. Gaillard; *Dalloz*, 2006, *Panorama* 3035, commentary by Th. Clay), *Rev. arb.*, 2007, p. 507, report by J.-P. Ancel, note by E. Gaillard; *JDI*, 2007, p. 1236, note by Th. Clay; *Petites Affiches*, 2007, no. 192, p. 20, note by M. de Boisséson; J.-P. Ancel, L'arbitrage comme juridiction internationale autonome, *Revue juridique de droit des affaires*, 2007, p. 883; Ph. Pinsolle, The Status of Vacated Awards in France: the *Cour de cassation* Decision in *Putrabali*, *Arbitration International*, 2008, p. 277 and, by the same author, L'ordre juridique arbitral et la qualification de la sentence arbitrale de décision de justice internationale. A propos de l'arrêt *Putrabali* du 29 juin 2007, *Les Cahiers de l'Arbitrage*, volume IV, Paris, Pedone, 2008, p. 110. For an English translation, see *Yearbook Commercial Arbitration*, 2007, p. 299.

[349] Cited *supra*, footnote 348.

提供了更加深厚的理论基础。[350]

128. 虽然在 Chromalloy[351] 一案中美国法院承认了一个在仲裁地撤销的裁决,但是今天美国案例法日益向着更加保守的方向发展。

在 Baker Marine[352] 一案中,第二巡回上诉法院拒绝承认在仲裁地撤销的裁决。在 Spier[353] 一案中纽约南区地区法院的决定如出一辙。同样,在 TermoRio[354] 一案中,哥伦比亚特区地区法院也作出了这样的决定,并且哥伦比亚特区上诉法院维持了原判。[355]

在这些案例中,美国法院都采用个案分析的方式,把它们的具体事实和 Chromalloy 的事实区分。在 TermoRio 案中地区法院作出的决定是一个典型例子。和先前的其他决定一样,地区法院没有回答当以下因素出现时,是否可以承认被仲裁地撤销的裁决。这些因素包括:一方当事人是美国当事人(仅仅涉及一家美国公司的子公司不满足这个要求)[356],放弃仲裁协议规定的救济方式就相当于承诺必须履行裁决[357],以及申请执行裁决的当事人比试图在仲裁地撤销裁决

---

[350] 关于这个决定对仲裁理论的影响,参见 supra, § 65。

[351] *Chromalloy Aeroservices v. Arab Republic of Egypt*, July 31, 1996, 939 F. Supp. 907 (D.D.C. 1996); *Rev. arb.*, 1997, p.439.

[352] *Baker Marine (Nig.) Ltd v. Chevron (Nig.) Ltd*, August 12, 1999, 191 F. 3d 194 (2d cir. 1999); *Rev. arb.*, 2000, p.135, note by E. Gaillard.

[353] *Spier v. Calzaturificio Tecnica, S. p. A.*, October 22, 1999, 71 F. Supp. 2d 279 (S.D.N.Y. 1999).

[354] *TermoRio S. A. E. S. P. et al. v. Electrificadora del Atlantico S. A. E. S. P. et al.*, March 17, 2006, 421 F. Supp. 2d 87 (D.D.C. 2006); *Yearbook Commercial Arbitration*, 2006, p.1457; *Rev. arb.*, 2006, p.786, note by J. Paulsson.

[355] Court of Appeals for the District of Columbia, *TermoRio S. A. E. S. P. and LeaseCo Group LLC v. Electranta S. P. et al.*, May 25, 2007, 487 F. 3d 928 (D. C. Cir. 2007); *Yearbook Commercial Arbitration*, 2008, p.955; *Rev. arb.*, 2007, p.553, note by J. Paulsson.

[356] 在 TermoRio 一案中,裁决对一家美国公司的当地子公司有利。在 Spier 中,起诉方本身是一个美国公司,但是这一点对案件结果没有任何影响。

[357] 在 Chromalloy 中,仲裁条款表明裁决是"最终的和有约束力的,不能受制于包括上诉在内的任何程序",这种条款在参考了与《ICC 仲裁规则》第 32 条第 2 款措辞类似的仲裁规则的仲裁协议中是非常普遍的。TermoRio 判决拒绝承认被哥伦比亚国务院(Consejo de Estado)撤销的 ICC 裁决,理由是国有主体不能接受 ICC 仲裁。但是该判决没有考虑《ICC 仲裁规则》对弃权的明确规定。

的当事人更早发动程序。*TermoRio* 一案的被告是一个国有单位,根据 *Chromalloy* 判定商事行为的标准,该国有单位从事的是商业活动。撇开这个标准带来的许多问题,因为这和我们的讨论相关与否还有待商榷[358],我们可以总结今天美国的案例法给承认被仲裁地撤销的裁决留下很小的空间。本质上,只有仲裁地撤销这个裁决的决定本身违反美国的公共政策,这种裁决才会在美国被执行。美国案例法清楚地表明了这一点。例如,在讨论了先前的案例和将它们和本案的事实区分开来以后,*TermoRio* 地区法院得出结论:

> 考虑到这些事实和前述的三个案例,除非哥伦比亚的国家法院的决定违反了美国的公共政策,否则原告不能要求执行他们的仲裁裁决。[359]

美国华盛顿哥伦比亚特区上诉法院在 *TermoRio* 案中作出的决定突出表明例外的范围是窄小的。法院确实仅仅关注哥伦比亚的国家法院撤销裁决的司法决定,而非审查裁决本身。法院在进一步的分析之前,就依据裁决已经被仲裁地的法院撤销的事实认定裁决不存在了。从这个角度看,只有当仲裁地所在国的法院作出的决定不能被执行国承认,仲裁裁决才可能会被执行国考虑。*Baker Marine*[360] 和 *Spier*[361] 暗示如果仲裁地法院撤销裁决的决定违反美国公共政策的话,结果可能不同。即使当美国法院尝试将本案和 *Chromalloy* 的事实区分,并坚持在后者中当事人已经放弃了任何救济途径,该方法始终依据美国公共政策来评价仲裁地法院撤销裁决的决定,而非裁决本身。如果一方当事人要求仲裁地的法院撤销裁决,他或者她这样做违反了不对裁决持有异议的合同义务,从而违背合同诚信,仲裁

---

[358] For a critical discussion of the four criteria selected by the District Court in *TermoRio*, see the observations by J. Paulsson, *Rev. arb.*, 2006, p. 792, at p. 801.

[359] Decision, *op. cit.* footnote 354, *Rev. arb.*, at p. 794, and *Yearbook Commercial Arbitration*, at p. 1468.

[360] *Baker Marine (Nig.) Ltd v. Chevron (Nig.) Ltd*, *op. cit.* footnote 352, at p. 197, § 3.

[361] Decision, *op. cit.* footnote 353, at p. 287.

地法院撤销裁决的决定有可能违反了美国的公共政策,所以这个被仲裁地法院错误撤销的裁决才有可能在美国被执行。这就是 *Bechtel* 案采用的逻辑。该案涉及一家美国公司和迪拜民用航空部门。[362] 迪拜法院撤销裁决的依据是证人没有根据迪拜法律宣誓作证,尽管双方当事人没有在仲裁过程中对此提出异议。虽然美国的联邦地区法院对迪拜法院作出的撤销裁决的决定的正确性持怀疑的态度,但是它拒绝无视迪拜法院的决定,原因是依据违反公共政策而拒绝承认外国司法决定的标准非常高,然而本案没有满足这个高标准。

从法学理论的角度看,与法国同行不同的是,美国法官仅仅考虑法院撤销裁决的决定而不是裁决本身。裁决仅仅是间接的考虑对象,而且是从仲裁地法院针对裁决的司法决定的角度进行考虑的。所以,在 *TermoRio* 案中,哥伦比亚特区上诉法院维持原判:

> 如果已经被仲裁所在国的适格的主体"撤销",该仲裁裁决就不存在了,也不能在其他缔约国被执行。这个原则决定应当如何处理本案。[363]

根据此方法,裁决不是执行地法院的主要研究对象。裁决的存在取决于仲裁地的法律秩序对其的承认,如果得不到这种承认,只有在仲裁地的司法决定依据执行地的公共政策得不到承认时,裁决才有可能被执行。裁决是仲裁地的法律秩序的一部分;国际仲裁的自治性是不存在的。从这个角度看,仲裁不过是审理案件的初级阶段,案件的最终决定权属于仲裁地的法院。然而,由于一方当事人通常正是仲裁地的国民,诉诸仲裁的原意正是要避免到该国法院寻求救济。晚近美国案例法和 1958 年《纽约公约》相比退步了,因为公约的

---

[362] US District Court for the District of Columbia, *International Bechtel Company Ltd v. Department of Civil Aviation of the Government of Dubai*, Decision of February 5, 2004, 300 F. Supp. 2d 112, and the decision of March 8, 2005, 360 F. Supp. 2d 136. 就对同样的案件法国法院采用的不同方法,参见 *supra*, footnote 345.

[363] *TermoRio S. A. E. S. P. and LeaseCo Group LLC v. Electranta S. P.*, *op. cit.* footnote 355, at p. 963.

主要成就是废除双重执行许可证制度,并且将承认仲裁裁决的条件从仲裁地的法律秩序中解放出来。[364]

129. 没有必要完整地重温涉及这个问题的法学辩论[365],被仲裁地撤销的裁决在法国和美国法中的命运有天壤之别,这足以说明,这种区别不是一个简单的技术性的争论,而代表了这两个国家的法律对国际仲裁的哲学表现形式有根本不同的看法。

这个结论也适用于反向问题——关于仲裁地拒绝撤销仲裁裁决的司法决定对执行国的影响——虽然法学著作很少涉及这个问题,但是它在实践中意义深远。

B. 仲裁地的法律秩序作出的不撤销裁决的决定的效力

130. 如果国际仲裁不是独立于仲裁地的法律秩序,如果执行国的法院主要考虑的是仲裁地法院就裁决有效性的司法决定,而不是裁决本身,仲裁地认为裁决有效的司法决定的影响力也值得分析。有一部分学者反对承认被仲裁地的法院撤销的裁决,对他们而言,承认和执行被仲裁地的法院撤销的裁决的逻辑也适用于承认和执行被仲裁地认定为有效的裁决:仲裁地作出的认为一个裁决有效的司法决定只要满足执行国承认外国判决的条件,就当导致该裁决在执行国的自动执行。

例如,在法国,Bollée教授已经尝试证明执行国应当承认仲裁地

---

[364] On this subject, see *supra*, § 33.
[365] 除了 *supra* footnote 335 的注解外,又见,对法国案例法的批判性分析,H. Muir-Watt's observations in *Rev. arb.*, 2006, p. 695; those of Ch. Seraglini, *JCP*, 2006, I-148, pp. 1174 and 1175; as well as S. Bollée, *Les méthodes de droit international privé à l'épreuve des sentences arbitrales*, *op. cit.* footnote 9, at §§ 369 *et seq.* 相反的,就对法国案例法的赞同观点,参见 Ph. Pinsolle, references *supra*, footnote 348; A. Mourre, *Stockholm International Arbitration Review*, 2005, p. 172; as well as the observations by E. Gaillard and J. Paulsson, *Rev. arb.*, 2006, p. 666 and p. 796 respectively.

作出的认为仲裁裁决有效的司法决定。[366] 他的分析从一个有说服力的观点开始,即"不对称地"看待针对撤销裁决的申请而作出的司法决定是"麻烦的"。然后,他表示:

> 通常而言,一个规则是否能够成为解决某个法律问题的基础不是取决于它主张的**结果**,而是它的**目的**。[367]

换句话说,如果其他法律秩序要承认仲裁地的法院撤销裁决的司法决定,同样它们也要承认仲裁地不撤销裁决的司法决定。根据这个逻辑,Bollée 教授总结道,执行地法院的审查应当仅仅涉及仲裁地的法院对仲裁的规范是否过于宽松这一点。[368]

Bollée 教授认为,如果一个外国法院决定采纳更低的标准,例如当一个外国法院拒绝决定仲裁员是否超越权限时,作为执行地的法国在其法律框架下仍然可以作出自己的决定。[369]

在英国学术著作中,国际私法学者 Roy Goode 教授提出了类似的见解。在一篇关于仲裁地法律的作用的文章中,作者批评了认为国际仲裁独立于仲裁地的法律的理论,他还讨论了仲裁地的法院拒绝撤销裁决的情况,并且也分析了当事人可以要求但是却没有要求仲裁地的法院撤销裁决的情况。他认为,在上述两种情况中,每个国家都应当尊重仲裁地法院的决定,相应地,没有在仲裁地的法院寻求救济的当事人应当被完全剥夺在另一个国家法院对裁决提出异议的能力:

---

[366] S. Bollée, *Les méthodes du droit international privé à l'épreuve des sentences arbitrales*, op. cit. footnote 9, at § § 402 et seq.

[367] Ibid., § 402, author's translation. 一旦我们同意不能区分对待仲裁地撤销裁决的决定和不撤销裁决的决定,问题就会变成:是否如 Bollée 教授建议的,其他国家的法院应当总是考虑仲裁地的决定,而不论决定的内容如何;或者,是否如本书的作者建议的,其他国家的法院就根本不应当考虑这种决定。

[368] 根据此,作者认为可撤销裁决的司法决定的标准,"据所谓的公共政策弱化效果理论(theory of the mitigated effect of public policy),应当毫无疑问的降低",ibid., § 418 in fine.

[369] Ibid., § 419.

无国籍裁决(stateless award)的概念的问题之一是它没有尊重被广泛接受的禁止反言理论。仲裁裁决的债务人决定在仲裁地的法院对裁决提出异议。如果他不成功的话,为什么他能够第二次——或者第三次或第四次——在其他国家的法院中对裁决提出异议呢? 为什么仲裁裁决的债务人已经根据仲裁地的法律对裁决提出异议后,不应当被要求接受异议的结果呢?[370]

131. 从审查仲裁裁决本身到审查国家法院就此裁决的决定,实质上改变了执行地审查的范围。例如,一个当事人质疑仲裁协议的有效性,但是仲裁员和随后仲裁地的国家法院都已经认定该协议是有效的。在所有的不允许审查外国判决的实体问题的法律秩序中,审查拒绝撤销裁决的司法决定不包括根据执行地的法律审查是否存在仲裁协议和协议是否有效的问题。执行地的法院通常仅仅审查外国法院的管辖权和法院的审判是否符合正当程序和国际公共政策的要求。因此问题是,如果仲裁地法院决定承认一个可能不以有效的仲裁协议为基础的裁决,该司法决定本身是否违反了执行国对国际公共政策的理解。为了回答此问题,一位赞同改变审查目标的学者,在法国法律框架下探讨了《法国民事诉讼法法典》第1502条和第1504条规定的对裁决的审查是否表现了法国法律秩序对外国裁决最大和最小的承认范围;或者,根据他支持的弱化的公共政策理论,执行地是否应当承认被仲裁地法院认可的裁决,虽然该裁决没有满足执行地对承认国际裁决的所有要求。[371] 这个方法的逻辑特别复杂,因为它首先包含根据通常适用于承认外国判决的规则审查外国法院的决定——这些规则不专门针对国际仲裁——然后,将这种审查的标准和通常适用于承认裁决的规则相比较,最后以根据国际公共政策的概念来决定,执行地的法律秩序是否可以接受仲裁地的

---

[370] R. Goode, The Role of the *Lex Loci Arbitri* in International Commercial Arbitration, *op. cit.* footnote 43, p. 35.

[371] See S. Bollée, *Les méthodes du droit international privé à l'épreuve des sentences arbitrales*, *op. cit.* footnote 9, at §§ 417—418.

法院对裁决的承认范围。分析不仅表明这个方法极其复杂,也表明在一定程度上该方法背离了《纽约公约》的逻辑。正相反的是,后者允许执行地的法院根据公约列明的条件直接审查裁决,以避免双重执行许可证制度。就如上述理论表示的,双重执行许可证制度认为裁决是一个私行为,所以除非它已经被仲裁地的法律秩序所承认,否则它没有约束力。[372]

132. 根据上述学者的观点,每个国家不是独立对裁决进行审查而是审查仲裁地的法院就裁决作出的司法决定,英国的案例法为这种审查在实践中是如何进行的提供了例子。2005年11月4日英国高院(High Court)根据这个观点审理了 *Svenska*[373] 一案,但是2006年11月13日上诉法院撤销了高院的决定。[374] 在那个案子中,立陶宛对受到它的一个国有公司签订的仲裁协议的约束表示异议。在丹麦作出的一个仲裁裁决却认为立陶宛受到该协议的约束。但是,立陶宛没有在丹麦法院中对该裁决提出异议。当这个裁决在英国被申请执行的时候,英国高院认为,既然立陶宛没有在丹麦对该裁决提出异议,它放弃了自己的权力,因此它不能在英国以不受仲裁协议约束为由拒绝执行该裁决。[375]

英国高院采用的方法在实践中会引起许多问题。首先,它鼓励

---

[372] On this subject, see *supra*, § 33.

[373] High Court of Justice, Queen's Bench Division, Commercial Court, *Svenska Petroleum Exploration AB v. Government of the Republic of Lithuania and AB Geonafta*, January 11, 2005, [2005] 1 All ER (Comm) 515, [2005] EWHC 9 (Comm); [2005] 1 Lloyd's Rep. 515; *Yearbook Commercial Arbitration*, 2005, p. 701.

[374] Court of Appeal, *Svenska Petroleum Exploration AB v. Government of the Republic of Lithuania and AB Geonafta*, [2006] All ER (D) 156 (Nov); [2006] EWCA Civ. 1529.

[375] High Court of Justice, Decision of January 11, 2005, *op. cit.* footnote 373, § 2:

> 我认为如果一个人已经参与了决定他是否是仲裁协议一方的仲裁程序,但是就此问题的仲裁结果对他不利,在他有机会在仲裁地的法院质疑该裁决的时候他却没有这样做,在这种情况下英国法院可以依据公约的第5条和法的第103章第2节(关于在何种情况下可以拒绝承认和执行仲裁裁决)行使自由裁量权来承认该裁决。

See also § 27 of the Decision.

对裁决不满意的一方当事人在仲裁地发动撤销仲裁的程序,即使它在那个国家没有财产可供执行。因此,这个解决方法在实践中会导致滥诉。其次,它鼓励第三国的法院中止执行程序以待仲裁地的法院决定是否撤销裁决。的确,这个逻辑要求仲裁失利的一方有义务首先在仲裁地所在国的法院对裁决提出异议,而不是等着执行地承认和执行程序的结果,这个要求是很奇怪的。最后,这个方法假设执行地的法院愿意接受仲裁地法院对裁决有效性的看法。这里,再次要问的是,如果仲裁地的司法决定得不到其他国家的认可,为什么要强迫仲裁失利的一方在仲裁地对裁决提出异议呢?这个逻辑不可避免地导致双层控制系统:仲裁地审查裁决之后,执行地的法院审查仲裁地就裁决作出的决定。撤销裁决的诉讼和执行撤销裁决的决定的诉讼重叠了,后者本质上只注重审查仲裁地的法院是否满足执行地公共政策的要求。虽然这种重叠不同于《纽约公约》的起草者们刻意避免的双重执行许可证制度[376],但是二者也相去不远。因此,幸运的是采用这个解决办法的唯一一个法院也被其上诉法院纠正了。[377]

英国高院作出的判决明显地反映了第一个国际仲裁的表现形式,与此截然相反的是,上诉法院在 *Svenska* 案件中采纳的解决方案是国际仲裁威斯特伐利亚表现形式的最好的例子。尽管该裁决没有被位于丹麦的仲裁地的法院撤销,英国仍然可以在《纽约公约》允许的范围内审查该裁决。认可存在仲裁法律秩序的仲裁的第三种表现形式也会带来同样的结论,因为每个国家都有权力自己审查国际仲裁裁决以决定是否承认和执行它。

---

[376] See *supra*, § 33.
[377] See the Decision issued by the Court of Appeal in *Svenska*, *supra*, footnote 374.

结　　论

133. 哲学的目的是提供一个认知世界的方法,同理,法律理论旨在认知其研究对象的哲学前提,以此帮助我们观察并且从批判性的角度评价与此研究对象有关的领域采纳的专业方法。

就国际仲裁而言,存在三大构建这个领域的表现形式:单独地区、威斯特伐利亚和跨国的表现形式,跨国的表现形式认可仲裁法律秩序的存在。不论问题涉及仲裁员的裁决权,还是整个仲裁程序,或者裁决的效力,每一种表现形式都能解答在仲裁领域可能遇到的所有问题。

134. 在每个案子中,对这些根本问题的回答来自每种表现形式特有的逻辑,尽管在某些情况下各种表现形式提供的回答可能是相同的。

在许多情况下,国际仲裁的每种表现形式导致不同的解决方法。例如,就决定用于解决争议的实体法而言,单独地区表现形式要求仲裁员适用仲裁地的法律选择规则;威斯特伐利亚模式倾向于适用仲裁员认为最合适的法律选择规则;认可仲裁法律秩序存在的表现形式允许仲裁员使用跨国的法律选择规则或者直接适用实体跨国规则。[378]

在其他情况下,不同表现形式所导致的解决方法可能有所交叉。例如,威斯特伐利亚的表现形式和仲裁法律秩序的表现形式都鼓励第三国的法院不要自动承认仲裁地撤销裁决的决定的效力。前者这样做是因为它强调每个法律秩序彼此独立;后者这样做的理由是,它认为无论该国是不是仲裁地,裁决的法律属性来自国际社会的集体

---

[378] See *supra*, § 105.

(collectivity of States),而不是单个国家的法律秩序。单独地区的表现形式恰与此观点相反,因为它认为仲裁地的法律秩序是裁决的"原产国"(State of "origin")[379]。这个例子表明每种表现形式提供的解决方式偶然也会重叠,但是它们采用这个解决方式的逻辑是各不相同的。在另一个例子中,就仲裁员适用强行规则问题而言,单独地区与威斯特伐利亚的表现形式看法类似。根据认可仲裁法律秩序存在的表现形式,只有当强行规则被广泛接受为跨国公共政策的时候,仲裁员才能无视合同准据法;另外两种表现形式,在某些情况下,也接受适用强行规则而不是合同准据法[380]。但是,每种表现形式这样做的原因不同。单独地区表现形式要求仲裁员适用仲裁地的国际私法体系,该体系指向的是仲裁地的强行规则或者"外国"强行规则。[381]鉴于准据法的多样性,威斯特伐利亚表现形式允许仲裁员自由适用合同准据法之外的强行规则,原因是为了保障裁决的有效性,或者便于仲裁员适用他们认为正当的规则。[382]

135. 因为所有三种国际仲裁的表现形式都能完全解释仲裁现象,读者不禁会问是不是存在客观的规则以供在这些表现形式中进行选择呢?然而,这个问题是毫无意义的,因为这些表现形式本来就是思想的产物,或者是对国际仲裁的主观看法,它们是信念(belief)——但不是信仰(faith)——也不是科学真理。一个思想的产物从来就无所谓对错;对它的评价只能看它是否前后一致,或者是否有效率。识别每一种表现形式的价值和评价它们对实践的启示来自别处:它们来自于这样一种愿望中,即完全理解仲裁法在某个历史时期标志性的特征,以掌握未来的趋势,并且能够在揭露某种偏见的同时评价仲裁法的整个演变过程。

---

[379] See *supra*, § 125. 对解决方式之间偶然重叠的另一个例子,参见双重诉讼是否可以适用于仲裁庭和国内法院之间,*supra*, § 83.

[380] See *supra*, § § 107 *et seq.*

[381] See *supra*, § 108.

[382] See *supra*, § § 110 *et seq.*

About the Author

Biographical Note

Emmanuel Gaillard, Born on January 1st, 1952 in Chambéry, France.
Agrégé des facultés de droit (1982).
Docteur en droit (Paris, 1981). *Diplômes d'études approfondies* in private law (Paris II, 1976) and criminal law (Paris II, 1977).

Professor at University of Lille II (1983—1987). Visiting Professor, Harvard Law School (1984). Professor at University of Paris XII (since October 1987, where he teaches private international law and international arbitration).

Secrétaire rédacteur, The Hague Conference on Private International Law (1980—1984).

Avocat, Paris Bar (since 1977).

President, International Commercial Arbitration Committee, International Law Association (ILA) (1989—1998).

Secretary-General of the French Branch of the International Law Association (ILA) (1989—1996).

Member of the French Committee on Private International Law.

Member of the French Arbitration Committee (CFA).

Member of the International Council for Commercial Arbitration (ICCA) (since 2007).

President of the International Arbitration Institute (IAI) (since 2001).

Member of the London Court of International Arbitration (LCIA) Arbitration Court (2002—2006).

Member of the Board of Trustees of the Foundation for International Arbitration Advocacy (since 2007).

Expert invited to participate in the work of the Organisation for Economic Co-operation and Development (OECD) and of the United Nations Conference on Trade and Development (UNCTAD) on international arbitration and investment law.

Observer to the United Nations Commission on International Trade Law (UNCI-

TRAL), invited to participate in the works on the revision of the UNCITRAL Arbitration Rules (2006—2010).

Member, appointed by France, of the Panel of Arbitrators of the International Centre for Settlement of Investment Disputes (ICSID) (2006—2012).

Counsel and arbitrator in numerous international arbitration proceedings (under the Arbitration Rules of the ICC, ICSID and UNCITRAL in particular).

Principal Publications

Books

Le pouvoir en droit privé, Paris, Economica, 1985.

Le Marché unique européen, Paris, Pedone, 1989 (co-author).

Insider Trading—The Laws of Europe, the United States and Japan, The Hague, Kluwer, 1992 (ed.).

Transnational Rules in International Commercial Arbitration, ICC Publication No. 480/4, 1993 (ed.).

Traité de l'arbitrage commercial international, Paris, Litec, 1996 (co-author).

Fouchard Gaillard Goldman On International Commercial Arbitration (E. Gaillard & J. Savage eds.), The Hague, Kluwer, 1999.

Annulment of ICSID Awards. IAI Series on International Arbitration No. 1, Huntington, Juris Publishing, 2004 (ed.)

La Jurisprudence du CIRDI, volume I, Paris, Pedone, 2004; volume II, Paris, Pedone, 2010.

Anti-Suit Injunctions in International Arbitration. IAI Series on International Arbitration No. 2, Huntington, Juris Publishing, 2005 (ed.).

Towards a Uniform International Arbitration Law? IAI Series on International Arbitration No. 3, Huntington, Juris Publishing, 2005 (ed.).

State Entities in International Arbitration. IAI Series on International Arbitration No. 4, Huntington, Juris Publishing, 2008 (ed.).

Precedent in International Arbitration. IAI Series on International Arbitration No. 5, Huntington, Juris Publishing, 2008 (ed.).

Enforcement of Arbitration Agreements and International Arbitral Awards, London, Cameron May Publishers, 2008 (co-ed.).

Aspects philosophiques du droit de l'arbitrage international, Leiden, Boston, Martinus Nijhoff, 2008.

The Review of International Arbitral Awards. IAI Series on International Arbitra-

tion No. 6, Huntington, Juris Publishing, 2010 (ed.).

Articles
International Arbitration in General

"L'interdiction de se contredire au détriment d'autrui comme principe général du droit du commerce international (Le principe de l'*estoppel* dans quelques sentences arbitrales récentes)", *Rev. arb.*, 1985, p. 241.

"L'affaire SOFIDIF ou les difficultés de l'arbitrage multipartite (à propos de l'arrêt rendu par Cour d'appel de Paris le 19 décembre 1986)", *Rev. arb.*, 1987, p. 275.

"The UNCITRAL Model Law and Recent Statutes on International Arbitration in Europe and North America", *ICSID Rev.*, 1987, p. 424.

"Le principe de confidentialité de l'arbitrage commercial international", *Dalloz*, 1987, Chr. 153.

"A Foreign View of the New Swiss Law on International Arbitration", *Arbitration International*, 1988, p. 25.

"L'arbitrage multipartite et la consolidation des procédures arbitrales connexes", *International Law Association*, *Report of the Sixty-third Conference*, Warsaw, 1988, p. 478.

"Précautions à prendre dans les contrats clés en mains", rapport du 19ème Congrès de l'Institut international de droit d'expression française (IDEF), Yaoundé, Cameroon, February 22—28, 1988, *Revue juridique et politique Indépendance et Coopération*, Paris, 1988, p. 810.

"La ley modelo de CNUDMI y la reciente legislación sobre arbitraje internacional en Europa y América del Norte", *Boletín de Información* (Ministerio de Justicia), Madrid, Ano XLII, March 15, 1988, n° 1485.

"The Use of Comparative Law in International Commercial Arbitration", *ICCA Congress Series No. 4. Arbitration in Settlement of International Commercial Disputes Involving the Far East and Arbitration in Combined Transportation* (P. Sanders ed.), Deventer, Kluwer, 1989, p. 283.

"Le nouveau droit de l'arbitrage international en Suisse", *JDI*, 1989, p. 905 (co-author).

"Les manœuvres dilatoires des parties et des arbitres dans l'arbitrage commercial international", *Rev. arb.*, 1990, p. 759.

"Laws and Court Decisions in Civil Law Countries", *ICCA Congress Series No. 5. Preventing Delay and Disruption of Arbitration/Effective Proceedings in Construction Cases* (A. J. van den Berg ed.), Deventer, Kluwer, 1991, pp. 65 and 104.

"La distinction des principes généraux du droit et des usages du commerce international", *Etudes offertes à Pierre Bellet*, 1991, p. 203.

"Trente ans de Lex mercatoria. Pour une application sélective de la méthode des principes généraux du droit", *JDI*, 1995, p. 5.

"Thirty Years of *Lex Mercatoria*: Towards the Selective Application of Transnational Rules", *ICSID Rev.*, 1995, p. 208.

"Aptitude des personnes publiques à compromettre et disparition de la notion de commercialité en matière internationale", Commentary of Paris Court of Appeal, June 13, 1996, *Société KFTCIC v. société Icori Estero et autre*, *Rev. arb.*, 1997, p. 251.

"L'exécution des sentences annulées dans leur pays d'origine", *JDI*, 1998, p. 645.

"Pour la suppression du contrôle de la contradiction de motifs des sentences arbitrales", Commentary of Paris Court of Appeal, March 5, 1998, *Société Forasol v. société mixte Franco-Kasakh CISTM*, *Rev. arb.*, 1999, p. 86.

"The Enforcement of Awards Set Aside in the Country of Origin", *ICSID Rev.*, 1999, p. 16.

"Un revirement de jurisprudence bienvenu: l'abandon du contrôle de la contradiction de motifs des sentences arbitrales", Commentary of Cass., 1re civ., May 11, 1999, *Société Rivers v. Fabre*, and Paris Court of Appeal, October 26, 1999, *J. Patou Parfumeur v. société Edipar*, *Rev. arb.*, 1999, p. 811.

"L'effet négatif de la compétence-compétence", *Etudes de procédure et d'arbitrage en l'honneur de Jean-François Poudret*, Lausanne, Payot, 1999, p. 387.

"Use of General Principles of International Law in International Long-Term Contracts", *International Business Lawyer*, May 1999, volume 27, no. 5, p. 214.

"L'arbitrage international: la valeur patrimoniale de la clause d'arbitrage", *Réalités industrielles (Annales des mines)*, August 1999, p. 36.

"*Baker Marine* and *Spier* Strike a Blow to the Enforceability in the United States of Awards Set Aside at the Seat", *International Arbitration Law Review*, April 2000, no. 2, p. 37 (co-author).

"The *Noga* case and the seizure of the *Sedov*. Observations on the Validity of Enforcement Measures in France Against Russian Federation Property", *Stockholm Arbitration Report*, 2000, no. 2, p. 119.

"Consécration de l'effet négatif du principe de compétence-compétence", Commentary of Cass., 1re civ., June 26, 2001, *Société American Bureau of Shipping v. Copropriété maritime Jules Verne et autres*, *Rev. arb.*, 2001, p. 529.

"Transnational Law: A Legal System or a Method of Decision Making?", *Arbitration International*, 2001, p. 59 (also published *in* K. P. Berger (ed.), *The Prac-*

tice of Transnational Law, The Hague, Kluwer, 2001, p. 53).

"The Negative Effect of Competence-Competence", *International Arbitration Report*, January 2002, p. 27.

"Arbitrating with Sovereigns: Commentary", *Arbitration International*, volume 18, no. 3, 2002, p. 247.

"The Consolidation of Arbitral Proceedings and Court Proceedings", *Complex Arbitrations Perspectives on their Procedural Implications*, ICC Bull., Special Supplement, 2003, p. 35.

"Institut pour l'Arbitrage International (IAI). Les premières applications du règlement de référé pré-arbitral de la CCI", *La Revue libanaise de l'arbitrage*, 2003, no. 25, p. 8.

"La nécessaire internationalisation des procédures arbitrales", *Journal des sociétés*, September 2003, p. 37.

"Regain de sévérité dans l'appréciation de l'indépendance et l'impartialité de l'arbitre", Commentary of Cass., $2^{\text{ème}}$ civ., December 6, 2001, *Fremarc v. ITM Entreprises*, Paris 1re ch. C., May 16, 2002 and April 2, 2003, *Rev. arb.*, 2003, p. 1231.

"*Anti-Suit Injunctions* et reconnaissance des sentences annulées au siège: une évolution remarquable de la jurisprudence américaine", *JDI*, 2003, p. 1105.

"Jonction de procédures arbitrale et judiciaire", *L'arbitrage complexe. Questions de procédure*, ICC Bull., Special Supplement, 2003, p. 37.

"Il est interdit d'interdire: réflexions sur l'utilisation des *anti-suit injunctions* dans l'arbitrage commercial international", *Rev. arb.*, 2004, p. 47.

"L'interférence des juridictions du siège dans le déroulement de l'arbitrage", *Liber Amicorum Claude Reymond. Autour de l'arbitrage*, Paris, Litec, 2004, p. 83.

"The ICC Pre-Arbitral Referee. First Practical Experiences", *Arbitration International*, volume 20, no. 1, 2004, p. 13 (co-author).

"Advocacy in International Commercial Arbitration in France", *The Art of Advocacy in International Arbitration* (R. D. Bishop ed.), Huntington, Juris Publishing, 2004, p. 133 (co-author).

"Impecuniosity of Parties and Its Effects on Arbitration: A French View", *Financial Capacity of the Parties. A Condition for the Validity of Arbitration Agreements?*, Frankfurt, Peter Lang, 2004.

"La reconnaissance, en droit suisse, de la seconde moitié du principe d'effet négatif de la compétence-compétence", *Global Reflections on International Law, Commerce and Dispute Resolution. Liber Amicorum in honour of Robert Briner* (G. Aksen, K.-H. Böckstiegel, M. J. Mustill, P. M. Patocchi, A. M. Whitesell eds.), Paris, ICC Publishing, 2005, p. 311.

"Reflections on the Use of Anti-Suit Injunctions in International Arbitration", *Pervasive Problems in International Arbitration* (L. A. Mistelis & J. D. M. Lew eds.), Alphen aan den Rijn, Kluwer Law International, 2006, p. 201.

"L'effet négatif de la compétence-compétence en droit comparé", Commentary of Cass., 1re civ., June 7, 2006, *Copropriété maritime Jules Verne v. American Bureau of Shipping (ABS)*, *Rev. arb.*, 2006, p. 945.

"Anti-Suit Injunctions Issued by Arbitrators", *ICCA Congress Series No. 13. International Arbitration 2006: Back to Basics?* (A. J. van den Berg ed.), Alphen aan den Rijn, Kluwer Law International, 2007, p. 235.

"The relationship of the New York Convention with Other Treaties and with Domestic Law", *Enforcement of Arbitration Agreements and International Arbitral Awards*, London, Cameron May Publishers, 2008, p. 69.

"The Role of the Arbitrator in Determining the Applicable Law", *The Leading Arbitrators' Guide to International Arbitration* (L. W. Newman & R. D. Hill eds.), Huntington, Juris Publishing, 2nd ed., 2008, p. 171.

"Negative Effect of Competence-Competence: The Rule of Priority in Favour of the Arbitrators", *Enforcement of Arbitration Agreements and International Arbitral Awards*, London, Cameron May Publishers, 2008, p. 257 (co-author).

"The Urgency of Not Revising the New York Convention", *ICCA Congress Series No. 14. 50 Years of the New York Convention* (A. J. van den Berg ed.), Alphen aan den Rijn, Kluwer Law International, 2009, p. 689.

"France", *Practitioner's Handbook On International Commercial Arbitration* (F.-B. Weigand ed.), Oxford, Oxford University Press, 2nd ed., 2009.

"Three Philosophies of International Arbitration", *Contemporary issues in International Arbitration and Mediation* (A. Rovine ed.), Huntington, Juris publishing, 2010, p. 305.

"L'ordre juridique arbitral: réalité, utilité et spécificité", *McGill Law Journal*, 2010, volume 55.

Investment Arbitration

Commentary of Cass., 1re civ., November 18, 1986, *Société Atlantic Triton v. République populaire révolutionnaire de Guinée et Société guinéenne de pêche (Soguipêche)*, *JDI*, 1987, p. 125.

"Quelques observations sur la rédaction des clauses d'arbitrage CIRDI", *Recueil Penant*, 1987, p. 291.

"Some Notes on the Drafting of ICSID Arbitration Clauses", *ICSID Rev.*, 1988,

p. 136.

"The Enforcement of ICSID Awards in France: The Decision of the Paris Court of Appeal in the *SOABI* Case", *ICSID Rev.*, 1990, p. 69.

Commentary of Cass., 1re civ., June 11, 1991, *Société Ouest-Africaine de Bétons Industriels (SOABI) v. Etat du Sénégal*, *JDI*, 1991, p. 1005.

"L'arbitrage sur le fondement des traités de protection des investissements", *Rev. arb.*, 2003, p. 853.

"The Meaning of 'and' in Article 42 (1), Second Sentence, of the Washington Convention: The Role of International Law in the ICSID Choice of Law Process", *ICSID Rev.*, 2003, p. 375 (co-author).

"La responsabilité des Etats du fait de leurs juridictions. L'affaire *Loewen c. Etats-Unis*", *DeCITA*, *Arbitraje*, 2004, volume 2, p. 257.

"The Extent of Review of the Applicable Law in Investment Treaty Arbitration", *IAI Series on International Arbitration No. 1. Annulment of ICSID Awards*, Huntington, Juris Publishing, 2004, p. 223.

"Investment Treaty Arbitration and Jurisdiction over Contractual Claims. The SGS Cases Considered", *International Investment Law and Arbitration: Leading cases from the ICSID, NAFTA, Bilateral Treaties and Customary International Law* (T. Weiler ed.), London, Cameron May, 2005, p. 325.

"Investment and Investors Covered by the Energy Charter Treaty", *Investment Arbitration and the Energy Charter Treaty* (C. Ribeiro ed.), Huntington, Juris Publishing, 2006, p. 54.

"The Effect of Broad Dispute Resolution Clauses in Investment Treaty Arbitration", *Arbitraje Internacional—Tensiones actuales* (F. Mantilla-Serrano ed.), Bogota, Legis, 2007, p. 23.

"Identify or define? Reflections on the evolution of the concept of investment in ICSID practice", *International Investment Law for the 21st Century. Essays in Honour of Christoph Schreuer* (C. Binder, U. Kriebaum, A. Reinisch, S. Wittich eds.), Oxford, Oxford University Press, 2009, p. 403.

Yearly commentaries on ICSID case law in *Journal du droit international* since 1986.

Private International Law

"Les conflits de lois relatifs au droit patrimonial à l'image aux Etats-Unis (à propos de la jurisprudence Groucho Marx)", *Revue critique de droit international privé*, 1984, p. 1.

"The Hague Conference Adopts a Convention for Trusts", *Trusts & Estates*,

February 1985, p. 23.

"La Convention de La Haye du 1er juillet 1985 relative à la loi applicable au trust et à sa reconnaissance", *Revue critique de droit international privé*, 1986, p. 1 (co-author).

"Trusts in Non-Trusts Countries: Conflict of Laws and The Hague Convention on Trusts", *American Journal of Comparative Law*, 1987, p. 307 (co-author).

"La réaction américaine aux lois de blocage étrangères", *L'application extraterritoriale du droit économique*, Cahiers du CEDIN, Paris, Montchrestien, 1987, p. 115.

"L'entrée en vigueur de la Convention de Vienne du 11 avril 1980 sur les contrats de vente internationale de marchandises", *Gazette du Palais*, 1988, Doctrine, p. 654-1.

"Les enseignements de la Convention de La Haye du 1er juillet 1985 relative à la loi applicable au trust et à sa reconnaissance", *Revue juridique et politique indépendance et coopération*, 1990, p. 304.

"Aspects de droit international privé de la restructuration de la dette privée des Etats", Communication du 8 mars 1989, *Travaux du Comité français de droit international privé*, CNRS, 1991, p. 77.

"Four Models for International Bankruptcy", *American Journal of Comparative Law*, 1993, p. 573 (co-author).

Public International Law

"Convention d'arbitrage, immunité d'exécution et émanations de l'Etat", Commentary of Rouen, June 20, 1996, *Société Bec Frères v. Office des céréales de Tunisie*, Rev. arb., 1997, p. 263.

"Recent Developments In State Immunity From Execution In France: Creighton v. Qatar", *International Arbitration Report*, October 2000, p. 49 (co-author).

"Convention d'arbitrage et immunités de juridiction et d'exécution des Etats et des organisations internationales", *ASA Bull.*, 2000, p. 471.

"L'immunité de juridiction des organisations internationales: restreindre ou contourner", *Souveraineté étatique et marchés internationaux à la fin du 20ème siècle. A propos de 30 ans de recherches du CREDIMI. Mélanges en l'honneur de Philippe Kahn*, Paris, Litec, 2000, p. 205 (co-author).

"International Organisations and Immunity From Jurisdiction: To Restrict or To Bypass", *International Comparative Law Quarterly*, 2002, p. 1 (co-author).

"Effectivité des sentences arbitrales, immunité d'exécution des Etats et autonomie des personnes morales dépendant d'eux. Réflexion sur trois principes incompatibles", *Droit des immunités et exigences du procès équitable*, Paris, Pedone, 2004, p.

119.

"Effectiveness of Arbitral Awards, State Immunity from Execution and Autonomy of State Entities. Three Incompatible Principles", *IAI Series on International Arbitration No. 4. State Entities in International Arbitration*, Huntington, Juris Publishing, 2008, p. 179.

Other

"Sanction du défaut de pouvoir", note sous Cass., Ass. pl., May 28, 1982, *Consorts Mégevant v. Consorts Depraz et autres*, *Dalloz*, 1983, p. 349.

"Les sanctions civiles des règles du contrôle des changes: un revirement partiel de jurisprudence", Commentary of Cass. com., May 9, 1983, *S. C. I. Les Jardins de Grimaud et autre v. Soc. d'études juridiques, fiscales et financières*, and Cass. com., November 22, 1983, *S. A. R. L. A. C. Scholaert et autre v. Etat Belge et autre*, *Dalloz*, 1984, p. 204.

"La double nature du droit à l'image et ses conséquences en droit positif français", *Dalloz*, 1984, Chr. 161.

"La représentation et ses idéologies en droit privé français", *Droits*, 1987, no. 6, p. 91.

"La libéralisation des transports aériens dans la Communauté Economique Européenne", *Revue française de droit aérien et spatial*, 1990, p. 9 (co-author).

"Le contrôle des concentrations d'entreprises dans la Communauté Economique Européenne", *Gazette du Palais*, 1990, no. 1, Doctrine, p. 126.

"Les opérations d'initiés dans la Communauté économique européenne", *Revue trimestrielle de droit européen*, 1990, p. 329 (co-author).

Numerous commentaries published in *Revue de l'arbitrage*, *Journal du droit international*, *Dalloz* and the *New York Law Journal* in particular, on international arbitration, private international law and legal theory.

Bibliography

Ancel, J.-P., "L'arbitrage comme juridiction internationale autonome", *Revue juridique de droit des affaires*, 2007, p. 883.

Aquinas, Th., *Summa Theologica*, 1.2, 9.96, al.

Archives de philosophie du droit. No. °7, *Qu'est-ce que la philosophie du droit?*, Paris, Sirey, 1962.

Arfazadeh, H., *Ordre public et arbitrage international à l'épreuve de la mondialisation*, Geneva, Schulthess, 2nd ed., 2006.

Atias, Ch., *Philosophie du droit*, Paris, PUF, 2nd ed., 2004.

Bachand, F., *L'intervention du juge canadien avant et durant un arbitrage commercial international*, Paris, LGDJ, 2005.

Baechler, J., *Qu'est-ce que l'idéologie?*, Paris, NRF coll. Idées, Gallimard, 1976.

Baizeau, D., "Modification de l'article 186 de la LDIP suisse: procédures parallèles et litispendance, clarification du législateur après la jurisprudence Fomento", *Les Cahiers de l'Arbitrage*, volume IV, Paris, Pedone, 2008, p. 226.

Barrington, L., "*Hubco v. WAPDA*: Pakistan Top Court Rejects Modern Arbitration", *The American Review of International Arbitration*, 2000, p. 385.

Batiffol, H., *Aspects philosophiques du droit international privé*, Paris, Dalloz, 1956.

Baum, A., "International Arbitration: The Path toward Uniform Procedures", *Global Reflections on International Law, Commerce and Dispute Resolution. Liber Amicorum in honour of Robert Briner* (G. Aksen, K.-H. Böckstiegel, M. J. Mustill, P. M. Patocchi, A. M. Whitesell eds.), Paris, ICC Publishing, 2005, p. 51.

Berger, K. P., *The Creeping Codification of the Lex Mercatoria*, The Hague, Kluwer Law International, 1999.

—(ed.), *The Practice of Transnational Law*, The Hague, Kluwer Law International, 2001.

Blessing, M., *Introduction to Arbitration—Swiss and International Perspectives*, Basel, Helbing & Lichtenhahn, 1999.

Boisséson (de), M., *Le droit français de l'arbitrage interne et international*, Paris, GLN Joly, 2nd ed., 1990.

Bollée, S., *Les méthodes du droit international privé à l'épreuve des sentences arbitrales*, Paris, Economica, 2004.

Bucher, A., *Le nouvel arbitrage international en Suisse*, Basel and Francfort-sur-le-Main, Helbing & Lichtenhahn, 1988.

—, "L'examen de la compétence internationale par le juge suisse", *La semaine judiciaire*, 2007, p. 153.

Carbonneau, Th., *The Law and Practice of Arbitration*, Huntington, Juris Publishing, 2nd ed., 2007.

—, "At the Crossroads of Legitimacy and Arbitral Autonomy", *The American Review of International Arbitration*, 2005, p. 213.

Cassese, A., *International Law and Politics in a Divided World*, Oxford, Oxford University Press, 1986.

Chedly, L., *Arbitrage commercial international & ordre public transnational*, Tunis, Centre de Publication Universitaire, 2002.

Chevallier, J., "L'ordre juridique", *Le droit en procès*, Paris, PUF, Publications du CURAPP, 1983, p. 7.

Chitty on Contracts, volume I, London, Sweet & Maxwell, 30th ed., 2008.

Clay, Th., *L'arbitre*, Paris, Dalloz, 2001.

Coe, J., *International Commercial Arbitration: American Principles and Practice in a Global Context*, Irvington-on-Hudson, Transnational Publishers, 1997.

Cohen, D., *Arbitrage et société*, Paris, LGDJ, 1993.

Combacau, J., "Le droit international: bric-à-brac ou système?", *Archives de philosophie du droit*. No. 31, *Le système juridique*, 1986, p. 85.

Court de Fontmichel, A., *L'arbitre, le juge et les pratiques illicites du commerce international*, Paris, Editions Panthéon-Assas, 2004.

Craig, L. W., Park, W., Paulsson, J., *International Chamber of Commerce Arbitration*, Paris and New York, Oceana Publications, Inc., 3rd ed., 2000.

Crivellaro, A., "International Arbitrators and Courts of the Seat—Who Defers to Whom?", *ASA Bull.*, 2003, p. 60.

Dalhuisen, J. H., "Legal Orders and Their Manifestation: The Operation of the International Commercial and Financial Legal Order and Its Lex Mercatoria", *Berkeley Journal of International Law*, 2006, p. 129.

David, R., "Droit naturel et arbitrage", *Natural Law and World Law. Essays to Commemorate the Sixtieth Birthday of Kotaro Tanaka*, Tokyo, Yuhikaku, 1954, p. 19.

—, *Arbitration in International Trade*, Deventer, Kluwer Law and Taxation Publishers, 1985.

De Ly, F., *International Business Law and Lex Mercatoria*, Amsterdam, North-Holland, 1992.

Derains, Y., "L'obligation de minimiser le dommage dans la jurisprudence arbitrale", *IBLJ*, 1987, p. 375.

—, "La pratique de l'administration de la preuve dans l'arbitrage commercial international", *Rev. arb.*, 2004, p. 781.

Deumier, P., *Le droit spontané*, Paris, Economica, 2002.

Dezalay, Y., Garth, B. G., *Dealing in Virtue: International Commercial Arbitration and the Construction of a Transnational Legal Order*, Chicago and London, The University of Chicago Press, 1996 (foreword by P. Bourdieu).

Dicey, Morris and Collins on the Conflict of Laws (L. Collins, A. Briggs, J. Harris, J. D. McClean, C. McLachlan, C. G. J. Morse eds.), London, Sweet & Maxwell, 14th ed., 2006.

Eisemann, F., "La *lex fori* de l'arbitrage commercial international", *Travaux du comité français de droit international privé*, 1973—1975, Paris, Dalloz, 1977, p. 189.

Fadlallah, I., "L'ordre public dans les sentences arbitrales", *Collected Courses*, volume 249, 1994, p. 369.

Fassò, G., *Histoire de la philosophie du droit. XIXe et XXe siècles*, Paris, LGDJ, 1976, translated from the third edition, *Storia della filosofia del diritto*. volume III, *Ottocento e Novecento*, Bologna, Società editrice il Mulino, 1974.

Fischer-Zernin, V., Junker, A., "Between Scylla and Charybdis: Fact Gathering in German Arbitration", *Journal of International Arbitration*, 1987, no. 2, p. 9.

Fouchard, Ph., *L'arbitrage commercial international*, Paris, Dalloz, 1965.

—, "L'autonomie de l'arbitrage commercial international", *Rev. arb.*, 1965, p. 99.

—, "La loi-type de la CNUDCI sur l'arbitrage commercial international", *JDI*, 1987, p. 861.

—, "La portée internationale de l'annulation de la sentence arbitrale dans son pays d'origine", *Rev. arb.*, 1997, p. 329.

—, "Anti-Suit Injunctions in International Arbitration—What Remedies?", *IAI Series on International Arbitration No. 2. Anti-Suit Injunctions in International Arbitration* (E. Gaillard ed.), Huntington, Juris Publishing, 2005, p. 153.

—, *Ecrits. Droit de l'arbitrage. Droit du commerce international*, Paris, Comité français de l'arbitrage, 2007.

Fouchard, Ph., Gaillard, E., Goldman, B., *Traité de l'arbitrage commercial international*, Paris, Litec, 1996.

Fragistas, Ch. N., "Arbitrage étranger et arbitrage international en droit privé", *Rev. crit. DIP*, 1960, p. 1.

Francescakis, Ph., "Droit naturel et Droit international privé", *Mélanges offerts à Jacques Maury*. volume I, *Droit international privé et public*, Paris, Dalloz, 1960, p. 113.

Gaillard, E., "The Use of Comparative Law in International Commercial Arbitration", *ICCA Congress Series No. 4. Arbitration in Settlement of International Commercial Disputes Involving the Far East and Arbitration in Combined Transportation* (P. Sanders ed.), Deventer, Kluwer, 1989, p. 283.

——, "La distinction des principes généraux du droit et des usages du commerce international", *Etudes offertes à Pierre Bellet*, Paris, Litec, 1991, p. 203.

——(ed.), *Transnational Rules in International Commercial Arbitration*, Dossiers of the ICC Institute of International Business Law and Practice, Paris, ICC Publishing, 1993.

——, "Thirty Years of *Lex Mercatoria*: Towards the Selective Application of Transnational Rules", *ICSID Rev.*, 1995, p. 208.

——, "L'exécution des sentences annulées dans leur pays d'origine", *JDI*, 1998, p. 645.

——, "Transnational Law: A Legal System or a Method of Decision Making?", *Arbitration International*, 2001, p. 59.

——, "General Principles of Law—More Predictable After All?", *New York Law Journal*, December 6, 2001.

——, "L'interférence des juridictions du siège dans le déroulement de l'arbitrage", *Liber Amicorum Claude Reymond. Autour de l'arbitrage*, Paris, Litec, 2004, p. 83.

——, "Il est interdit d'interdire: Réflexions sur l'utilisation des *anti-suit injunctions* dans l'arbitrage commercial international", *Rev. arb.*, 2004, p. 47.

——, *La Jurisprudence du CIRDI*, volume I, Paris, Pedone, 2004.

——, "Du bon usage du droit comparé dans l'arbitrage international", *Rev. arb.*, 2005, p. 375.

——, "La reconnaissance, en droit suisse, de la seconde moitié du principe d'effet négatif de la compétence-compétence", *Global Reflections on International Law, Commerce and Dispute Resolution. Liber Amicorum in honour of Robert Briner* (G. Aksen, K.-H. Böckstiegel, M. J. Mustill, P. M. Patocchi, A. M. Whitesell eds.), Paris, ICC Publishing, 2005, p. 311.

—(ed.) , *IAI Series on International Arbitration No. 2. Anti-Suit Injunctions in International Arbitration*, Huntington, Juris Publishing, 2005.

—, "Reflections on the Use of Anti-Suit Injunctions in International Arbitration", *Pervasive Problems in International Arbitration* (L. Mistelis & J. Lew eds.) , Alphen aan den Rijn, Kluwer Law International, 2006, p. 201.

—, "Switzerland Says *Lis Pendens* Not Applicable to Arbitration", *New York Law Journal*, August 7, 2006.

—, "Souveraineté et autonomie: réflexions sur les représentations de l'arbitrage international", *JDI*, 2007, p. 1163.

—, "Anti-suit Injunctions Issued by Arbitrators", *ICCA Congress Series No. 13. International Arbitration 2006: Back to Basics?* (A. J. van den Berg ed.) , Alphen aan den Rijn, Kluwer Law International, 2007, p. 235.

—, "L'ordre juridique arbitral: réalité, utilité et spécificité", *McGill Law Journal*, 2010, volume 55.

—, (ed.) , *IAI Series on International Arbitration No. 6. The Review of Arbitral Awards*, Huntington, Juris Publishing, 2010.

Gaillard, E., Savage, J. (eds.) , *Fouchard Gaillard Goldman On International Commercial Arbitration*, The Hague, Kluwer, 1999.

Gaillard, E., Banifatemi, Y., "Negative Effect of Competence-Competence: The Rule of Priority in Favour of the Arbitrators", *Enforcement of Arbitration Agreements and International Arbitral Awards* (E. Gaillard & D. di Pietro eds.) , London, Cameron May, 2008, p. 257.

Gentinetta, J., *Die lex fori internationaler Handelsschiedsgerichte* (The *Lex Fori* of International Commercial Arbitration Tribunals) , Bern, Verlag Stämpfli & Cie, 1973.

Gharavi, H. G., *The International Effectiveness of the Annulment of an Arbitral Award*, The Hague, Kluwer Law International, 2002.

Goldman, B., "Les conflits de lois dans l'arbitrage international de droit privé", *Collected Courses*, volume 109 (1963) , p. 347.

—, "Frontières du droit et 'lex mercatoria'", *Archives de philosophie du droit*. No. 9, *Le droit subjectif en question*, 1964, p. 177.

—, "Une bataille judiciaire autour de la *lex mercatoria*. L'affaire Norsolor", *Rev. arb.*, 1983, p. 379.

—, "Nouvelles réflexions sur la *Lex Mercatoria*", *Etudes de droit international en l'honneur de Pierre Lalive*, Basel, Helbing & Lichtenhahn, 1993, p. 241.

Goode, R., "The Role of the *Lex Loci Arbitri* in International Commercial Arbitration", *Arbitration International*, 2001, p. 19.

Grigera Naón, H. A., "Competing Orders Between Courts of Law and Arbitral Tribunals: Latin American Experiences", *Global Reflections on International Law, Commerce and Dispute Resolution. Liber Amicorum in honour of Robert Briner* (G. Aksen, K.-H. Böckstiegel, M. J. Mustill, P. M. Patocchi, A. M. Whitesell eds.), Paris, ICC Publishing, 2005, p. 335.

Gurvitch, G., *L'expérience juridique et la philosophie pluraliste du droit*, Paris, Pedone, 1935.

Hancock, M., "Three Approaches to the Choice-of-Law Problem: the Classificatory, the Functional and the Result-Selective", XXth *Century Comparative and Conflicts Law. Legal Essays in Honor of Hessel E. Yntema*, Leiden, A. W. Sythoff, 1961, p. 365.

Hanotiau, B., "L'arbitrabilité", *Collected Courses*, volume 296, 2002, p. 25.

Hart, H. L. A., *The Concept of Law*, Oxford, Oxford University Press, 2nd ed., 1994.

Hascher, D., "Principes et pratique de procédure dans l'arbitrage commercial international", *Collected Courses*, volume 279, 1999, p. 51.

——, "L'influence de la doctrine sur la jurisprudence française en matière d'arbitrage", *Rev. arb.*, 2005, p. 391.

——, "The Review of Arbitral Awards by Domestic Courts—France", *IAI Series on International Arbitration No. 6. The Review of Arbitral Awards* (E. Gaillard ed.), Huntington, Juris Publishing, 2010.

Hauriou, M., *La théorie de l'institution et de la fondation*, Paris, Coll. Cahiers de la nouvelle journée, Bloud & Gay, 1925.

Heuzé, V., "La morale, l'arbitre et le juge", *Rev. arb.*, 1993, p. 179.

Hirsch, A., "The Place of Arbitration and the Lex Arbitri", *The Arbitration Journal*, Sept. 1979, volume 34, no. 3, p. 43.

Holmes, O. W., "The Path of the Law", *Harvard Law Review*, 1897, p. 457.

Horsmans, G., "Actualité et évolution du droit belge de l'arbitrage", *Rev. arb.*, 1992, p. 417.

Jarrosson, Ch., *La notion d'arbitrage*, Paris, LGDJ, 1987.

Jarvin, S., "The sources and limits of the arbitrator's powers", *Arbitration International*, 1986, volume 2, no. 1, p. 140.

Jestaz, P., "L'avenir du droit naturel ou le droit de seconde nature", *RTD civ.*, 1983, p. 233.

Kahn, Ph., "Droit international économique, droit du développement, lex mercatoria: concept unique ou pluralisme des ordres juridiques?", *Le droit des relations économiques internationales. Etudes offertes à Berthold Goldman*, Paris, Litec,

1982, p. 97.

—, "Les principes généraux du droit devant les arbitres du commerce international", *JDI*, 1989, p. 305.

—, " A propos de l'ordre public transnational: quelques observations ", *Mélanges Fritz Sturm offerts par ses collègues et ses amis à l'occasion de son soixante-dixième anniversaire*, volume II, Liège, Ed. Jur. Univ. Liège, 1999, p. 1539.

Kalinowski, G., *Introduction à la logique juridique. Eléments de sémiotique juridique, logique des normes et logique juridique*, Paris, LGDJ, 1965.

Kassis, A., *Théorie générale des usages du commerce*, Paris, LGDJ, 1984.

—, *L'autonomie de l'arbitrage commercial international. Le droit français en question*, Paris, L'Harmattan, 2005.

Kaufmann-Kohler, G., "Identifying and Applying the Law Governing the Arbitration Procedure—The Role of the Law of the Place of Arbitration", *ICCA Congress Series No. 9. Improving the Efficiency of Arbitration Agreements and Awards—40 Years of Application of the New York Convention* (A. J. van den Berg ed.), Deventer, Kluwer Law International, 1999, p. 336.

—, "Mondialisation de la procédure arbitrale", *Le droit saisi par la mondialisation* (Ch.-A. Morand ed.), Brussels, Bruylant, 2001, p. 269.

—, "Globalization of Arbitral Procedure ", *Vanderbilt Journal of Transnational Law*, 2003, volume 36, no. 4, p. 1313.

Kaufmann-Kohler, G., Bärtsch, P., "Discovery in International Arbitration: How Much is Too Much?", *SchiedsVZ*, 2004, no. 1, p. 13.

Kelsen, H., *Pure Theory of Law*, Union, N. J., Lawbook Exchange, transl. Max Knight, 2002.

Kessedjian, C., "Transnational Public Policy", *ICCA Congress Series No. 13. International Arbitration 2006: Back to Basics?* (A. J. van den Berg ed.), Alphen aan den Rijn, Kluwer Law International, 2007, p. 857.

Keutgen, G., Dal, G.-A., *L'arbitrage en droit belge et international*. volume I, *Le droit belge*, Brussels, Bruylant, 2nd ed., 2006.

Klein, F.-E., *Considérations sur l'arbitrage en droit international privé*, Basel, Editions Helbing & Lichtenhahn, 1955.

—, "Autonomie de la volonté et arbitrage", *Rev. crit. DIP*, 1958, p. 255.

Knoepfler, F., " L'article 19 LDIP est-il adapté à l'arbitrage international?", *Etudes de droit international en l'honneur de Pierre Lalive*, Basel, Helbing & Lichtenhahn, 1993, p. 531.

Kopelmanas, L., " La place de la Convention européenne sur l'arbitrage commercial international du 21 avril 1961 dans l'évolution du droit international de l'arbitrage", *Annuaire français de droit international*, 1961, p. 331.

Lagarde, P., "Approche critique de la *lex mercatoria*", *Le droit des relations économiques internationales. Etudes offertes à Berthold Goldman*, Paris, Litec, 1982, p. 125.

Lalive, P., "Problèmes relatifs à l'arbitrage commercial international", *Collected Courses*, volume 120, 1967, p. 569.

——, "Les règles de conflit de lois appliquées au fond du litige par l'arbitre international siégeant en Suisse", *Rev. arb.*, 1976, p. 155.

——, "Transnational (or Truly International) Public Policy and International Arbitration", *ICCA Congress Series No. 3. Comparative Arbitration Practice and Public Policy in Arbitration* (P. Sanders ed.), Deventer, Kluwer, 1987, p. 257.

——, "Le droit applicable au fond par l'arbitre international", *Droit international et droit communautaire*, Colloquium Proceedings, Paris, April 5—6, 1990, Fondation Calouste Gulbenkian, 1991, p. 33.

——, "On the Transfer of Seat in International Arbitration", *Law and Justice in a Multistate World. Essays in Honor of Arthur T. von Mehren* (J. A. R. Nafziger & S. C. Symeonides eds.), Ardsley, Transnational Publishers, Inc., 2002, p. 515.

——, "L'ordre public transnational et l'arbitre international", *New Instruments of Private International Law. Liber Fausto Pocar*, Milan, Giuffrè Editore, 2009, volume II, p. 599.

Lalive, P., Poudret, J.-F., Reymond, C., *Le droit de l'arbitrage interne et international en Suisse*, Lausanne, Payot, 1989.

Leben, Ch., "De quelques doctrines de l'ordre juridique", *Droits*, 2001, no. 33, p. 19.

Lew, J., *Applicable Law in International Commercial Law. A Study in Commercial Arbitration Awards*, New York, Oceana Publications and Sijthoff & Noordhoff, 1978.

——, "Achieving the Dream: Autonomous Arbitration", *Arbitration International*, 2006, p. 179.

——, "Control of Jurisdiction by Injunctions Issued by National Courts", *ICCA Congress Series No. 13. International Arbitration 2006: Back to Basics?* (A. J. van den Berg ed.), Alphen aan den Rijn, Kluwer Law International, 2007, p. 185.

Lew, J., Mistelis, L., Kröll, S., *Comparative International Commercial Arbitration*, The Hague, Kluwer Law International, 2003.

Loquin, E., "L'application de règles anationales dans l'arbitrage commercial international", *L'apport de la jurisprudence arbitrale*, ICC Publication No. 440/1, 1986, p. 67.

—, "La réalité des usages du commerce international", *Revue internationale de droit économique*, 1989, p. 163.

—, "Les manifestations de l'illicite", *L'illicite dans le commerce international* (P. Kahn & C. Kessedjian eds.), Paris, Litec, 1996, p. 247.

—, "Où en est la *lex mercatoria*?", *Souveraineté étatique et marchés internationaux à la fin du 20ème siècle. A propos de 30 ans de recherches du CREDIMI. Mélanges en l'honneur de Philippe Kahn*, Paris, Litec, 2000, p. 23.

—, "Les règles matérielles du commerce international", *Rev. arb.*, 2005, p. 443.

—, "Les règles matérielles internationales", *Collected Courses*, volume 322, 2006.

Luhmann, N., "L'unité du système juridique", *Archives de philosophie du droit*. No. 31, *Le système juridique*, 1986, p. 163.

Malinvaud, Ph. *Droit des obligations*, Paris, Litec, 10th ed., 2007.

Mann, F. A., "*Lex Facit Arbitrum*", *International Arbitration. Liber Amicorum for Martin Domke* (P. Sanders ed.), The Hague, Martinus Nijhoff, 1967, p. 157, reprinted in *Arbitration International*, 1986, p. 241.

—, "England Rejects 'Delocalised' Contracts and Arbitration", *International and Comparative Law Quarterly*, 1984, p. 193.

Matray, L., "Arbitrage et ordre public transnational", *The Art of Arbitration. Essays on International Arbitration. Liber Amicorum Pieter Sanders* (J. C. Schultsz & A. J. van den Berg ed.), Deventer, Kluwer Law and Taxation Publishers, 1982, p. 241.

Mayer, P., "L'autonomie de l'arbitre international dans l'appréciation de sa propre compétence", *Collected Courses*, volume 217, 1989, p. 319.

—, "La règle morale dans l'arbitrage international", *Etudes offertes à Pierre Bellet*, Paris, Litec, 1991, p. 379.

—, "The Trend Towards Delocalisation in the Last 100 Years", *The Internationalisation of International Arbitration. The LCIA Centenary Conference* (M. Hunter, A. Marriott, V. V. Veeder eds.), London/Dordrecht/Boston, Graham & Trotman/Martinus Nijhoff, 1995, p. 37.

—, "L'arbitre et la loi", *Etudes offertes à Pierre Catala. Le droit privé français à la fin du XXe siècle*, Paris, Litec, 2001, p. 225.

—, "Revisiting *Hilmarton* and *Chromalloy*", *ICCA Congress Series No. 10. International Arbitration and National Courts: The Never Ending Story* (A. J. van den Berg ed.), The Hague, Kluwer Law International, 2001, p. 165.

—, "Effect of International Public Policy in International Arbitration?", *Pervasive Problems in International Arbitration (L. Mistelis & J. Lew eds.), Alphen aan den Rijn, Kluwer Law International, 2006, p. 61.

Mebroukine, A., "Le choix de la Suisse comme siège de l'arbitrage dans les clauses d'arbitrage conclues entre entreprises algériennes et entreprises étrangères", *ASA Bull.*, 1994, p. 4.

Motulsky, H., *Ecrits.* volume II, *Etudes et notes sur l'arbitrage*, Paris, Dalloz, 1974.

Mustill, M., "The New *Lex Mercatoria*: The First Twenty-five Years", *Liber Amicorum for the Rt. Hon. Lord Wilberforce* (P. Bos & I. Brownlie eds.), Oxford, Clarendon Press, 1987, p. 149, reprinted in *Arbitration International*, 1988, p. 86.

Mustill, M., Boyd, S., *The Law and Practice of Commercial Arbitration in England*, London and Edinburgh, Butterworths, 2nd ed., 1989; *Commercial Arbitration. 2001 Companion Volume to the Second Edition*, London, Butterworths, 2001.

Nancy, J.-L., *Etre singulier pluriel*, Paris, Galilée, 1996.

Oetiker, C., "The Principle of *Lis Pendens* in International Arbitration: The Swiss Decision in *Fomento* v. *Colon*", *Arbitration International*, 2002, p. 137.

Oppetit, B., "La notion de source du droit et le droit du commerce international", *Archives de philosophie du droit.* No. 27, "*Sources*" *du droit*, 1982, p. 43.

—, "Philosophie de l'arbitrage commercial international", *JDI*, 1993, p. 811.

—, *Théorie de l'arbitrage*, Paris, PUF, 1998.

—, *Philosophie du droit*, Paris, Dalloz, 1999.

Osman, F., *Les principes généraux de la lex mercatoria. Contribution à l'étude d'un ordre juridique anational*, Paris, LGDJ, 1992.

Ost, F., Kerchove (van de), M., *De la pyramide au réseau? Pour une théorie dialectique du droit*, Brussels, Publications des Facultés universitaires Saint-Louis, 2002.

Pamboukis, Ch., "La *lex mercatoria* reconsidérée", *Le droit international privé: esprit et méthodes. Mélanges en l'honneur de Paul Lagarde*, Paris, Dalloz, 2005, p. 635.

Park, W. W., "The *Lex Loci Arbitri* and International Commercial Arbitration", *International and Comparative Law Quarterly*, 1983, p. 21.

—, *International Forum Selection*, The Hague, Kluwer, 1995.

—, *Arbitration of International Business Disputes. Studies in Law and Practice*, Oxford, Oxford University Press, 2006.

Partasides, C., "Solutions Offered by Transnational Rules in Case of Interference by the Courts of the Seat", *IAI Series on International Arbitration No. 3. Towards a Uniform International Arbitration Law?* (E. Gaillard ed.), Huntington, Juris Publishing, 2005, p. 149.

Paulsson, J., "Delocalisation of International Commercial Arbitration: When and Why it Matters", *International and Comparative Law Quarterly*, 1983, p. 53.

—, "Enforcing Awards Notwithstanding a Local Standard Annulment (LSA)", *ICC Bull.*, May 1998, p. 14.

—, "Interference by National Courts", *The Leading Arbitrators' Guide to International Arbitration* (L. W. Newman & R. D. Hill eds.), Huntington, Juris Publishing, 2nd ed., 2008, p. 119.

—, *Denial of Justice in International Law*, London, Cambridge University Press, 2005.

Pellet, A., *Recherche sur les principes généraux de droit en droit international*, Doctoral Thesis, Paris II University, 1974.

—, "La *lex mercatoria*, 'tiers ordre juridique'? Remarques ingénues d'un internationaliste de droit public", *Souveraineté étatique et marchés internationaux à la fin du 20ème siècle. A propos de 30 ans de recherches du CREDIMI. Mélanges en l'honneur de Philippe Kahn*, Paris, Litec, 2000, p. 53.

Perelman, Ch., *Logique juridique. Nouvelle rhétorique*, Paris, Dalloz, 2nd ed., 1999.

Petrochilos, G., *Procedural Law in International Arbitration*, Oxford, Oxford University Press, 2004.

Pinsolle, Ph., "The Status of Vacated Awards in France: the Cour de Cassation Decision in *Putrabali*", *Arbitration International*, 2008, p. 277.

—, "L'ordre juridique arbitral et la qualification de la sentence arbitrale de décision de justice internationale. A propos de l'arrêt *Putrabali* du 29 juin 2007", *Les Cahiers de l'Arbitrage*, volume IV, Paris, Pedone, 2008, p. 110.

Poncet, Ch., "Swiss Parliament Removes *Lis Pendens* as an Obstacle to International Arbitrations in Switzerland", *World Arbitration & Mediation Report*, 2006, volume 17, no. 12, p. 395.

Poudret, J.-F., "Quelle solution pour en finir avec l'affaire *Hilmarton*? Réponse à Philippe Fouchard", *Rev. arb.*, 1998, p. 7.

—, "Exception d'arbitrage et litispendance en droit suisse. Comment départager le juge et l'arbitre?", *ASA Bull.*, 2007, p. 230.

Poudret, J.-F., Besson, S., *Droit comparé de l'arbitrage international*, Zurich, Schulthess, 2002.

—, *Comparative Law of International Arbitration*, London, Sweet & Maxwell, 2007.

Racine, J.-B., *L'arbitrage commercial international et l'ordre public*, Paris, LG-

DJ, 1999.

——, "Réflexions sur l'autonomie de l'arbitrage commercial international", *Rev. arb.*, 2005, p. 305.

Radicati di Brozolo, L. G., "Arbitrage commercial international et lois de police. Considérations sur les conflits de juridictions dans le commerce international", *Collected Courses*, volume 315, 2005, p. 265.

Reale, M., *Teoria Tridimensional do Direito: preliminares históricas et sistemáticas*, São Paulo, Saraiva ed., 4th ed., 1986.

——, "La situation actuelle de la théorie tridimensionnelle du droit", *Archives de philosophie du droit*. No. 32, *Le droit international*, 1987, p. 369.

Redfern, A., Hunter, M., Blackaby, N., Partasides, C., *Redfern and Hunter on International Arbitration*, Oxford, Oxford University Press, 5th ed., 2009.

Rigaud, M.-C., *La procédure arbitrale transnationale*, Doctoral Thesis, Paris XII University, 2008.

Rigaux, F., *Introduction à la science du droit*, Brussels, Ed. Vie ouvrière, 1974.

Robinet, J.-B., *Dictionnaire universel des sciences morale, économique, politique et diplomatique, ou Bibliothèque de l'homme-d'Etat et du citoyen*. volume 16, *Droit naturel*, London, Libraires associés, 1780.

Romano, S., *L'ordinamento giuridico*, Pisa, Spoerri, 1st ed., 1918; in French, *L'ordre juridique*, transl. L. François & P. Gothot, with an introduction by Ph. Francescakis, Paris, Dalloz, 1st ed., 1975; 2nd ed., 2002, foreword by P. Mayer.

Ross, A., *On Law and Justice*, London, Stevens & Sons Ltd., 1958.

Sanders, P., *Quo Vadis Arbitration? Sixty Years of Arbitration Practice*, The Hague, Kluwer Law International, 1999.

Sandrock, O., "To Continue Nationalizing or to De-nationalize? That is Now the Question in International Arbitration", *The American Review of International Arbitration*, 2001, p. 301.

Sauser-Hall, G., Institute of International Law, Report on the Amsterdam Resolution, *Yearbook*, volume 44, 1952, part I, p. 469.

Scelle, G., International Law Commission, Report on arbitral procedure, *Yearbook of the International Law Commission*, volume II, 1950, p. 114.

Scherer, M., "When Should an Arbitral Tribunal Sitting in Switzerland Confronted with Parallel Litigation Abroad Stay the Arbitration?", *ASA Bull.*, 2001, p. 451.

——, "The Place or 'Seat' of Arbitration (Possibility, and/or Sometimes Necessity of its Transfer?)—Some Remarks on the Award in ICC Arbitration n° 10′623",

ASA Bull. , 2003, p. 112.

—, "The Recognition of Transnational Substantive Rules by Courts in Arbitral Matters", *IAI Series on International Arbitration No. 3. Towards a Uniform International Arbitration Law*? (E. Gaillard ed.), Huntington, Juris Publishing, 2005, p. 91.

Schmitthoff, C. , "The Law of International Trade, its Growth, Formulation and Operation", *The Sources of the Law of International Trade*, London, Stevens & Sons, 1964, p. 3.

—(ed.), *The Sources of the Law of International Trade*, London, Stevens & Sons, 1964.

Schwartz, E. A. , "Do International Arbitrators Have a Duty to Obey the Orders of Courts at the Place of the Arbitration? Reflections on the Role of the *Lex Loci Arbitri* in the Light of a Recent ICC Award", *Global Reflections on International Law, Commerce and Dispute Resolution. Liber Amicorum in honour of Robert Briner* (G. Aksen, K.-H. Böckstiegel, M. J. Mustill, P. M. Patocchi, A. M. Whitesell eds.), Paris, ICC Publishing, 2005, p. 795.

Schwebel, S. M. , *International Arbitration. Three Salient Problems*, Cambridge, Grotius Publications Ltd. , 1987.

—, "Anti-Suit Injunctions in International Arbitration. An Overview ", *IAI Series on International Arbitration No. 2. Anti-Suit Injunctions in International Arbitration* (E. Gaillard ed.), Huntington, Juris Publishing, 2005, p. 5.

Seidl-Hohenveldern, I. , " Chronique de jurisprudence autrichienne", *JDI*, 1998, p. 1003.

Seraglini, Ch. , *Lois de police et justice arbitrale internationale*, Paris, Dalloz, 2001.

Sériaux, A. , *Le droit naturel*, Paris, Coll. Que sais-je?, PUF, 2nd ed. , 1999.

Söderlund, C. , " *Lis Pendens, Res Judicata* and the Issue of Parallel Judicial Proceedings", *Journal of International Arbitration*, 2005, p. 301.

Sperduti, G. , "Les lois d'application nécessaire en tant que lois d'ordre public", *Rev. crit. DIP*, 1977, p. 257.

Tao, J. , von Wunschheim, C. , " Articles 16 and 18 of the PRC Arbitration Law: the Great Wall of China for Foreign Arbitration Institutions", *Arbitration International*, 2007, p. 309.

Terré, F. , " L'arbitrage, essence du juridique", *Liber Amicorum Claude Reymond. Autour de l'arbitrage*, Paris, Litec, 2004, p. 309.

Treitel, G. , *The Law of Contract*, London, Sweet & Maxwell, 12th ed. (by E. Peel), 2007.

Van den Berg, A. J., *The New York Arbitration Convention of 1958. Towards a Uniform Judicial Interpretation*, Deventer, Kluwer Law and Taxation, 1981.

——, "Enforcement of Annulled Arbitral Awards?", *ICC Bull.*, Nov. 1998, p. 15.

Vanderelst, A., "Increasing the Appeal of Belgium as an International Arbitration Forum? ——The Belgian Law of March 27, 1985 Concerning the Annulment of Arbitral Awards", *Journal of International Arbitration*, no. 2, 1986, p. 77.

Van Houtte, H., "La loi belge du 27 mars 1985 sur l'arbitrage international", *Rev. arb.*, 1986, p. 29.

Virally, M., "Un tiers droit? Réflexions théoriques", *Le droit des relations économiques internationales. Etudes offertes à Berthold Goldman*, Paris, Litec, 1982, p. 373.

Von Mehren, A. T., "Limitations on Party Choice of the Governing Law: Do They Exist for International Commercial Arbitration?", The Mortimer and Raymond Sackler Institute of Advanced Studies, Tel Aviv University, 1986.

——, Institute of International Law, Report on the Santiago de Compostela Resolution, *Yearbook*, volume 63, 1989, part I, p. 35.

——, "Arbitration Between States and Foreign Enterprises: The Significance of the Institute of International Law's Santiago de Compostela Resolution", *ICSID Rev.*, 1990, p. 54.

Wald, A., "La résolution, par l'arbitrage, des conflits entre l'administration publique et les entreprises privées en droit brésilien", *Les Cahiers de l'Arbitrage*, volume IV, Paris, Pedone, 2008, p. 175.

Wengler, W., "Les principes généraux du droit en tant que loi du contrat", *Rev. crit. DIP*, 1982, p. 467.

Table of Abreviations

AAA	American Arbitration Association
AC	The Law Reports, Appeal Cases
ALI	American Law Institute
All ER	All England Law Reports
ASA Bull.	Bulletin ASA (Association Suisse d'Arbitrage)
ATF	Arrêts du Tribunal Fédéral Suisse
Bull. civ.	Bulletin des arrêts de la Cour de cassation (chambres civiles)
Cass. com.	Cour de cassation, chambre commerciale
Cass., 1re civ.	Cour de cassation, première chambre civile
Cass., 2ème civ.	Cour de cassation, deuxième chambre civile
Chr.	Chroniques (Dalloz)
Ed. G	Edition Générale (JCP)
EU	European Union
EWCA	England and Wales Court of Appeal
EWHC	England and Wales High Court
F. 3d	Federal Reporter 3d Series
F. Supp.	Federal Supplement
HKCU	Hong Kong Cases Unreported
IBA	International Bar Association
IBLJ	International Business Law Journal
ICC	International Chamber of Commerce
ICCA	International Council for Commercial Arbitration
ICC Bull.	The ICC International Court of Arbitration Bulletin
ICDR	International Centre for Dispute Resolution
ICSID	International Centre for the Settlement of Investment Disputes
ICSID Rev.	ICSID Review—Foreign Investment Law Journal
JCP	Juris-Classeur Périodique (La Semaine Juridique)
JDI	Journal du droit international
LCIA	London Court of International Arbitration

Lloyd's Rep.	Lloyd's Law Reports
OECD	Organisation of Economic Co-operation and Development
OJEC	Official Journal of the European Communities
OJEU	Official Journal of the European Union
PILS	Swiss Private International Law Statute
QB	The Law Reports, Queen's Bench
Rev. arb.	Revue de l'arbitrage
Rev. crit. DIP	Revue critique de droit international privé
Rev. dr. com. belge	Revue de droit commercial belge
RTD civ.	Revue trimestrielle de droit civil
RTD com.	Revue trimestrielle de droit commercial et de droit économique
UNCITRAL	United Nations Commission on International Trade Law
UNIDROIT	International Institute for the Unification of Private Law
Unif. L. Rev.	Uniform Law Review

索　引

（索引中数字指的是段落编号）

Aggravating the dispute，加剧争端　98
Agreement to agree，同意签约的意向书　62
Algeria，阿尔及利亚　58，62，113，126
ALI（American Law Institute），美国法律学会（ALI）　99
Anti-Suit Injunctions，禁诉令
　　Anti-anti-suit，禁—禁诉令　75
　　—at the seat，—在仲裁地　76—81
　　—in a place other than the seat，—在仲裁地之外的地方　73—75
　　Definition，定义　34，72
　　Non-compliance with international law，和国际法不符　75
　　Proliferation，广泛的采用　22，72
　　Unsuitability，不合适　75
Applicable law，准据法
　　Autonomy，自治　103
　　Choice of law，法律的选择
　　　　—method（static nature），—方法（静态本质）　57—58
　　　　—rules of the seat，—仲裁地的规则　101，103

　　—as regards arbitral proceedings，—关于仲裁程序　88—99
　　False conflicts，假冲突　22
　　Governmental interests，政府利益　113
　　Institute of International Law Resolutions，国际法研究所决议　89—91，101—103
　　Law or rules of law，法律或者法律的规则　42，60
　　Mandatory rules，强行规则　see Mandatory rules
　　Party autonomy，当事人自治　103
　　Substance of competing laws，相互竞争的法律的实质内容　58
　　Voie directe，直接的法律途径　104
　　See also ICC，ICDR，LCIA，Representation，UNCITRAL
Arbitrability，可仲裁性　14，38，69
　　See also New York Convention
Arbitral case law，仲裁案例法　60，62
Arbitral legal order，仲裁法律秩序
　　A-national character，非国家的特点　43，51
　　Aptitude to reflect on own sources，说明自己的渊源　62

—and anti-suit injunctions,—和禁诉令 76
—and arbitral procedure,—和仲裁程序 98
—and arbitrator's freedom,—和仲裁员的自由 95
—and autonomy,—和自治 43
—and award not set aside,—和不被撤销的裁决 132
—and award set aside,—和被撤销的裁决 125, 134
—and law applicable to the merits,—和适用于实体问题的法律 105, 134
—and *lex mercatoria*,—和商人习惯法 42
—and *lis pendens*,—和平行程序 83
—and mandatory rules,—和强行规则 118, 134
—and transnational public policy,—和跨国公共政策 115
Comprehensive character,全面的特点 62, 123
In general,一般来说 40—67
Jusnaturalist trend,自然法学派 46—49
Positivist trend,实证派 50—58
Recognition in arbitral case law,在仲裁案例法中承认 60—62
Recognition in national legal orders,在国家法律秩序中承认 63—67
Terminology,术语 43
Arbitral procedure,仲裁程序
    Ambulatory nature,漂移的本质 31

Arbitrators' freedom,仲裁员的自由 88—98
Autonomy,自治 92
Document production,文证提供 99
Evolving sources,演变进化中的渊源 89—93
Law or rules of law,法或者法律的规则 42
Liberalization,自由化 94
Parties' freedom,当事人自由 92
Transnational rules,跨国的规则 42
Witnesses,证人 98
Arbitration,仲裁
    Adjudicating differently,裁决不同 48
    agreement,协议 *see* Arbitration agreement
    Autonomy,自治
        Acknowledgement,承认 62
        First manifestations,首次表现 87, 101
        Terms of the debate,辩论的术语 9, 42
    Contractual nature,合同属性 9, 42
    Favoring-,支持— 84
    International-(misnomer),国际的—（用词不当）13
    Juridicity,法律属性 35—39, 43, 81
    Jurisdictional nature,管辖权的本质 9
    Mistrust of-,怀疑— 69
    Modernization of legislation,立法的现代化 22

Normal means of dispute resolution, 争端解决的常用方式 36, 69, 84
Sui generis nature, 独一无二的本质 9
Arbitration agreement, 仲裁协议
 Autonomy of-, 自治— 56, 58
 Existence and validity, 存在和效力 14, 30, 34, 60, 72, 83, 131
 Prima facie assessment, 表面审核 see Competence-competence
 Severability of-, 可分割原则的— 56, 58
Arbitrator, 仲裁员
 Conception of their role, 对仲裁员作用的认识 59
 Duty to the parties, 对当事人的职责 80
 Equated with national judge, 等同于国内法官 13, 41
 Extent of freedom, 自由的程度 86
 International judge, 国际法官 62
 Legal training, 法律培训 98
 Occasional organ of a State, 国家的临时代言人 76
 Power to adjudicate, 裁决权 9, 22, 23, 41, 42, 50, 53, 54, 68, 69, 87, 133
 Subjectivity, 主观性 49
 Truncated tribunal, 缺员仲裁庭 79
Argentina, 阿根廷 73
Atias, 阿蒂亚斯 6
Austin, 奥斯汀 31
Austria, 奥地利 126

Autonomy, 自治
 —of arbitration, —仲裁的 see Arbitration
 —of arbitration agreement, —仲裁协议的 see Arbitration agreement
 Party-, 当事人— 9, 33, 42
Award, 裁决
 "Colombian"-, "哥伦比亚的"— 11, 23
 Decision of international justice, 国际司法裁断 65
 Enforceable character, 可以执行的特点 38, 39
 Final-, 终局— 33
 Floating-, 漂浮的— 27
 "Foreign"-, "外国的"— 9, 33
 International-, 国际的— 11, 23, 33
 Juridicity, 法律属性 2, 11, 23, 29, 33, 36, 65, 133
 Non-existent-, 不存在的— 78
 Non-integrated-, 不与……结合的— 65
 Place of enforcement, 执行地 36
 Ripert-Panchaud— 126
 Set aside-, 撤销—
  Austria, 奥地利 126
  Belgium, 比利时 126
  European Convention of 1961, 1961年《欧洲公约》 126
  France, 法国 127
  Netherlands, 荷兰 126
  New York Convention of 1958, 1958年《纽约公约》 33
  United States, 美国 128

Stateless-,无国籍的— 130

Baechler 6
Baker Marine 128
Bangladesh,孟加拉 78
Bank guarantee,银行担保 98
Bank Mellat 27
Bankruptcy proceedings,破产程序 38
Bargues Agro Industries 65, 127
Bastardization,杂交 99
Batiffol 1
Bechtel 97, 127, 128
Belgium,比利时
 Award set aside at the seat,在仲裁地被撤销的裁决 126
 Waiver of action to set aside,放弃撤销裁决的诉讼 66
Belief,信念 125, 132, 135
Besson 7, 14, 18
Bolivia,玻利维亚 22
Bollée 21, 130—131
Boycott,联合抵制 111, 121
Brazil,巴西 72, 73
Bribery,贿赂 *see* Corruption
Business ethics,商业道德 64, 113

Casa v. Cambior 38
Cassese 32
Change in circumstances doctrine,情势变更原则 61
Chaos,混乱 21, 22
Chedli 116
Chemical weapons,化学武器 55
China,中国 70
Choice of law,法律选择 *see* Applicable law
Chromalloy 65, 128

Clay 43, 48
Cohen 43
Coherence,连贯一致 6, 35, 43, 49, 62, 135
Collectivity,集体 *see* Plurality
Colombia,哥伦比亚 128
Competence-competence,仲裁庭自裁管辖权
 —and *lis pendens*,—和平行程序 84
 In general,一般而言 75
 Negative effect of-,消极影响— 7, 84
 Positive effect of-,积极影响— 75, 83
 Prima facie,表面上 83, 84
Competition law,竞争法 38
Conflict of laws,冲突法 *see* Applicable law
Conservatism,保守主义 22
Contract adaptation,合同调整 52
Contractual good faith,合同诚信 4, 61, 62, 128
Cooperation between parties,当事人之间的合作 52
Cooperation between States,国家之间的合作 32, 107
Coordination between systems,制度之间的协调 21, 22
COPEL 73
Copernican revolution,哥白尼革命 24
Corruption,腐败 38, 49, 57, 112, 113, 115, 117
Court de Fontmichel, Fontmichel 法院 5, 111
Cuba,古巴 121
Cuban Liberty and Democratic Solidarity

Act,《古巴自由和民主联盟法》 121

D'Amato Act,《达马托法》 111
Darwinism (legal),达尔文主义（法律的） 52
David 48
Decision refusing to set aside an award, 不撤销裁决的决定 130—132
Denial of justice, 拒绝司法 79
Discovery, 证据开示 see Arbitral procedure (document production)
Desuetude, 弃之不用 5
Doctrine, 学说 6
Double exequatur, 双重执行许可证制度 see New York Convention
Dow Chemical 52
Drug trafficking, 贩毒 see Trafficking
Dubai, 迪拜 97, 128

Effectiveness, 有效性 5
Efficiency, 效率 6, 35, 135
Eisemann, Eisemann 116
Embargo, 禁运 61, 115, 121
England, 英格兰
    Autonomy of the arbitration agreement, 仲裁协议自治 56, 58
    Awards not set aside at the seat, 没有在仲裁地被撤销的裁决 132
    Floating awards, 漂浮的裁决 32
    Lois de police, 强行规则 109
    See also agreement to agree
Environment, 环境 57, 122
Ethics, 道德 see Business ethics
Ethiopia, 埃塞俄比亚 80
European Convention of 1961, 1961年《欧洲公约》
    Awards set aside at the seat, 在仲裁地被撤销的裁决 126
    Procedure, 程序 91
European Gas Turbines 64

Faith, 信仰 20, 135
Fiona Trust 58
Fomento 85
Forum, 管辖地
    No-for arbitrators, 不一对仲裁员而言 1, 23, 31, 49, 66
    See also Seat
Fouchard, Fouchard 7, 13, 75, 102
Fougerolle 64
Fragistas 13
France, 法国
    Action to set aside, 撤销裁决的诉讼 66
    Arbitrator as an international judge, 仲裁员作为国际法官 65
    Awards not integrated, 裁决没有与仲裁地的法律秩序相结合 65
    Awards set aside at the seat, 在仲裁地被撤销的裁决 65, 127
    Voie directe (law applicable to the merits), 直接的法律途径（适用于实体问题的法律） 104
Francescakis 1
Freedom, 自由
    Contractual-, 合同的— 113
    —gained, —争取的 95
    —granted, —获准的 95
    In general, 一般而言 2
    See also: Applicable law, Arbitral procedure

Gaillard，盖拉德 7，23，24，36，56，61，84
General Principles，一般原则
    Article 38 of International Court of Justice Statute,《国际法院规约》第38条 54
    Distinguished from transnational rules，与跨国规则的区别 61
    —of law，—法律的 54
    Increasing specialization，日益细化 61
Geneva Convention of 1927，1927年《日内瓦公约》 33
Geneva Protocol of 1923，1923年《日内瓦议定书》 89
Goldman 1，7，13，65，102
Good faith，诚信 see Contractual good faith
Goode 9，14，28，130
Götaverken 66
Gothot 117
Governmental interests，政府利益 113
Grundnorm 18
Gurvitch 2

Harmony（international-of solutions），和谐（国际—解决方法的） 17，19，21，22
Hart 2，5，18，62
Hauriou 3
Helms-Burton Act,《赫尔姆斯—伯顿法》 121
Hilmarton 65，113
Himpurna 79
Holmes 5
Hong Kong，香港 74
Hubco 73

IBA（International Bar Association），国际律师协会（IBA） 99
ICC（International Chamber of Commerce），国际商会（ICC）
    1953 preliminary draft，1953年初稿 33
    Arbitration Rules，仲裁规则
        Challenge of arbitrators，要求仲裁员回避 78，80
        Law applicable to the merits，适用于实体问题的法律 104
        Legally enforceable awards，法律上可以执行的裁决 38，80
        Procedure，程序 93
        Transnational approach，跨国方式 116
ICDR（International Center for Dispute Resolution），国际争端解决中心
    Law applicable to the merits，适用于实体问题的法律 104
    Procedure，程序 93
Ideology，意识形态 6，135
IDI（Institut du Droit International），国际法研究所（法语，IDI） see Institute of International Law
Idiosyncrasies，违反主流
    Acceptance of-，接受— 97
    Disregarding-，不理会— 106
    Exacerbation，加剧 22，54
    Examples，例子 62，106
Imprévision，不可预见 see Change in circumstances doctrine
In defavorem arbitrandum，对仲裁无益 39
India，印度 72

Indifference as a virtue, 互不干涉值得提倡 34
Indonesia, 印度尼西亚 72, 74, 79
Injustice or chaos, 非正义或者混乱 22
Institute of International Law, 国际法研究所
    Amsterdam Resolution of 1957, 1957 年《阿姆斯特丹决议》 1, 89—90, 92, 101—103
    Basel Resolution of 1991, 1991 年《巴塞尔决议》 112
    Santiago de Compostela Resolution of 1989, 1989 年《圣地亚哥德孔波斯特拉决议》 92, 103, 116
    Siena Resolution of 1952, 1952 年《锡耶纳决议》 9, 89, 90
Institution theory, 制度主义理论 see Legal order
Intermediaries (prohibition of-), 中介人（禁止—） 58, 62, 113
International arbitration, 国际仲裁 see Arbitration
International commerce (specific needs of), 国际商事交易（的特别需要） 105
Iran, 伊朗 114, 121
Iran-Libya Sanctions Act, 《伊朗—利比亚制裁法》 111, 121
Iraq, 伊拉克 121

Juridicity, 法律属性
    Ability to sanction, 制裁的能力 28
    —of arbitration, —仲裁的 2, 14, 27, 28, 35—39, 40—41, 3, 50, 81, 125

—of the award, —裁决的 see Award
—of *lex mercatoria*, —商人习惯法的 5
—of transnational rules, —跨国规则的 3
Notion, 观点 2, 3, 5, 28
Standpoint of the arbitrators, 仲裁员的视角 41
Jus cogens, 强行规则 118
Jusnaturalism, 自然法学 see Natural law

Kahn 116
Kassis 21
Kaufmann-Kohler 94
Kelsen 2, 3, 18, 43
Kerchove (de) 5, 43, 62
Kompetenz-Kompetenz: see Competence-competence, *Kompetenz-Kompetenz*
Kopelmanas 102

Lagarde 3, 21
Lagergren 90
Laissez-faire, 自由放任原则 61
Lalive 94, 102, 116
Law of nations, 万国公法 55
LCIA (London Court of International Arbitration), 伦敦国际仲裁院
    Law applicable to the merits, 适用于实体问题的法律 104
    Procedure, 程序 93
Le Créole 55
Legal Darwinism, 法律达尔文主义 see Darwinism
Legal Force, 法的效力 see Juridicity, Award

Legal Nature，法的性质 *see* Juridicity
Legal order，法律秩序
  Institution theory，制度理论 3
  —distinguished from body of rules，—区别于一系列规则 61
  —distinguished from legal system，—区别于法律制度 62
  Notion，观点
  Validation role of-，确认的角色— 62
  See also Arbitral legal order
Legal system，法律制度 *see* Legal order
Legal theory (object)，法律理论(研究对象) 133
Legality (pole of)，合法性(支柱的) 5
Legitimacy，正当性 2, 5, 27, 40, 49, 75, 112, 121
Lex arbitri，仲裁法 13, 14, 18, 20, 94
Lex arbitrii，仲裁法 14
Lex executionism，执行法主义 37—39, 111
Lex fori，裁判地法 14
  See also Forum，又见管辖地
Lex loci arbitri，仲裁地法 14, 28
Lex mercatoria，商人习惯法
  Belief，信念 98
  Illusion，错觉 6
  Inadequacy of national legal orders (theme of)，国家法律秩序的不足(的主题) 52
  Juridicity，法律属性 5
  —and legal order，—和法律秩序 42
  Phenomenon，现象 5
  Pseudo-legal caprice，伪法律且善变 6
  Quarrel，争论 3, 5
  Subject of legal theory，法学理论的研究对象 3
Liberalization，自由化
  Law applicable to the merits，适用于实体问题的法律 100—106
  Procedure，程序 88
Liberty，自由 *see* Freedom
Limitation of liability clause，限制责任的条款 58, 106
Lis pendens，平行程序
  In general，一般而言 7, 82—85
  See also Competence-competence
Litigiousness，好讼 72
Localization of the arbitration，把仲裁当地化
  Hotels，旅馆 36
  Monolocal，单独地区的 *see* Monolocal representation
  Multilocal，多地区的 *see* Westphalian representation
  Place of enforcement，执行地 36
  Seat，仲裁地 36
  Transnational approach，跨国方式 *see* Arbitral legal order
Lois de police，强行规则 *see* Mandatory rules
Loquin 43, 52, 116
Loyalty in business，商业忠诚 52

Majoritarian Principle，多数原则 54—56
Mandatory rules，强行规则
  Conflict of-，冲突的— 113
  Cumulative approach，累加的方法 111

In general, 一般而言 107—123
　—and moral rule, —和道德规范 49
　—and transnational public policy, —和跨国公共政策 118
　Rome I Regulation, 《罗马条例I》 108, 109
　Seat, 仲裁地 36
Mann 13, 14, 18, 20, 89, 109
Matray 116
Mayer 29, 49, 55, 56
Mitigation of damages (duty of), 减小损失（的义务） 62
Model of law, 法律的模式 see Pyramidal model of law, Network
Modernization of legislation, 立法的现代化 see Arbitration
Monolocal Representation, 单独地区的表现形式 see Representation (monolocal)
Montego Bay Convention of 1982, 1982年《蒙特哥贝公约》 122
Moral rule, 道德规范 4, 49, 55
Multilocal, 多地区的 see Westphalian representation
Multiple or collective, 多个的或者集体的 41
Myth, 神话 6

National Grid 73
National legal orders, 国家法律秩序
　Inadequacy of-(theme), 不足—（主题） 52—53
　Plurality, 多个 36, 41, 50, 134
Nationalism, 民族主义 22
Natural Law, 自然法
　Ambiguous relationships, 界线模糊 49
　David 48
　Definition, 定义 48—49
　Discreet manifestation, 谨慎的表现 47
　Oppetit 48
　Representation, 表现形式 46—49
　Trends, 学派 47
Needs of international commerce, 国际商事交易的需要 105
Netherlands (The), 荷兰
　Awards set aside at the seat, 在仲裁地被撤销的裁决 126
　Voie directe (Law applicable to the merits), 直接的法律途径（适用于实体问题的法律） 104
Network model of law, 法律的网状模式 3, 5
New York Convention of 1958, 1958年《纽约公约》
　Arbitrability, 可仲裁性 33, 125
　Arbitral proceedings (conduct of), 仲裁程序（进行） 91, 97
　Award (notion), 裁决（看法） 66
　Double exequatur (abolition), 双重执行许可证制度（废除） 33, 36, 128, 131, 132
　More favorable regime, 更有利的制度 80
　Multiple proceedings, 多个程序 74
　Public policy, 公共政策 125
　Seat (role of), 仲裁地（的角色） 33
　Westphalian representation, 威斯

特伐利亚的表现形式 33,
　34, 125
Normative activity of States, 国家的规
　范性活动 41, 50, 53, 62
Norsolor 127
Nuclear weapons, 核武器 55

OECD Convention of 1997, 1997年《经
　济合作和发展组织公约》 57, 120
Oppetit 3, 6, 47, 48
Order, 秩序 20—22
Organ trafficking, 贩卖器官 *see* Traf-
　ficking
Ost 5, 43, 62
Outdated rules, 过时的规则 54
Overriding mandatory rules, 高于一切
　的强行规则 *see* Mandatory rules

Pakistan, 巴基斯坦 72, 73
Panama, 巴拿马 66
Park 13
Particularism, 特殊主义 *see* Idiosyn-
　crasy
Party Cooperation, 当事人合作 *see* Co-
　operation between parties
Passions, 激情 6
Paulsson 79
Pertamina 74
Peru, 秘鲁 66
Petrobangla 78
Place of arbitration, 仲裁地 *see* Seat
Plurality or collectivity, 多个的或者集
　体的 41
Polish Ocean Line 127
Portugal, 葡萄牙 58, 106
Positivism, 实证主义
　　Glowing-, 蓬勃日上— 47

—and ability to impose sanctions,
　—进行制裁的能力 28
—and legal order, —和法律秩序
　50—58
State-, 国家— 18—19, 27—29
Postulates, 前提 7
Poudret 7, 14, 18
Power to adjudicate, 裁决权 *see* Arbi-
　trator
Price determination, 确定价格 62
Prima facie, 表面 *see* Arbitration agree-
　ment
　　Competence-competence, 仲裁庭
　　　自裁管辖权
Private justice, 私人的正义 2, 3,
　27, 31, 40, 67, 86, 107, 124, 131
Procedure, 程序 *see* Arbitral procedure
Public policy, 公共政策
　　Mitigated effect of-, 弱化效果的—
　　　130
　　Transnational-, 跨国的—
　　　Corruption, 腐败 117, 120
　　　Embargo and boycott, 禁运和
　　　　联合抵制 121
　　　Environment, 环境 122
　　　Evolving nature, 不断演变的
　　　　本质 122
　　　Notion, 观点 115
　　　Exclusive distributorship agree-
　　　　ments, 独家分销协议 117
　　　—and mandatory rules, —和
　　　　强行规则 118
　　　—in national case law, —在
　　　　国家案例法中 64
　　　See also Trafficking
　　Truly international-, 真正国际的—
　　　5, 64

Putrabali 65, 127
Pyramidal model of law, 法律的金字塔模式 3, 5

Quebec, 魁北克 108

Racial discrimination, 种族歧视 49, 55
Racine 43, 116
Radicati di Brozolo 112
Reale 5
Recourse to one's own law to avoid arbitration, 诉诸自己的法律以避免仲裁 75, 80
Religious discrimination, 宗教歧视 49
Representation, 表现形式
    Mental-, 思想的 7
    Monolocal-, 单独地区的—
        —and anti-suit injunctions, —和禁诉令 75, 76
        —and awards set aside, —和撤销裁决 125, 134
        —and law applicable to the merits, —和适用于实体问题的法律 101—104, 105, 134
        —and law applicable to procedure, —和适用于程序问题的法律 94, 8
        —and *lis pendens*, —和平行程序 83
        —and mandatory rules, —和强行规则 108, 134
        —and refusal to set aside award, —和拒绝撤销裁决 132
        —and transfer of seat, —和转移仲裁地 78
    Notion, 观点 11, 23, 41
        Objectivist trend, 客观主义的观点 13
        Subjectivist trend, 主观主义的观点 14
    Terminology, 专门用语 21, 41, 51
    Stakes, 风险 68
    Structuring-, 构建— 10, 68, 133
    Transnational, 跨国的 *see* Arbitral legal order
    Westphalian-, 威斯特伐利亚的—
        Essentially unstable character, 本质上不稳定的特点 41, 70, 76
        Terminology, 专门用语 21, 41, 51
        —and anti-suit injunctions, —和禁诉令 75, 76
        —and awards set aside, —和撤销裁决 125, 134
        —and law applicable to the merits, —和适用于实体问题的法律 105, 134
        —and *lis pendens*, —和平行程序 83
        —and mandatory rules, —和强行规则 110, 134
        —and refusal to set aside award, —和拒绝撤销裁决 132
        —and transfer of seat, —和转移仲裁地 78
Right or wrong, 对或者错 6, 35, 135
Ripert 102

Romano 3,43,62
Ross 5
Rule,规则 see Moral rule, Outdated rules, Rules of law
　　Transnational rules,跨国规则
Rules of law,法律的规则 42,60

Saipem 78
Salini 80
Sanders 66
Sandrock 7
Sauser-Hall 1,89,101
Schmitthoff 90
Schwebel 75,79
Seat(of arbitration),仲裁地
　　Fiction,虚构 94
　　—and decision refusing to set aside an award,—和拒绝撤销裁决的决定 130—132
　　—and decision setting aside an award,—和撤销裁决的决定 125—129
　　—and law applicable to the merits,—和适用于实体问题的法律 101—104
　　—and procedure,—和程序 89—99
　　Perceived as a forum,被当做仲裁管辖地 11,20,41
　　Source of juridicity of arbitration,仲裁法律属性的渊源 14
　　Title,资格 36
　　Transfer of-,转移— 78
Security of transactions,交易安全 52
SEEE 126
Seraglini 112
Severability of arbitration agreement:,仲裁协议的可分割性:
　　see Arbitration agreement
Slavery,奴隶制 55,57,58
Society of merchants,商人社会 52
Sociology,社会学 3
Sources,渊源
　　Fruitfulness,丰硕成果 2
　　Theory of-,的理论— 2
　　See also Juridicity, Arbitrator (power to adjudicate)
Sperduti, Sperduti 117
Spier 128
State contract,政府合同 73,103
Stateless award,无国籍的裁决 see Award
Strategic choice of philosophical references,策略性的选择哲学参考文献 5
Sweden,瑞典 66
Switzerland,瑞士
　　Competence-competence,仲裁庭自裁管辖权 85
　　Lis pendens,平行程序 85
　　Mandatory rules,强行规则 85,109
　　New dangers,新危险 109
　　Waiver of action to set aside,放弃撤销裁决的诉讼 66
Svenska 132

TermoRio 128
Territoriality,地域性 9
　　See also Representation (monolocal)
Thomas Aquinas 22
Trade usages,贸易惯例 52
Trafficking,贩卖
　　Drug-,毒品— 115

—of human organs, 一人体器官 115

—of slaves, 一奴隶 55

Transnational Public Policy, 跨国公共政策

    see Public policy (transnational)

Transnational rules, 跨国规则

    Arbitral case law, 仲裁案例法 60

    Comparative law method, 比较法方法 60

    Dynamic nature, 动态本质 57—58, 62

    Evolving nature, 演变的本质 122

    List or method, 清单或方法 61, 62

    Method, 方法 54, 57

    Philosophy, 哲学 56

    Predictability, 可预见性 62

    Procedural-, 程序的— 99

    Public policy-, 公共政策— 54

    Substantive-, 实体的— 54

    Transnational choice of law rules, 跨国的法律选择规则 105

    —and trade usages, —和贸易惯例 52

    Unanimity requirement (false), 全体一致的要求（错误的）55

Tridimensional legal theory, 三维的法律理论 5

Truly international public policy, 真正的国际公共政策 *see* Public policy

Truncated tribunal, 缺员仲裁庭 *see* Arbitrator

Tunisia, 突尼斯 66, 108

UN (United Nations), 联合国 121

UNCITRAL (United Nations Commission on International Trade Law), 联合国国际贸易法委员会

    Arbitration Rules,《仲裁规则》

        Hearings, 审讯 78

        Law applicable to the merits, 适用于实体问题的法律 105

        Procedure, 程序 93

    Model Law,《示范法》22, 104

UNIDROIT principles,《国际统一私法协会国际商事合同通则》

    Hardship, 艰难情形 61

    Procedure, 程序 99

United States, 美国

    Anti-suit injunction, 禁诉令 74—75

    Awards set aside at the seat, 在仲裁地被撤销的裁决 128

Validation, 确认 *see* Legal order

Values, 价值 4, 6, 46, 48, 49, 55, 115

Von Mehren 31, 92, 103

Wengler 6

Westland 64

Westphalian representation, 威斯特伐利亚的表现形式

    see Representation (Westphalian)

Witnesses, 证人 *see* Arbitral procedure

Yukos 126

译 后 记

本书的原作为法语书 *Aspects philosophiques du droit de l'arbitrage international*,2008 年出版后,在欧洲好评如潮,但是书中提出的仲裁法律秩序的观点也引起广泛争议。在此后两年中,该书被先后翻译成英、中、西班牙和阿拉伯语出版。作为译者,能够参与这样的翻译项目,我深感荣幸,但是同时诚惶诚恐。经过一年的辛勤努力,中文版终于面世了。

在翻译过程中,对于"representation"的中文翻译,请教了母语为法语、英语或者中文的多位法学教授,最后定为"表现形式"。同样经过多方咨询,在本书中"forum"被统一翻译成"管辖地","seat"为"仲裁地"。对于"place where the arbitration procedure is conducted","place where the arbitration took place,"或者"place where the arbitration was held,"根据上下文,有的翻译成了"仲裁进行地",有的翻译成了"仲裁地"。因为"仲裁进行地"有可能是"仲裁地",但是也可能不是的。例如,举行审讯(hearing)的地点就可以称为"仲裁进行地",但是不一定是"仲裁地"。本书赞同的观点是,国际仲裁没有管辖地,如果一定要给他找个管辖地的话,这个地点是全世界;国际仲裁的管辖地而并不仅仅局限于仲裁地和仲裁进行地。对于"lex arbitri"和"lex arbitrii"的翻译,译者特别和作者讨论过。作者采纳了译者的意见在英文版中加了注释 58,说明这二者的区别,同理参见中文版的注释 58。在本书中,"lex arbitri"意为"仲裁法",强调在某个特定案件中适用的仲裁法(the law of the arbitration in question, not the law of arbitration in general)。对于"a decision of international justice"中"justice"的翻译,译者也征询了作者的意见,作者表示这里的"justice"和"国际法院"(International Court of Justice)中的"justice"同义,所以翻译成"国际司法的裁断"。至于文中其他地方出现的"justice"，译者根据上下文，有的翻译成"司法"，有的翻译成"公正"，有的翻译成"正义"。对于"juridicity"的翻译，译者曾经考虑过"司法属性"，但是最终决定采用"法律属性"。翻译是一门精深的学问，虽然译者尽力精益求精，但是唯恐百密一疏。因此，诚心求教方家，望指正。

在此，我特别感谢恩师 Peter D. Trooboff 的指导，陈晶莹教授的大力支持，陈治东教授和数位匿名专家的批评指正，以及华劼博士、史岩林博士、龙威狄博士、Stephen McIntyre 博士和吴婵小姐的帮助。同时感谢 Yas Banifatemi 博士和编辑王晶女士为本书的出版工作作出的努力。

本书献给我的父亲和母亲。

黄洁
美国北卡罗来纳州达勒姆市杜克大学法学院
2010 年 5 月 12 日